D0688856

CLUB
CUISINE

CLUB CUISINE

Cooking with a Master Chef

E D W A R D   G .   L E O N A R D , CMC

PHOTOGRAPHS BY RON MANVILLE

WILEY

John Wiley & Sons, Inc.

This book is printed on acid-free paper. ⊗

Copyright © 2007 by John Wiley & Sons, Inc. All rights reserved

Published by John Wiley & Sons, Inc., Hoboken, New Jersey
Published simultaneously in Canada

No part of this publication may be reproduced, stored in a retrieval system, or transmitted in any form or by any means, electronic, mechanical, photocopying, recording, scanning, or otherwise, except as permitted under Section 107 or 108 of the 1976 United States Copyright Act, without either the prior written permission of the Publisher, or authorization through payment of the appropriate per-copy fee to the Copyright Clearance Center, Inc., 222 Rosewood Drive, Danvers, MA 01923, (978) 750-8400, fax (978) 750-4470, or on the web at www.copyright.com. Requests to the Publisher for permission should be addressed to the Permissions Department, John Wiley & Sons, Inc., 111 River Street, Hoboken, NJ 07030, (201) 748-6011, fax (201) 748-6008, e-mail: permcoordinator@wiley.com.

Limit of Liability/Disclaimer of Warranty: While the publisher and author have used their best efforts in preparing this book, they make no representations or warranties with respect to the accuracy or completeness of the contents of this book and specifically disclaim any implied warranties of merchantability or fitness for a particular purpose. No warranty may be created or extended by sales representatives or written sales materials. The advice and strategies contained herein may not be suitable for your situation. You should consult with a professional where appropriate. Neither the publisher nor author shall be liable for any loss of profit or any other commercial damages, including but not limited to special, incidental, consequential, or other damages.

For general information on our other products and services or for technical support, please contact our Customer Care Department within the United States at (800) 762-2974, outside the United States at (317) 572-3993 or fax (317) 572-4002.

Wiley also publishes its books in a variety of electronic formats. Some content that appears in print may not be available in electronic books. For more information about Wiley products, visit our web site at www.wiley.com.

Library of Congress Cataloging-in-Publication Data:

Leonard, Edward G.
  Club cuisine / Edward G. Leonard.
    p. cm.
  Includes index.
  ISBN-13: 978-0-471-74171-8 (cloth)
  ISBN-10: 0-471-74171-X (cloth)
  1. Cookery—Clubs—United States. 2. Cookery, American. I. Title: Guide to culinary competitions. II. Title.
  TX648.L46 2006
  641.5'079'73—dc22

                                                                                      2005008657

Printed in the United States of America

10 9 8 7 6 5 4 3 2

To Ariadna for the artistic talent, contributions, and guidance

To Chefs Brad Barnes, Joachim Buchner, Fritz Sonnenschmidt, Steve Jilleba, and Dan Scannell, friends behind the stoves and in the heat of life.

To Chef Rosendale—your youth, passion, and talent have pushed me to a time of 10 years earlier in my life.

To my brigade and colleagues, Victor, Jose, Big Joey T, Chris, Seymour, Marco, Jaime, Fast Eddie, Carias, Natalie, Jennifer, Mike, Michael, Moose, Jean, Matt, and Trish—always cook from the heart.

To my championship culinary team of 2004, Russell, Dan, Trish, Rich, James, and Joachim—we cooked with character.

CONTENTS

PREFACE

A Labor of Love

Food is one of the few items that touch us all in many ways. It brings people together at happy times, such as holidays and celebrations, and sad times, such as after a funeral. Business deals are made over meals; people get engaged, and weddings are usually celebrated over sit-down dinners, elaborate or simple buffets, or a reception of finger foods. The importance of food in culture and society cannot be underestimated.

In the world of culinary arts, we hear all the latest buzzwords and phrases: passion, dedication, my dream job, I always wanted to cook, I always wanted to be a chef, etc. The truth is that the art of cooking comes down to respecting a craft that is so special, so intense that it consumes your life when done properly and correctly.

Many people work in the foodservice industry, and many cook daily in kitchens across the country. The majority work hard to make a living, but for many of them cooking is just a job. Other people have talent and work hard in their chosen venue; they enjoy what they do and look forward to it. They go beyond the call of duty by getting involved in industry associations and charities; they give of themselves and their time for what they enjoy doing.

Then there is the minority: those who give of their soul, who commit their life to the quest of cooking and serving great food in the most demanding venues. Those in this minority never settle for second best. They never follow the easy path, which takes them away from what is really deep down in the heart: the passion to cook and lead a kitchen that has a standard few others are willing to uphold.

These special cooks and chefs give back; they teach, they share, and they live and breathe all things culinary at an extraordinary level. They are the few who live the passion that is today's cooking industry. They are the leaders of this industry by virtue of their reputation as very good cooks and chefs and not by awards bestowed within set groups. These leaders set a standard and pace for others to imitate and follow. They bang the pans every day and run their kitchen like a well-oiled machine. They do not veer from the path that leads us to what is in their heart, which is working a quality kitchen.

My toque is off to those in this minority, those who cook with their heart and push the envelope. These gifted people spend 12 to 15 hours a day, every day, in a kitchen, developing new menus, new creations, and a culture of culinary pride in their operations.

I truly hope that you enjoy my labor of love, a book that reflects the many dishes my culinary team and I prepare and cook daily for our club members. This book features my cuisine, my belief in a total quality focus, a style that varies with the ingredients, and my quest to exceed the expectations of today's diners.

The pictures are of actual dishes prepared by a chef who loves his work. They bring to life the reality, the flavors, the imperfections, and the mouthwatering feel we can get from well-prepared and attractively presented food.

Club Cuisine is a labor of love created to share with those who appreciate the craft of cookery, whether as a professional or as a fan. Enjoy the recipes and savor the pictures, but use this book as a guide and an influence that encourages you to create, to dream, and to be consumed by food.

FOREWORD

Cooking, the Most Refined Love. . . .

I have been a cook for most of my life, and no matter where my career goes, the thing that never changes is my love for food. More importantly, neither does my insatiable need to understand more completely how I may be able to make food taste and look better, as well as how I may help our profession progress into the new century. Of course, I share this passion with many of the world's cooks, but none quite as closely as with Chef Edward Leonard.

Ed has been my colleague, confidant, and partner in crime through many challenges, almost all of which have been connected to food and cooking. I know Ed shares my intense passion for our career and industry, as I have learned much of it from him. I have been fortunate.

To really know what Ed is about, you should understand that he has spent more than 14 hours a day, seven days a week for I don't know how long working in the culinary industry. I say *industry* because Ed's pursuit does not finish at the kitchen door; it extends to all who work in the world's kitchens, to anyone who cares about food, and to any segment of our business that needs knowledge.

Ed shares selflessly. He makes it his business and his true passion to develop our profession into what he feels it should be. My friend has spent more of his time than anyone I have ever known working to bring the culinary business into the future and to share his love with culinarians.

It should also be said that much of his work is done at great personal cost—the absence of loved ones and, I am sure, the quiet loneliness that comes with constant travel. Nevertheless, he pushes on and does whatever is necessary to fulfill his mission.

I am pleased to see the pages that follow. They demonstrate how lucky the club industry is to have Edward Leonard as a leader.

A cook who reads this book and absorbs the style and most of all the heart with which it is written will as a professional be changed. He or she will see that the need to know food, feel its value, and understand what it does best is paramount to being a skilled cook.

The cook who reads this book will want to challenge his or her own skills and attain a new level of cooking. That cook will know that to be a craftsman is to be truly successful in the kitchen and will come to believe that cooking is, indeed, the most refined love.

Bradley Barnes
Certified Master Chef
Vice President, B&B Solutions
National Certification Chair for the
American Culinary Federation

MY PHILOSOPHY OF CUISINE

Cuisine, as defined by the dictionary, is "a characteristic manner or style of preparing food." So when chefs speak of "my cuisine" or "my philosophy of cuisine," it means their manner and style of preparing the food they serve.

Sometimes *cuisine* is easily defined. For example, *Italian cuisine* is the style and manner of preparing Italian food using Italian food products. A chef at a restaurant can have a defined cuisine as she drives that one operation and features her food.

Ultimately, one's philosophy of cuisine is one's personal cooking style regardless of the type of food.

To be honest, I am not sure when exactly my personal cuisine emerged, but I do know that it is not complicated or overbearing in presentation and preparation. I formed a strong philosophy in the course of many years of hard training, world travel, and interaction and cooking with other chefs, together with a strong culinary competition background. Experience and continued studying about food have helped develop my beliefs about what cuisine should and should not be.

The most important questions I ask chefs, cooks, and students who wish to work and study in my kitchens is "What are your philosophies and your belief in cuisine?" It is a question that provokes, unfortunately, little to no response most times.

A serious student of cookery and a person who has passion for the culinary arts has a firm understanding of what they do and why they do it. This foundation, I believe, is one ingredient that separates great cooks from good ones.

I adjust my style from time to time when I learn new concepts or lessons. However, my basic principles, my philosophy of food and the foundation that trained me, never change regardless of what trends come and go. My foundation has always been my steady rock as I moved forward in my quest to cook, prepare, and serve high-quality food.

What happens in a professional kitchen is a sight to behold. The effort it takes to produce high-quality food for many people in the time given is underestimated and underappreciated.

I do enjoy that there are foodies and fans of chefs and cookery magazines out there. However, most cannot conceive the amount of work and stress that go into operating top dining facilities. Spending a day cooking a dinner party for eight by following steps and recipes from a cooking magazine is nice, but it is not what professional cooking is like.

Take those eight hours and get ready for 200 to 300 meals of the highest quality. Orchestrating a brigade of cooks, chefs, and servers who will follow through on your vision and philosophy each and every night to make your customers happy requires detailed organization and precision. Only then can you feel the heat of a professional kitchen. High-quality food, while at the top of the list, is not the sole ingredient of an exemplary dining experience.

While my cuisine crosses many borders—classical French, Italian, Spanish, Mexican, American, and so on—years ago I learned the two most important things in creating a great dish are using the freshest ingredients you can find and cooking them properly. I do not ever cut corners when it comes to these points.

The *proper* preparation of food means many things to many people. For me, it means executing the fundamentals of cooking exactly, no shortcuts, no ignoring a process or step. This is the first part of my philosophy on cuisine: to sauté, roast, grill, fry, and bake properly and correctly. Some may think on a busy night it is okay to place food in the pan before it is hot enough to properly sauté, to have the heat so high the caramel is burned, or to skip deglazing the pan. However, this is wrong, as every step you do when cooking creates flavor. Proper preparation builds the flavor profile to ensure a finished product whose quality one can smell, feel, and taste;

there is no other way and no shortcut in preparing good food. Period.

The second part of my philosophy is to respect the food; food is a product that must be handled with care. It frustrates me when I see people mistreat food by storing it improperly, handling it too many times, or making it go through too many temperature changes, for example. Once a fresh food product is received in the kitchen, it should be handled with care, kept at the appropriate temperature, and used within a short time for optimum flavor and freshness. When preparing the product, butcher, fillet, cut, dice, or chop carefully, and handle it with as few steps as possible. This consideration goes a long way and is the start of serving pleasing food to the guest.

The third part of my philosophy is to ensure the cooking process and accoutrements selected complement and showcase the main featured item.

For example, Dover sole is one of the finest flat fish there is. The cost is high, but the quality and flavor are something special. If one were to sauté this delicate, neutral-tasting fish and then cook a spicy Creole sauce to go over it, then the customer would never get to experience the texture, the taste of a great fish. If, however, one lightly seasons the fish and sautés it in brown butter, teams it with asparagus poached in butter and a delicate soufflé of potatoes, and presents it with sea salt, creamy butter, and fresh lime, then one creates both a memorable dish and a memorable dining experience.

The presentation of food is also important, as people eat as much with the eyes as with the mouth. In my view, however, some presentations go to the extreme, and so much is focused on the presentation—the stunning height, the gimmick—that focus on the flavor of the actual food is lost. I have seen some incredible presentations that looked amazing, but the food was served cold and lacked substance. Often, such food is not prepared with a fundamental cooking procedure. Perhaps casseroles and braised and roasted foods are disappearing because they cannot be presented stunningly.

Many of my most memorable dishes are those presented in a simple and elegant way. Take, for example, a cassoulet. This stew of beans, duck, sausage, and vegetables is cooked slowly for 12 to 16 hours, placed in a casserole dish, covered with a sautéed bread crumb crust, and baked to seal in all the flavors and juices. It is presented to the guest in an elegant dish placed on a special folded napkin. When the guest breaks open the crust, allowing the aromatic steam to emerge, he knows immediately that he is in for something special.

SPECIAL THANKS

In my life I been fortunate to do for a living what I truly love to do and to gain experiences in all things culinary that will forever stay with me.

It would be remiss of me not to mention and thank those who have supported this effort, my passion, and the book, *Club Cuisine*, a project I have loved every step of the way.

First, my family, Ariadna, Giancarlo, Cosette, and Edward, for the sacrifice they make in not having me at home as much as they need and would like, not only while I wrote this book but with my life as a chef driven to cook and pursue all things culinary at an intense level. They do not always agree but understand that I know no other way.

Melissa Oliver, who took the chance and had the patience to assist me every step of the way in writing this book. John Wiley and Sons, for publishing a book of cookery that recognizes the cuisine of private clubs and the chefs who cook every day in a unrecognized venue. They understand the real meaning of a certified master chef and not the unearned titles given by the press.

The Westchester Country Club, the canvas for my art, and Robert James and William Minard, two special people in an industry of many.

The American Culinary Federation, the leader of all things culinary. Being a member has influenced my career in countless ways.

Ron Manville, a photographer whose true passion is the magic created when his craft and mine meet. This is amazing: He shot all the pictures for this book in only four and a half days. I hope we collaborate again on another culinary endeavor.

Natalie and Moose, for their dedication and help on this project, which required so much hard effort to meet the timetables given. Moose, for prepping and organizing all the foodstuffs, and Natalie, for editing, writing, and organizing the recipes of a crazy chef.

The rest of my culinary team, especially Mike Pillarella and Mike Ruggiero, who put in the long hours for the fast-paced photo shoot. My friends, chefs Joachim, Joe, Charles, and Reimund, who are featured in the guest chefs chapter. They love to cook, put themselves in the minority I describe in the preface, and gladly gave of their time for no other reason than to cook with a friend.

Last but not least, the ACF Culinary Team USA and its members, for the cooking, sharing, friendships, and inspiration that still drive me to stay in competition.

1

Breakfast the Elegant Way

Breakfast is the most important meal of the day. It should offer great taste and nourishment and be worth getting out of bed for, whether you are looking forward to a busy or a relaxing day. Many private clubs serve breakfast, whether for banquets, member events, or everyday service in the clubhouse and restaurant. It is my belief that the breakfast menu should offer the same quality and variety as the lunch and dinner menus. The goal and philosophy of my kitchen is to exceed guest and member expectations.

This chapter features breakfast items that start the day with panache and excitement. In many places, the standard breakfast menu is fruit and Danish, perhaps in a buffet setting; eggs, bacon, and toast; and perhaps an old-fashioned favorite such as Eggs Benedict. I like to enhance the typical breakfast menu with items such as Brioche French Toast with Pumpkin Butter and a hearty breakfast sandwich that combines eggs, corned beef hash, and Welsh rarebit sauce.

I employ the same plate development practices and methodology for breakfast as I do for first plates for dinner and special events. Textures, flavors that harmonize, and seasonal products are all part of the development of every meal. These simple breakfast dishes are presented elegantly and tastefully.

Enjoy the next six recipes, which are a far cry from the usual standard breakfast fare. Club members taking a meal before work, golf, tennis, or a meeting of friends will love this special start to their day.

MENU

My Breakfast Sandwich

*Toasted English Muffins, Corned Beef Hash with
Fried Egg, Welsh Rarebit Sauce, and Broiled Tomato*

Autumn-Style French Toast

*Brioche Bread with Cinnamon Egg Batter,
Pumpkin Butter, and Maple Syrup with Cloves*

The Breakfast Cristo

*Fried Egg, Smoked Ham, Cheese Sandwich
Dipped in an Egg Batter and Grilled*

Ricotta Blintzes with Fruit
Compote Mascarpone Cream

Banana Cinnamon Waffles
with Bananas Brûlée

Eggs and Bacon Profiterole

My Breakfast Sandwich

An exceptional breakfast sandwich that can utilize the previous night's roasted meats and vegetables. You can use corned beef with potatoes and onions, roasted turkey with beets or apples, or pork loin with caramelized root vegetables. The possibilities are endless.

HASH

1 onion, small, diced ¼ in.

1 Tbsp butter, unsalted

1 tsp Chefnique Pâté Spice or other poultry spice blend

1¼ cups corned beef brisket or other roasted meat, diced ¼ in.

½ cup mixed roasted or boiled vegetables, diced ¼ in.

1 Tbsp bacon fat or unsalted butter (or use nonfat vegetable-based spray, if desired)

BROILED TOMATOES

2 tomatoes, medium size, ripe

3 Tbsp extra-virgin olive oil

Salt

Freshly ground black pepper

ASSEMBLY

4 eggs, large

1 Tbsp butter, unsalted

4 English muffins, toasted and buttered

Salt

Freshly ground black pepper

8 oz Welsh Rarebit Sauce (see Chef's Pantry)*

HASH

1. In a small sauté pan, sauté the onion in the butter until it becomes translucent.

2. Add the spice blend and season with salt and pepper. Transfer to a mixing bowl and cool to room temperature. Add the meat and vegetables and mix very well.

3. Portion the mixture into 4 equal patties, using buttered ring molds, if desired.

4. In a large cast iron or nonstick sauté pan, heat the bacon fat over medium heat. Sauté the patties for 3 minutes on each side or until a golden crust develops.

BROILED TOMATOES

1. Using a serrated knife, trim the top and bottom of each tomato so they are flat at both ends. Cut each tomato in half horizontally and place the pieces in a small mixing bowl. Toss with 3 Tbsp olive oil, salt, and pepper.

*All references to pantry refer to Chapter 15, Chef Leonard's Pantry.

2. Place the pieces in a baking dish and set under the broiler for 3 minutes or until the tomatoes just begin to soften. Remove the dish from the broiler and allow the tomatoes to cool for 5 minutes.

3. Using a small knife, remove a small portion of the center of each tomato half to form a small well. Reserve the tomato centers for service.

4. In a small mixing bowl, combine the panko with the remaining olive oil and Italian seasoning. Fill each tomato half with an equal amount of the bread crumb mixture.

5. At time of service, place the tomatoes and reserved tomato cuttings onto a baking dish and place under a preheated broiler for 3–5 minutes or until the bread crumbs are nice and golden brown.

6. Serve each sandwich with 1 stuffed tomato and a portion of the heated tomato cutting.

ASSEMBLY

1. In a large cast iron or nonstick pan, fry the eggs in the butter.

2. Place the toasted English muffin bottoms on a plate and stack with tomato, hash, and egg.

3. Pour the sauce over the sandwich fillings. Cover with the English muffin tops.

Autumn-Style French Toast

SERVES: 4

This French toast is made with cinnamon, pumpkin butter, and maple syrup with cloves and is a perennial fall favorite at my club. The pumpkin butter is a fall staple; it can also be served with soft rolls at dinner or on top of your favorite risotto, or used to finish winter vegetable soups.

CINNAMON BATTER

1 tsp ground cinnamon

1 tsp vanilla extract

¼ tsp freshly ground nutmeg

2 Tbsp Cinnamon Honey (see Chef's Pantry)

½ cup heavy cream

6 eggs, large

MAPLE SYRUP WITH CLOVES

8 whole cloves

1 cinnamon stick

2 star anise

8 oz maple syrup

ASSEMBLY

4 Tbsp butter, unsalted

8 slices brioche

4 oz Pumpkin Butter, sliced in rounds (see Chef's Pantry)

confectioner's sugar, for dusting

CINNAMON BATTER

1. In a saucepan, place the cinnamon, vanilla, nutmeg, honey, and cream. Bring to a boil.

2. Stir to dissolve the honey, remove from heat, and allow the mixture to steep for 20 minutes.

3. Once the mixture is cooled to room temperature, transfer it to a large bowl, add the eggs, and mix well. Refrigerate the batter until needed.

MAPLE SYRUP WITH CLOVES

1. Make a sachet by placing the cloves, cinnamon stick, and star anise in a piece of cheesecloth or small coffee filter and tying it closed with kitchen string.

2. Place the sachet and the maple syrup in a small saucepan. Bring to a boil and remove from heat. Allow to steep 20 minutes or longer to develop flavors.

3. Remove the sachet and reserve the syrup.

ASSEMBLY

1. In a large sauté pan, melt the butter over medium heat until foamy.

2. Dip the brioche into the cinnamon egg batter and coat both sides thoroughly.

3. Fry the brioche for 2–3 minutes on each side or until it is golden and cooked through. Remove from the pan.

4. Place the toast on plates, slice diagonally, top with pumpkin butter and syrup, and dust with confectioner's sugar.

The Breakfast Cristo

SERVES: 4

EGG BATTER

4 eggs, large

1 Tbsp sugar

1 tsp potato starch

½ tsp cinnamon

1 tsp vanilla extract

1–2 Tbsp milk

ASSEMBLY

8 slices brioche or Texas-style toast

1 Tbsp Dijon honey mustard

4 eggs, large

4 Tbsp butter, unsalted

4 slices smoked ham

*4 oz Vermont cheddar cheese or top-quality cheddar,
    sliced into 4 pieces*

2 Tbsp butter, unsalted

confectioner's sugar, for dusting

EGG BATTER

1. In a medium stainless-steel mixing bowl, combine the eggs, sugar, potato starch, cinnamon, vanilla extract, and milk.

2. Using a wire whisk, whip the mixture gently to incorporate all ingredients.

3. Reserve the batter in the refrigerator until needed.

ASSEMBLY

1. Lay out 4 slices of brioche on a work surface or cutting board.

2. Spread each with a thin coat of Dijon honey mustard.

3. Fry the eggs in 4 Tbsp butter over medium heat.

4. Top each prepared brioche slice with an egg, slice of ham, slice of cheese, and the remaining slices of bread.

5. In a large nonstick pan, melt 2 Tbsp butter until foamy.

6. Dip the sandwiches into the batter and coat both sides thoroughly.

7. Place the sandwiches in the pan and fry 2–3 minutes on each side until golden brown.

8. Remove to a warm plate and sprinkle with confectioner's sugar.

Ricotta Blintzes with Fruit Compote Mascarpone Cream

SERVES: 4

The ricotta filling can be flavored with liqueurs or simple syrups to complement the fruit compote and change with the seasons.

BLINTZES

1 cup milk

½ cup heavy cream

3 whole eggs, large

1 egg yolk

1 Tbsp granulated sugar

1 cup all-purpose flour

4 Tbsp butter, melted

4 Tbsp butter, solid

RICOTTA FILLING

12 oz fresh whole-milk ricotta, hand packed, room
   temperature

4 oz mascarpone cheese, softened

2 Tbsp confectioner's sugar

1 Tbsp kirschwasser or other flavored brandy

1 tsp lemon juice

¼ cup heavy cream

FRUIT COMPOTE

3 whole cloves

1 cinnamon stick

1 vanilla bean, split

⅓ cup dried cherries

⅓ cup dried cranberries

1 pear, peeled and diced ¼ in.

¼ cup strawberry preserves

¼ cup brown sugar

¼ cup port wine

2 cups apple juice

Juice and zest of ½ lemon

BLINTZES

1. In a blender or food processor, process the milk, cream, eggs, egg yolk, sugar, flour, and melted butter until smooth. Let mixture rest in refrigerator for ½ hour or up to 24 hours.

2. Pass the mixture through a chinois.

3. In a 7–8-in. crepe pan or large nonstick sauté pan, heat 1 tsp of the solid butter. Make the first blintz to test the amount of batter you need, its consistency, and the temperature of the pan.

4. Using a 2-oz ladle, drop 1½ oz of the batter into the pan and immediately swirl it with the ladle so it covers the entire surface. Return the pan to the heat and cook for about 45 seconds or until the edge of the blintz is golden and flips easily. Use a rubber spatula to carefully flip the blintz. Cook for an additional 1–2 minutes or until the blintz is golden. Transfer to a wire rack to cool. Repeat with the remaining batter.

5. Stack the cooled blintzes between sheets of parchment paper and reserve in the refrigerator. The blintzes can be made up to 1 day in advance.

RICOTTA FILLING

1. Using a rubber spatula, combine by hand in a stainless-steel mixing bowl the ricotta, sugar, marscapone, kirschwasser, lemon juice, and cream. Blend until smooth.

2. Place the mixture in a piping bag fitted with a round tip.

FRUIT COMPOTE

1. Place the cloves, cinnamon stick, and vanilla bean in small piece of cheesecloth or coffee filter, and tie with kitchen string to make a sachet.

2. Place the sachet, cherries, cranberries, pear, strawberry preserves, sugar, wine, and apple juice in a small saucepan.

3. Simmer over low heat until the liquid is reduced to a syrup and the fruit is tender yet still firm enough to hold its shape.

Remove the sachet and add lemon juice and zest. Keep warm to serve or reserve for up to 1 week.

ASSEMBLY

1. Lay 1 blintz on a cutting board and place 2 oz of the ricotta filling in the center. Fold the right and left side of the blintz over slightly and roll the blintz from bottom to top to form an enclosed cylinder. Place the rolled blintz onto a greased baking sheet. Repeat for the remaining blintzes.

2. Place the baking sheet with the rolled blintzes in a 350°F oven. Bake until heated through, 5–7 minutes.

3. Preheat 4 serving plates. Place 2 blintzes on each plate and top each with 1 Tbsp of the warm fruit compote. Serve immediately, with extra fruit compote on the side.

Banana Cinnamon Waffles with Banana Brûlée

SERVES: 4

This elegant breakfast item can be transformed into a delicious dessert with the addition of sweetened whipped cream.

WAFFLE MIX

1½ cups milk

1 banana, extra-ripe, cut into pieces

1 vanilla bean, split

2 Tbsp butter, unsalted

½ cup sugar

3 eggs

1 tsp baking powder

1½ cups all-purpose flour, sifted

Pinch kosher salt

2 Tbsp sugar

1 tsp cinnamon

1 Tbsp butter, unsalted, melted

CARAMELIZED BANANAS

1 banana

¼ cup sugar

ASSEMBLY

As needed, maple syrup, warm

As needed, whipped sweet butter

WAFFLE MIX

1. In a small saucepan, combine the milk, banana, vanilla bean, butter, and ½ cup sugar. Bring the milk to a boil, lower heat, and simmer for 5 minutes. Remove the vanilla bean, scrape out the seeds, and return the seeds to the milk. Place the milk-banana mixture in a blender and puree until smooth. Allow to cool, blend in eggs, and mix well.

2. In a large mixing bowl, place the baking powder, flour, and salt; stir to combine. Slowly mix in the milk mixture to form a batter. Allow to rest for ½ hour.

3. Preheat a waffle iron and brush with 1 Tbsp melted butter.

4. Pour batter into the iron until it is almost full. Cook until steam stops coming out of the side. Reserve the waffle on a warm plate.

CARAMELIZED BANANAS

1. Peel the banana and cut it into ¾-in. slices.

2. Place the bananas in a shallow baking dish and top them with sugar to a depth of ¼ in. Brûlée with a torch or under a broiler until the sugar caramelizes. Do not allow to burn.

ASSEMBLY

1. Preheat 4 service plates.

2. Place 1 warm waffle on each plate. Divide the caramelized banana slices equally among the plates, setting them on top of the waffles.

3. Serve with warm maple syrup and whipped sweet butter on the side.

Eggs and Bacon Profiterole

SERVES: 4

7 eggs

¾ cup heavy cream

4 slices bacon, cooked and chopped

2 Roma tomatoes, small, seeded, diced

2 oz butter, unsalted, melted, room temperature

¼ tsp freshly ground nutmeg

To taste, kosher salt

To taste, freshly ground black pepper

1 cup shredded Gruyère cheese

As needed, butter

½ cup dried bread crumbs

ASSEMBLY

8 Profiteroles, medium (see Chef's Pantry)

2 Tbsp chopped parsley

1. In a large mixing bowl, combine the eggs, cream, bacon, tomatoes, butter, nutmeg, salt, and pepper. Fold in ¾ cup of the Gruyère cheese.

2. Coat 4 ramekins with butter, then with the bread crumbs. Reserve the remaining bread crumbs.

3. Place the ramekins in a 2-in.-deep baking dish or hotel pan. Carefully fill the pan 1 in. deep with warm water.

4. Fill the ramekins three-quarters full with the egg mixture. Top with the remaining Gruyère and bread crumbs.

5. Bake at 350°F until just firm in the center, 6–8 minutes. Allow to stand in the oven with the door ajar for 2 minutes.

ASSEMBLY

1. Cut the profiteroles in half horizontally.

2. Use a spoon to remove the egg custard from the ramekins and place in the bottom half of the profiteroles.

3. Sprinkle with parsley, place the profiterole tops over the eggs, and serve.

2

Lunch

Many people approach lunch thinking "I am busy and just need to eat quickly." Some eat at their desk; others munch fast food while running errands. It is difficult to take the time to savor the tasty soups, sandwiches, and salads chefs prepare for today's lunch menu.

Many club members and their guests, however, do take the time to enjoy lunch. They relish the view of the golf course on a nice spring day as they dine on the terrace, or perhaps they seek an elegant dining room setting when a business lunch is needed to close a deal. They may lunch with a bridge group, at the end of a morning golf game, or sitting by the pool. Whatever the occasion, good food is wanted and expected at a top club.

Lunch, like breakfast, is often a menu of standard items including the club sandwich, chicken soup, chef's salad, and the classic Reuben sandwich. These tried-and-true items are, in fact, featured daily at many clubs. However, that does not stop the chef from trying new items or putting a new spin on the classics.

For example, consider the club sandwich, an old favorite consisting of turkey, bacon, lettuce, tomato, and mayonnaise stacked on three slices of bread. Create the same sandwich concept with lobster, artichoke, avocado, bacon, lettuce, and tomato on vanilla brioche. This lobster club can quickly become a new favorite. Substitute salmon for the turkey; with honey lime mayonnaise, this takes the standard club sandwich to a new level.

Lunch can and does include more than soup, salad, and sandwiches. The next three chapters feature innovative lunch items, showing variety and creativity while respecting the old favorites.

Soups

I once worked for a regional manager whose first priority when visiting a chef's kitchen would be to taste the soup. He believed the sign of a good chef was the high quality and excellent flavor of the soup or soups being offered.

A good soup excites the palate. It calls forth warm memories of growing up and enjoying mom's homemade soup on a cold winter's day. A fresh tomato soup can remind you of eating a fresh sun-warmed tomato straight off the vine.

I have learned through the years that making a good soup requires much skill. Here are a few rules to the making of a lick-the-bowl-clean soup:

- Base most soups on a foundation of stock or broth of meat, fish, poultry, or vegetables. Great soups start with a great-tasting foundation, plain and simple.

- Make sure the soup garnish—vegetables, diced meat, pasta, clams—is small enough to fit on the soupspoon and plentiful enough to be eaten with every spoonful.

- Cook pasta or rice for soups separately in a broth, cool, and then add to the soup bowl when serving. This prevents the starch from absorbing the soup liquid and getting mushy.

- Add appropriate fresh herbs to the soup as it is poured into the bowl to infuse it with fresh flavor. Adding fresh herbs too early results in a poor flavor profile and, sometimes, a bitter taste.

- Finish cream or pureed soups with cold, diced butter for a silky finish and soft flavor.

- Enhance soups with a high-quality flavored oil added just prior to service.

   One of the soups in this chapter reflects the flavor of a BLT sandwich; another takes traditional clam chowder to Hawaii. Tomatoes star in summer soups. In the fall, try truffle, egg, and potato, and move on to wild mushrooms.

MENU

BLT Soup with Rye Croutons

Butternut Squash Soup
with Duck Confit, Pecan Syrup,
and Brioche Croutons

Big Island Clam Chowder

Country Potato Soup with Truffle

Naples Roasted Tomato Soup

Wild Mushroom Soup
with Tarragon Cream

BLT Soup
with Rye Croutons

SERVES: 8

RYE CROUTONS

4 slices rye bread, trimmed and cubed

SOUP

8 oz veal bacon, diced

2 oz pork bacon, diced

1 sweet onion, chopped

1 garlic clove, minced

4 oz butter, unsalted

1 head romaine lettuce, chiffonade

4 oz all-purpose flour

1 qt Chicken Brodo (see Chef's Pantry)

1 cup light cream, heated

1 cup milk, heated

4 Roma tomatoes, peeled, seeded, diced

⅓ cup high-quality mayonnaise

4 Tbsp high-quality mayonnaise

2 Tbsp fresh sage, chopped

To taste, kosher salt

To taste, freshly ground black pepper

10 oz butter, unsalted

RYE CROUTONS

1. Arrange the diced rye bread in an even layer on a baking sheet. Place the baking sheet in a preheated 375°F oven.

2. Remove from the oven and stir to encourage even browning. Return to the oven until all the moisture is removed and the bread begins to brown, about 3 more minutes.

SOUP

1. Render the bacon. Drain the grease into a soup pot. Hold the bacon for later use.

2. Heat the grease in the soup pot. Sauté the onions and garlic. Add the butter.

3. Reserve 8 oz of the romaine. Add the remaining romaine to the pot and sauté 2–3 minutes.

4. Add the flour and cook until it is light brown.

5. Add the broth and bring to a simmer. Add the cream, milk, half the tomatoes, and half the reserved bacon. Simmer for 5–6 minutes.

6. Whip in ⅓ cup mayonnaise. Simmer 2 more minutes, then remove from stove.

ASSEMBLY

1. Finish the soup with salt, pepper, and butter. Pour into bowls. Garnish soup bowls with the remaining romaine, croutons, reserved bacon, remaining tomato, 4 Tbsp mayonnaise, and sage.

Butternut Squash Soup with Duck Confit, Pecan Syrup, and Brioche Croutons

SERVES: 4

SOUP

1 butternut squash, large, peeled, seeded, diced medium

3 Tbsp extra-virgin olive oil, plus more as needed

To taste, salt

To taste, freshly ground black pepper

2 oz butter

½ onion, small, finely diced

½ carrot, small, finely diced

1 celery rib, finely diced

1 pt high-quality chicken stock

1 pt apple juice

2 oz chestnuts, peeled

1 tsp cinnamon

2 oz honey

1 pt heavy cream

2 oz butter

CURE

3 Tbsp coarse sea salt

2 Tbsp brown sugar

3 garlic cloves, crushed

1 shallot, peeled and sliced

3 sprigs thyme

2 sprigs rosemary

2 bay leaves

6 duck legs, trimmed

2 Tbsp Cinnamon Honey (see Chef's Pantry)

½ tsp cracked black pepper

CONFIT

4 cups duck fat

4 garlic cloves

4 shallots, peeled

PECAN SYRUP

2 cups granulated sugar

1 cup water

½ cup chopped pecans

1 tsp maple flavoring

¼ cup butter, unsalted

BRIOCHE CROUTONS

4 slices brioche

¼ cup clarified butter

SOUP

1. Preheat oven to 300°F. Lightly coat the squash dice with olive oil and place on a baking sheet. Season lightly with salt and pepper. Roast until the squash is very soft, about 45 minutes.

2. In a large soup pot, heat 2 oz butter and sauté the carrots, onion, and celery until lightly caramelized. Add the chicken stock, apple juice, and chestnuts and simmer for 10 minutes, stirring occasionally.

3. Add the roasted squash to the soup pot and simmer for a few more minutes.

4. Puree the soup with a blending stick until smooth.

5. Add the cinnamon, honey, heavy cream, and butter. Adjust the seasoning with salt and pepper.

CURE

1. Sprinkle 1 Tbsp of the sea salt and 1 Tbsp of the brown sugar in the bottom of a dish large enough to hold the duck legs. Evenly distribute half of the garlic, shallot, and herbs over the salt mixture. Arrange the duck, skin side up, over the cure mixture.

2. Sprinkle the duck legs with the remaining sea salt, sugar, garlic, shallot, herbs, honey, and pepper. Cover with plastic wrap and place in the refrigerator for 1 to 2 days to cure.

CONFIT

1. Remove the duck legs from the dish and brush off the cure. Preheat the oven to 225°F.

2. In a saucepan, melt the duck fat.

3. Arrange the clean duck pieces in a single snug layer in an ovenproof vessel with the garlic and shallots. Pour the melted duck fat over the duck legs. The duck legs should be covered completely by fat.

4. Cover the vessel with aluminum foil. Place the confit in the preheated oven and cook at a very slow simmer—just an occasional bubble—until the duck is tender and easily pulled from the bone, 2–3 hours. Remove the confit from the oven and allow to cool.

5. Remove the duck legs from the fat and gently remove the meat from the bones. Place the meat into a container and cover with the fat. Store in the refrigerator; the confit will keep for several weeks if covered by fat.

PECAN SYRUP

1. In a stainless-steel saucepan, bring the sugar and water to a boil over medium heat. When the sugar is dissolved, add the pecans and maple flavoring, reduce the heat to low, and allow the pecans to simmer for 3 minutes.

2. Turn off the heat and add the butter slowly until incorporated. Reserve for service.

BRIOCHE CROUTONS

1. Using a serrated knife, cut the brioche into ¼-in. cubes.

2. In a medium-size sauté pan, melt the clarified butter. Remove from the heat and add the cubed brioche. Toss gently to distribute the butter evenly throughout the brioche. Evenly spread the brioche cubes on a baking sheet and bake at 350°F for 7 minutes or until golden brown. Remove the bread from the oven and allow to cool. Reserve for service.

ASSEMBLY

1. Heat the soup to at least 165°F.

2. Gently heat the duck in the oven until warmed through.

3. Divide the soup evenly among 4 heated soup bowls. Place 2 oz duck confit in each bowl. Drizzle lightly with pecan syrup and top with a few brioche croutons. Serve immediately.

Big Island
Clam Chowder

SERVES: 4

POACHING LIQUID

1 pt coconut milk

One 15-oz can cream of coconut

2 shallots, diced small

3 lemon leaves

¼ cup Chinese chili sauce

1 qt Seafood Brodo (see Chef's Pantry)

SOUP

1 Tbsp olive oil

3 slices smoked bacon, chopped small

½ cup celery, small dice

1 garlic clove, sliced thin

½ cup onion, small dice

1 tsp lemongrass, finely minced

2 oz all-purpose flour

3 cups high-quality clam broth

2 cups Idaho potatoes, diced small

1 cup heavy cream

6 drops Tabasco Sauce

1 oz anise honey

1 Tbsp finely chopped thyme

To taste, salt

To taste, freshly ground black pepper

ASSEMBLY

24 Manilla clams

6 oz butter, unsalted

12 leaves sage, fried

¼ cup toasted coconut

Zest of 1 lemon

POACHING LIQUID

1. In a 4-qt saucepan, combine the coconut milk, cream of coconut, shallots, lemon leaves, chili sauce, and Seafood Brodo. Bring to a simmer over medium heat and allow to simmer for 5 minutes to combine flavors. Turn off heat; leave the pan on the stove.

SOUP

1. Place the oil and bacon in a heavy-bottomed saucepot. Cover the pot and set over low heat. Render the bacon until it begins to crisp, stirring occasionally. Add the celery, garlic, and onions. Cover and sweat over low heat until the vegetables are translucent.

2. Add the lemongrass and cook for 2 additional minutes.

3. Add the flour and cook for 3 additional minutes, stirring constantly.

4. Add the clam broth and stir until smooth. Bring to a light simmer and continue to cook, stirring occasionally, for 5 minutes.

5. Add the potatoes and half of the cream. Simmer gently until the potatoes are just cooked, 7–10 minutes.

6. Add the Tabasco, honey, and thyme. Season with salt and pepper to taste.

1. At time of service, bring the poaching liquid to a strong simmer. Add the clams and cook gently until they open.

2. Remove the clams from their shells and place in a small amount of the warm broth for service.

3. Heat 4 soup bowls. Finish the chowder with cold diced butter and divide among the bowls.

4. Spoon 2 Tbsp poaching liquid along with 6 clams into each soup bowl. Garnish with 3 fried sage leaves, toasted coconut, and lemon zest.

Country Potato Soup with Truffle

SERVES: 4

8 oz butter

2 leeks, white part only, diced small

¼ cup finely diced onion

5 potatoes, peeled

1 qt white chicken stock

1 Tbsp salt

1 cup heavy cream

1 Tbsp finely chopped thyme

1 oz white truffle oil

To taste, kosher salt

To taste, cracked black pepper

1 egg, cooked medium, chopped

16 slices truffle

1 tsp finely chopped chives

1. In a medium, heavy-bottomed stockpot, melt 4 oz of the butter over low heat. Add the leeks and onions. Cook over low heat, stirring occasionally, until the onions are translucent.

2. Roughly chop 4 of the potatoes and add to the pot. Sauté for 2 minutes.

3. Add the chicken stock and bring to a strong simmer over medium heat. Allow to simmer until the potatoes are tender, 10–15 minutes.

4. Cut the remaining potato into ¼-in. dice. Place in a small saucepan with 1 Tbsp salt and enough cold water to cover. Cook over medium heat until the potato is tender, about 10 minutes. Strain and reserve for service.

5. Puree the chicken stock and rough-cut potatoes with a blending stick or in a blender. Return the soup to the stove and place over low heat. Add the heavy cream, remaining 4 oz butter, thyme, and truffle oil. Season with salt and pepper to taste.

6. At time of service, heat 4 soup bowls. Add the diced potatoes to the soup and divide the soup evenly among the bowls. Garnish each bowl with chopped egg, 4 truffle slices, and chopped chives. Serve immediately.

Naples Roasted Tomato Soup

SERVES: 4

ROASTED TOMATOES

2 oz extra-virgin olive oil

2 lb Roma tomatoes, ripe, cut in half

1 sweet onion, small, peeled, sliced thin

4 garlic cloves, peeled

2 tsp honey

1 tsp brown sugar

8 basil leaves, blanched

To taste, sea salt

Pinch crushed red pepper flakes

SOUP

2 cups Chicken Brodo (see Chef's Pantry)

1 cup tomato puree

2 oz butter, unsalted, cold, diced small

2 Tbsp aged balsamic vinegar

GARNISH

4 Tbsp fresh ricotta cheese

4 slices crostini, small

8–12 cherry tomatoes, peeled

4 Tbsp extra-virgin olive oil

4 leaves basil

ROASTED TOMATOES

1. Preheat oven to 350°F.

2. Put the oil in a small roasting pan and place in the oven until very hot.

3. Remove the pan from the oven and carefully add the Roma tomatoes, onion, and garlic, turning to coat all the vegetables with oil.

4. Drizzle the honey over the vegetables, sprinkle the sugar on them, and then add the blanched basil leaves. Sprinkle with sea salt and red pepper flakes.

5. Roast in the oven for 20–25 minutes, stirring twice.

SOUP

1. In a stainless-steel pan, bring the broth and the tomato puree to a boil, reduce the heat, and simmer for 20 minutes. Add the contents of the roasting pan to the broth mixture, including the pan scrapings and all juices. Simmer for 10 minutes.

2. In a blender, puree the mixture 1 cup at a time.

3. Strain the pureed soup into a stainless-steel pot. Whisk in the butter and vinegar; adjust the seasoning with salt if needed.

GARNISH

1. Divide the ricotta into 4 spoon shapes, place on crostini, and put into 4 soup bowls.

2. In a sauté pan, lightly fry the cherry tomatoes in the oil for 1–2 minutes. Pour the soup into the bowls and garnish with the cherry tomatoes and basil leaves.

NOTE: *The key to soup—and any other dish—is the freshness and quality of the ingredients. Use the finest-quality butter, cold-pressed extra-virgin olive oil, ripe tomatoes, fresh hand-beaten ricotta, and fragrant fresh basil.*

Wild Mushroom Soup with Tarragon Cream

SERVES: 4

CRISPY MUSHROOMS

½ cup sugar

½ cup water

1 portobello cap, gills removed

TARRAGON CREAM

1 cup heavy cream

½ cup tarragon leaves

SOUP

1 Tbsp olive oil

5 Tbsp butter, unsalted

½ cup chopped shallots

12 oz assorted wild mushrooms, chopped

8 oz button mushrooms, sliced

3 garlic cloves, minced

3 tsp chopped tarragon

1½ oz dried porcini mushrooms or morels, soaked overnight in 1 cup broth

3½ cups mushroom broth or chicken broth

4 tsp all-purpose flour

2 cups heavy cream

To taste, kosher salt

To taste, cracked black pepper

2 Tbsp butter, cold, diced

2 tsp truffle oil

CRISPY MUSHROOMS

1. In a heavy-bottomed saucepan, combine sugar and water. Bring to a boil over medium heat and cook until sugar is dissolved. Remove from heat.

2. Cut the portobello into ⅛-in. slices. Dip each slice into the sugar syrup and lay on a Silpat.

3. Bake the portobello slices at 200°F until dry and crisp, about 30 minutes. Reserve for service.

TARRAGON CREAM

1. Combine the heavy cream and tarragon in a small saucepan. Bring to a slow simmer over medium heat and simmer for 10 minutes.

2. Puree the cream in a high-speed blender. Strain through a fine sieve and reserve for service.

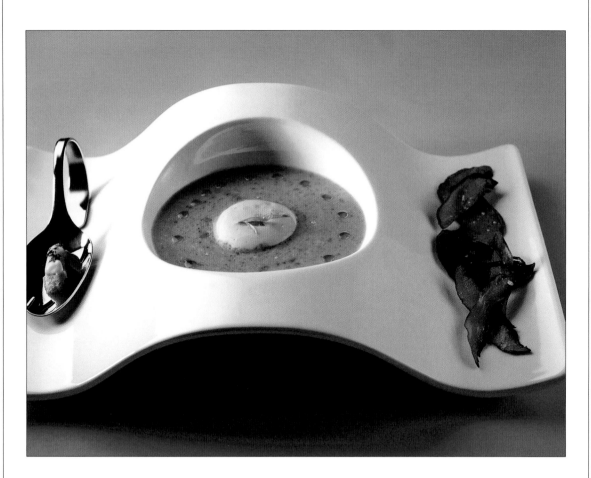

SOUP

1. In a large heavy-bottomed stockpot, heat the olive oil and butter over medium heat. Add the chopped shallots and sauté until tender.

2. Add the wild and button mushrooms and sauté until brown and tender, about 8 minutes.

3. Drain the soaked porcini mushrooms, reserving the soaking liquid. Add the garlic, tarragon, and porcini mushrooms to the stockpot and sauté for 2 minutes.

4. Sprinkle the flour over the mushrooms and continue to cook while stirring for 1 minute.

5. Gradually whisk in reserved porcini liquid, mushroom broth, and heavy cream. Bring to a boil over medium heat, stirring frequently. Reduce heat and simmer until the soup thickens slightly, about 12 minutes.

6. Transfer 1½ cups of the soup to a blender and puree until smooth.

7. Return the puree to the pot and bring the soup back to a simmer.

8. Season to taste with salt and pepper. At time of service, whisk in the cold butter, and check the seasoning; adjust if necessary.

9. Place the tarragon cream in a foaming bottle with 2 charges. If you do not have a foaming bottle, gently whip the cream until it begins to thicken slightly.

10. Ladle the soup into preheated bowls. Garnish with truffle oil, tarragon cream, and crisp mushrooms.

3

Salads

When one thinks about salad, one pictures a variety of fresh, crisp, and flavorful ingredients tossed with a dressing or vinaigrette. Salad serves many purposes: It can be a palate cleanser during a multi-course meal, a lunch entrée, a first plate at dinner, or a light bite during the day.

Salad, like all good food, starts with the freshest ingredients possible. The greens, lettuce, or vegetables featured in a salad often stand on their own, so their flavor and freshness are critical for success.

Dressings and vinaigrettes should be flavorful, complementing the salad without overpowering it. They should gently coat the salad and add flavor without weighing down the ingredients and pooling in the bottom of the bowl or plate.

Salads today are limited by the imagination only. Be inspired by the selection of greens, microgreens, traditional lettuce, and specialty items to create wonderful, memorable salads.

In this chapter, we fuse ingredients to develop wonderful flavor profiles, put a spin on traditional and popular salads, and offer light and flavorful summer treats.

Contemporary Caesar Salad

French Bean, Artichoke, and Olive
Oil Tomato Salad

Warm Spinach Salad with Beets,
Apples, Warm Bacon Vinaigrette,
Fried Egg, and Petite Grilled
Cheddar Cheese Sandwich

Lobster and Duck Confit Salad

Mixed California Greens with
Balsamic Strawberries, Fresh
Ricotta, and Brioche

Heirloom Tomato Carpaccio
with Roasted Cipolline Onions,
Poached Pears, Arugula,
and Pear Vinaigrette

Contemporary Caesar Salad

SERVES: 4

DRESSING

1½ tsp garlic, minced

3 white anchovy filets

Pinch salt

Pinch freshly ground black pepper

2 Tbsp pasteurized egg yolks

2 Tbsp lemon juice

2 Tbsp water

½ cup extra-virgin olive oil

¼ cup finely grated Parmigiano-Reggiano

BRIOCHE

4 slices brioche

To taste, kosher salt

To taste, freshly ground black pepper

As needed, clarified butter, melted

ROMAINE

1 heart of romaine, large

PARMIGIANO COOKIES

1 cup grated Parmigiano-Reggiano

ASSEMBLY

12 white anchovies

To taste, extra-virgin olive oil

DRESSING

1. In a small food processor, add garlic, anchovy filets, and a pinch of salt and pepper. Puree until smooth.

2. Add the pasteurized yolks, lemon juice, and water. Process for 30 seconds.

3. While the processor is running, slowly add the oil to form an emulsion. Remove the mixture from the processor and place in a small bowl.

4. Stir in the Parmigiano-Reggiano. Adjust the seasoning with salt and pepper if needed. Place the dressing in a squirt bottle and reserve.

BRIOCHE

1. Season both sides of each brioche slice with kosher salt and pepper and drizzle with melted clarified butter.

2. Place the brioche slices on a wire rack and the rack on a baking sheet. Toast in a 350°F oven until golden brown. Reserve for service.

ROMAINE

1. Holding the heart of romaine lettuce upright, dress the inside and outside of the lettuce using the dressing in the squirt bottle.

2. Tightly wrap the dressed romaine heart in plastic wrap to form a cylinder. Refrigerate ½ hour so the romaine holds its shape.

1. Place a Silpat on a baking sheet. Use a 4-in. round mold to form 4 circles of Parmigiano-Reggiano on the Silpat.

2. Bake the circles in a 350°F oven for 5–7 minutes or until the cheese is slightly browned. Allow to cool. Remove from Silpat.

ASSEMBLY

1. Place the brioche slices in the center of 4 plates.

2. Cut the head of romaine into 4 equal slices, 1½ to 2 in. thick. Place a romaine round on top of each brioche slice.

3. Top each romaine round with a Parmigiano cookie.

4. Roll up each white anchovy and place 3 on each plate. Drizzle with remaining Caesar dressing and olive oil to taste.

French Bean, Artichoke, and Olive Oil Tomato Salad

SERVES: 4

1 gal water

1 cup kosher salt

12 oz haricots verts, cleaned

2 heads frisée

13 prepared artichokes, halved

2 cups grapeseed oil

1 Tbsp mixed Italian seasoning

1 cup all-purpose flour

To taste, kosher salt

¼ cup aged red wine vinegar

Pinch kosher salt

Pinch cracked black pepper

24 petals Olive Oil Tomatoes (see Chef's Pantry)

1. In a medium stockpot, combine the water and salt. Bring to a rapid boil over high heat.

2. Add the haricots verts to the boiling water and cook until al dente, 3–5 minutes. Drop into an ice water bath to shock the beans and stop the cooking process. After 2 minutes, remove the beans from the ice water bath and blot dry with paper towels. Reserve.

3. Clean the frisée by removing the bottom and trimming off the dark green outer leaves. Cut into smaller pieces and wash in very cold water. Spin dry in a salad spinner or pat dry with paper towels. Reserve for service.

4. Remove the leaves from one of the prepared artichokes. Pat dry with paper towels.

5. In a 2-qt saucepan, bring the grapeseed oil to approximately 325°F.

6. Combine the Italian seasoning with the flour. Toss the artichoke leaves with the seasoned flour. Shake off excess flour and place in the heated oil. Fry for 1 to 2 minutes until crisp. Remove the artichoke leaves from the oil and drain on paper towels. Season lightly with kosher salt and reserve for service.

7. To make the dressing, place the vinegar in a small bowl with a pinch of salt and pepper. Whisking constantly, slowly add ¾ cup of the oil from the olive oil tomatoes to form an emulsion.

8. At time of service, combine the tomato petals, frisée, haricots verts, and the halved artichokes in a medium-size bowl. Season lightly with salt and Pepper. Toss the mixture lightly with the dressing. Divide the salad among 4 chilled service plates. Garnish with the artichoke chips.

Warm Spinach Salad with Beets, Apples, Warm Bacon Vinaigrette, Fried Egg, and Petite Grilled Cheddar Cheese Sandwich

SERVES: 4

DRESSING

2 slices apple-smoked bacon, diced small

1 shallot, small, sliced thin

¼ cup apple cider

¼ cup applesauce or apple puree

¼ cup apple cider vinegar

1 Tbsp Dijon mustard

1 cup grapeseed oil

To taste, kosher salt

To taste, cracked black pepper

BEETS

2 red beets, small (or 1 large)

1 Tbsp extra-virgin olive oil

To taste, kosher salt

To taste, cracked black pepper

GRILLED CHEESE

2 oz Vermont cheddar, sliced very thin

4 slices Pullman loaf

1 Tbsp butter, unsalted, softened

ASSEMBLY

4 eggs, medium

1 Tbsp butter, unsalted

1 green apple, large

12 oz baby spinach with stems removed

DRESSING

1. In a small saucepan, render the diced bacon over low heat. Once it begins to turn light brown, add the shallot and cook until translucent.

2. Add the cider and the puree and reduce by half over medium heat, stirring often to avoid burning. Add the cider vinegar and remove from the heat. Cool the mixture completely over an ice bath.

3. Add the Dijon mustard and combine well with a whisk. Slowly add the grapeseed oil while whisking.

4. Season to taste with kosher salt and pepper. Reserve for service.

BEETS

1. Preheat the oven to 350°F.

2. Toss the beets in the olive oil and season with salt and pepper. Place in a small roasting pan, pour in ½ in. water, and cover with foil. Bake for 40 minutes or until fork tender.

3. Remove the beets from the pan and cool slightly before peeling. They are easier to peel when still warm. Allow the peeled beets to cool completely and reserve.

GRILLED CHEESE

1. Arrange the cheese evenly on the slices of bread. Close to form 2 sandwiches and use the softened butter to coat each outside face.

2. Toast in a nonstick pan until the sandwich is golden and the cheese is melted. Reserve in a warm place.

ASSEMBLY

1. Heat the dressing gently in a small saucepan.

2. Fry the eggs in a nonstick skillet with the butter to desired doneness. (It is recommended but not essential that you leave the yolks soft.) Place on paper towels to drain.

3. Julienne the apple and beets on a mandoline, starting with the apple. (Do this at the last moment so the apple does not brown and no lemon is required.) Place the spinach, apples, and beets in a large bowl and toss with the warm dressing.

4. Working quickly, place the dressed mixture in the center of 4 salad plates. Remove the crusts from the sandwiches and cut each sandwich into 8 equal pieces. Arrange the mini sandwiches neatly on the plates next to the salad.

5. Place 1 egg on top of each salad. Serve immediately.

Lobster and Duck Confit Salad

SERVES: 4

1 butternut squash, small

As needed, olive oil

6 oz butter, unsalted

12 oz picked lobster meat

½ cup white balsamic vinegar

1 tsp lavender honey

¼ cup heavy cream

Pinch kosher salt

Pinch cracked black pepper

1 Tbsp chopped tarragon

1 ½ cups grapeseed oil

2 heads frisée

4 legs Duck Confit (see Chef's Pantry)

To taste, kosher salt

To taste, cracked black pepper

1. Peel the butternut squash and remove the seeds. Cut into ¼-in. cubes. Toss lightly with the olive oil and season with salt and pepper. Place on a baking sheet and roast in a preheated 350°F oven for 20 to 25 minutes or until caramelized and tender. Reserve for service.

2. Melt the butter in a small saucepan. Add the picked lobster meat and mix well. Cover and reserve in a warm place until service.

3. In a medium mixing bowl, place the vinegar, honey, heavy cream, salt, pepper, and chopped tarragon. While whisking constantly, slowly add the olive oil. Adjust seasoning with salt and pepper and reserve for service.

4. Trim the dark green outer leaves and remove the core from the frisée. Cut into bite-size pieces and wash thoroughly in very cold water. Dry the frisée and reserve for service.

5. At time of service, place the duck confit under the broiler and heat until the meat is warmed through and the skin is crisp. Heat the dressing slightly over low heat. Place the frisée and the butternut squash in a mixing bowl and toss lightly with the dressing and salt and pepper to taste.

6. Divide the mixture among 4 salad plates. Evenly distribute the lobster meat among the salads. Place 1 duck leg on top of each salad. Serve immediately.

Mixed California Greens with Balsamic Strawberries, Fresh Ricotta, and Brioche

Serves: 4

½ cup champagne

1 cup mixed berries

2 Tbsp Cinnamon Honey (see Chef's Pantry)

1 oz butter, unsalted

½ cup champagne vinegar

1½ cups grapeseed oil

1 Tbsp chopped mint

To taste, kosher salt

To taste, cracked black pepper

12 strawberries, quartered

3 Tbsp 12-year-old balsamic vinegar

4 mini brioche rolls

4 Tbsp fresh ricotta

12 oz mesclun greens

1. In a stainless-steel saucepan, combine the champagne, mixed berries, Cinnamon Honey, and butter. Bring to a boil and let simmer for 5 minutes. Remove from heat and allow to cool slightly. Puree in blender and strain. Cool liquid completely in an ice bath.

2. In a medium mixing bowl, combine the cooled liquid and the champagne vinegar. While whisking, slowly add the grapeseed oil to form an emulsion. Add the chopped mint and season to taste with salt and pepper. Reserve for service.

3. In a small bowl, combine the strawberries with the balsamic vinegar. Toss gently and allow to stand for 30 minutes.

4. Cut a small *V*-shape into the top of each brioche roll. Lightly toast the brioche in a 350°F oven for 3–4 minutes. Allow to cool before adding ricotta. Place 1 Tbsp ricotta into the top of each brioche. Reserve for service.

5. At time of service, gently toss the greens with the berry dressing and season with salt and pepper. Divide the greens evenly among 4 chilled salad plates. Add an equal amount of the marinated strawberries to each plate. Place 1 ricotta brioche on each salad and serve immediately.

Heirloom Tomato Carpaccio with Roasted Cipolline Onions, Poached Pears, Arugula, and Pear Vinaigrette

SERVES: 4

12 cipolline onions, peeled

2 sprigs thyme

1 Tbsp brown sugar

1 Tbsp honey

To taste, kosher salt

To taste, cracked black pepper

2 Tbsp butter, unsalted

2 cups Chicken Brodo (see Chef's Pantry)

3 cups port wine

1 cup orange juice

1 cinnamon stick

¼ cup honey

1 star anise

2 pears

¼ cup pear puree

½ cup pear balsamic vinegar

1½ cups grapeseed oil

To taste, extra-virgin olive oil

2 heirloom tomatoes, large, or 4 small

12 oz arugula, picked over and washed

1. In a shallow ovenproof container, place the onions, thyme sprigs, and brown sugar; mix gently. Drizzle with 1 Tbsp honey, salt, and pepper. Dice the butter and distribute evenly over the onions. Add the chicken broth to barely cover the bottom of the baking dish. Place into a preheated 400°F oven. Roast onions 20 to 25 minutes, stirring and basting every 3 to 5 minutes, until tender and glazed. Add more chicken broth as necessary. Remove from the oven and allow to cool. Reserve for service.

2. In a stainless-steel 2-qt saucepan, combine the port wine, orange juice, cinnamon stick, ¼ cup honey, and star anise. Peel the pears, cut in half, and core. Place pears in the wine mixture, bring to a simmer over medium heat for 15 to 20 minutes or until fork tender. Cool the pears and the liquid over an ice bath. Dice the pears small and reserve for service. Save the poaching liquid, as it can be used again in other applications.

3. In a medium mixing bowl, combine the pear puree, pear balsamic vinegar, and ¼ cup of the poaching liquid from the pears. Mix thoroughly. Slowly add the grapeseed oil, whisking constantly to form an emulsion. Season to taste with salt and pepper. Reserve for service.

4. At time of service, slice the tomatoes as thin as possible and arrange to cover the inside of 4 chilled salad plates.

5. Lightly drizzle the tomatoes with olive oil and season with salt and pepper. Gently toss the arugula with the pear vinaigrette and place approximately 3 oz in the center of each plate.

6. Arrange 3 onions and some of the poached pears around the arugula. Serve immediately.

4

Main Plate Salads

Main plate salads are receiving newfound culinary attention and these days are often seen on the dinner menu as well as the lunch menu. The need for a more casual dinner meal, one that can be served quickly, has encouraged many chefs to develop these salads. Whether for lunch or dinner, a main plate salad is a good alternative to having a full meal.

What exactly is a main plate salad? Aren't chef salads and Cobb salads main plate salads? They are in the sense that they offer protein and offer a full plate of food. The primary difference between these and a main plate salad is that the latter focuses on vegetables, fruits, or proteins rather than salad greens.

These diced, sliced, or otherwise prepared items are typically tossed with dressing, then placed so as to dominate the presentation from the top and side views, covering the greens underneath. A perfect example is my club's Executive Chef Seafood Salad. It includes four types of seafood, salad greens wrapped in asparagus ribbons, other vegetables, a light dressing, and a white tartar sauce.

Try the generous salads in this chapter, or be inspired to create your own main plate salads for a special dining treat.

MENU

Executive Chef Salad

*Romaine Lettuce, Bibb and Endive, Cinnamon-Spiced
Skirt Steak, Beet and Potato Salad, French Beans,
Crispy Goat Cheese, and Apple Cider Dressing*

Lobster Cobb Salad

*Romaine, Frisée, and Bibb Lettuce with Lobster,
Avocado, Pancetta, Egg, Spiced Ricotta,
and Vanilla Vinaigrette*

Executive Chef Seafood Salad

*Mixed Greens, Grilled Shrimp, Petite Crab Cake,
Marinated Lobster, Mignon of Salmon with Fingerlings,
and Honey Thyme Dressing*

Pomegranate Crab Salad
with Cucumbers, Asparagus,
and Crab Cake

Grilled Portobello, Heirloom
Tomato, Cipolline, Artichoke,
and Asparagus

Executive Chef Salad

SERVES: 4

Four 4-oz skirt steaks

3 Tbsp Master's Steak Seasoning

1 Tbsp cinnamon

2 golden beets

2 Tbsp kosher salt

To taste, extra-virgin olive oil

To taste, kosher salt

To taste, cracked black pepper

2 Yukon Gold potatoes

2 Tbsp kosher salt

12 oz haricots verts

1 cup kosher salt

8 oz goat cheese

1 cup all-purpose flour

2 eggs, beaten lightly

1 cup panko bread crumbs

1 head Bibb lettuce

1 head romaine

1 head Belgian endive

As needed, Apple Cider Dressing (see Chef's Pantry)

1. Remove all fat and sinew from the steaks. Combine the steak seasoning and cinnamon. Gently rub into both sides of meat and reserve for service.

2. Place the beets in a medium saucepan and cover with cold water. Add 4 Tbsp kosher salt and bring to a simmer over medium heat. Allow the beets to cook until a knife can be inserted and removed easily. Place cooked beets in an ice bath to stop the cooking process; let cool. Use a small knife to remove the skin from the beets. Slice them into 16 even slices, about ⅛ in. thick. Toss lightly with olive oil, kosher salt, and pepper, then reserve for service.

3. Cook the potatoes in the same way as the beets, but do not peel them. Slice the cooked and cooled potatoes into 16 even slices, marinate as for the beets, and reserve for service.

4. Bring 1 gal water and 1 cup kosher salt to a rolling boil over high heat. While you are waiting for the water to boil, trim both ends of the haricots verts using a small knife. Add the haricots verts to the boiling water and and cook until al dente. Plunge the beans into an ice bath to stop the cooking process. Drain, then marinate with olive oil, kosher salt, and black pepper. Reserve for service.

5. Cut the goat cheese into 8 equal portions. Toss the cheese with the flour and shake off excess. Place the floured cheese in the beaten egg. Remove from the egg and toss with panko bread crumbs to coat evenly. Remove from bread crumbs and reserve for service.

6. Remove the brown leaves from the Bibb lettuce and the romaine and trim the bottoms. Cut into medium-size pieces. Wash in very cold water, dry using a salad spinner, and reserve for service.

7. Trim the bottom end of the Belgian endive and remove 8 leaves. Cut the leaves into 1-in. pieces. Reserve for service.

8. At time of service, grill the steak to the desired temperature and place on a wire rack to rest for at least 10 minutes.

9. While the meat is resting, deep fry the goat cheese until golden brown. Drain on paper towels and sprinkle lightly with kosher salt.

10. Combine the salad greens in a medium mixing bowl. Toss with the dressing and season with kosher salt and pepper. Divide the salad evenly among 4 salad plates. Arrange the beet and potato slices in a half-moon shape to one side of the salad greens, alternating beets and potatoes. Place equal portions of the haricots verts in a small bundle at the top of the beets and potatoes. Slice the skirt steak into 5 slices and place on top of the salad greens. Garnish each salad with 2 pieces of fried goat cheese. Serve immediately.

Lobster Cobb Salad

SERVES: 4

VANILLA VINAIGRETTE

1 vanilla bean, split and scraped

¼ cup sugar

¼ cup water

1 tsp vanilla extract

2 oz rice wine vinegar

1 Tbsp Dijon mustard

6 oz grapeseed oil

To taste, kosher salt

To taste, freshly ground black pepper

SALAD

Two 1¼-lb lobsters

As needed, Court Bouillon (see Chef's Pantry)

12 oz mixed greens (baby romaine, Bibb lettuce, frisée)

1 zucchini, small, thinly sliced lengthwise to form ribbons

4 slices pancetta

4 Tbsp fresh ricotta

1 tsp Spice de Cosette

2 eggs, hard-boiled, cut in half

1 avocado, quartered and sliced

4 flatbread pieces

2 vanilla beans, split

2 Tbsp lemon zest

VANILLA VINAIGRETTE

1. Combine the vanilla bean and seeds, sugar, and water in a small saucepan. Bring to a boil, remove from heat, and allow to steep for 20 minutes. Cool and reserve.

2. In a bowl, combine the vanilla syrup, vanilla extract, vinegar, and mustard. Whisk until incorporated.

3. Slowly stream in the oil while whisking continuously to form an emulsion.

4. Season to taste with kosher salt and pepper; reserve.

SALAD

1. Poach the lobster in the Court Bouillon for 10 minutes. Drain.

2. Remove the lobster meat from the shell and divide it into 4 portions.

3. Divide the lettuce into 4 bunches and wrap with zucchini ribbon.

4. Place the pancetta on a Silpat and cover with another Silpat; place a sheet pan on top, and bake at 350°F until crisp, about 15 minutes.

5. Mix the ricotta with the Spice de Cosette. Form quenelles and place on flatbreads.

6. Place the lettuce bundles in the center of 4 large plates. Arrange the lobster around the bundles and top with egg, avocado, and flatbread. Drizzle 1½ oz Vanilla Vinaigrette over each salad. Garnish each with ½ vanilla bean and ½ Tbsp lemon zest.

Executive Chef Seafood Salad

SERVES: 4

HONEY THYME DRESSING

2 oz honey

2 oz lemon juice

1 tsp thyme, picked

To taste, salt

To taste, freshly ground black pepper

¾ cup extra-virgin olive oil

LOBSTER AND POTATO

One 1¼-lb lobster

As needed, Court Bouillon (see Chef's Pantry)

8 oz salmon filet

8 fingerling potatoes

CRAB CAKES

1 tsp minced shallot

1 tsp Dijon mustard

1 tsp chopped parsley

1 egg

4 oz jumbo lump crabmeat

2 oz bread crumbs, or as needed

ASSEMBLY

12 oz mixed greens (butter lettuce, frisée, mesclun)

1 zucchini, sliced paper-thin

2 Tbsp extra-virgin olive oil

4 jumbo shrimp

As needed, Tomato Syrup (see Chef's Pantry)

MARINADE FOR SHRIMP AND SALMON

1 tsp Spice de Cosette

6 Tbsp extra-virgin olive oil

2 Tbsp lemon juice

DRESSING

1. Combine the honey, lemon juice, thyme, salt, and pepper in a bowl and whisk together until incorporated.

2. Whisking vigorously, slowly drizzle in the olive oil to form an emulsion. Reserve.

LOBSTER AND POTATO

1. Poach the lobster in Court Bouillon for 10 minutes.

2. Remove the lobster meat from shell and reserve.

3. Cut the salmon into 4 equal portions. Toss the salmon and shrimp with marinade ingredients and allow to sit for 15 minutes.

4. In a small saucepan, cook the potatoes in heavily salted water until tender. Peel while hot and reserve.

CRAB CAKES

1. Place the shallot, mustard, parsley, and egg in a bowl and mix thoroughly. Gently fold in the crabmeat and then add bread crumbs as needed to tighten mixture. Divide the mixture into 4 portions and form into small patties.

ASSEMBLY

1. Divide the salad greens into 4 bundles and wrap each with a zucchini ribbon.

2. Heat the olive oil in a large sauté pan over medium-high heat. Sear the salmon for 30 seconds on one side, turn over, and cook for another 30 seconds.

3. Add the crab cakes to the pan and cook until browned on both sides. Add the shrimp. When all are cooked through, reserve.

4. Place the greens in the center of 4 large salad plates. Arrange the seafood and potato as shown. Top with a crab cake. Drizzle dressing over the salad greens. Dot plate with Tomato Syrup.

Pomegranate Crab Salad with Cucumbers, Asparagus, and Crab Cake

SERVES: 4

POMEGRANATE DRESSING

2 Tbsp lime juice

4 Tbsp pear vinegar

1 tsp Dijon mustard

2 tsp Spice de Cosette

3 Tbsp Anise honey

½ cup mayonnaise

To taste, kosher salt

To taste, freshly ground black pepper

¼ cup pomegranate juice

2 Tbsp olive oil

SALAD

12 oz picked lump crabmeat

½ cup pomegranate seeds

¼ cup roasted corn, cut from the cob

4 Tbsp almond oil

1 Tbsp champagne vinegar

2 tsp chopped basil

CRAB CAKES

½ tsp minced thyme

½ cup high-quality or house-made mayonnaise

1 Tbsp worcestershire sauce

⅓ tsp Chipotle sauce

⅓ oz dry mustard

1 tsp whole-grain mustard

1 tsp Spice de Cosette (see Chef's Pantry)

1 lb lump crabmeat

1 avocado, diced

⅓ cup seasoned fresh bread crumbs

1 tsp salt

½ tsp ground white pepper

3 tsp Old Bay Seasoning

1 Tbsp chopped parsley

As needed, canola oil

ASSEMBLY

24 spears white or green asparagus, blanched

1 cucumber, sliced thin lengthwise

To taste, Pomegranate Syrup (see Chef's Pantry)

DRESSING

1. Blend all items well and reserve.

SALAD

1. Toss all items together, let marinate for 30 minutes.

CRAB CAKES

1. In a bowl, combine the thyme, mayonnaise, Worcestershire sauce, chipotle sauce, dry mustard, whole-grain mustard, and Spice de Cosette. Mix well.

2. Gently fold the lump crabmeat and avocado into the thyme mixture. Shape into 4-oz cakes.

3. Dredge the crab cakes in the bread crumbs, salt, white pepper, Old Bay Seasoning, and chopped parsley.

4. Sauté the crab cakes in a minimal amount of canola oil until golden brown. Finish in a 350°F oven for 10–12 minutes.

ASSEMBLY

1. Wrap 6 asparagus spears in cucumber slices to make 4 bundles. Place on plates.

2. Add 1 crab cake, 3 oz crab salad, and remaining cucumber ribbons. Drizzle with dressing and Pomegranate Syrup.

Grilled Portobello, Heirloom Tomato, Cipolline, Artichoke, and Asparagus

SERVES: 4

4 portobello caps, stem removed and black scraped off inside

3 Tbsp olive oil

1 Tbsp balsamic vinegar

1 yellow heirloom tomato, sliced medium

1 red heirloom tomato, sliced medium

16 grape tomatoes, yellow and red, peeled

2 cooked Roma artichokes

8 spears grilled asparagus

12 roasted cipolline onions

1 loaf semolina bread, with crust removed and sliced

2 Tbsp extra virgin olive oil

4 slices Carrot Bacon (see Chef's Pantry)

1 zucchini, sliced thin

2 lemons

½ cup extra virgin olive oil

2 minced garlic cloves

2 sprigs thyme, picked

2 Tbsp simple syrup

1 Tbsp olive oil

½ cup fresh fava beans

2 shallots, sliced thin

6 Tbsp soft Brie cheese

To taste, kosher salt and ground black pepper

2 Tbsp Balsamic Reduction (see Chef's Pantry)

1. Mix oil and vinegar, and brush the mixture on the portobello caps. Grill for 3–4 minutes on each side. Reserve.

2. Ensure that the tomatoes, onions, asparagus and artichokes are at room temperature, and place them on a baking tray.

3. Brush the bread slices with olive oil, and grill 1–2 minutes per side. Reserve.

4. Grill thin zucchini slices for 1–2 minutes per side.

5. For dressing, in a stainless steel bowl add lemon juice, olive oil, garlic, thyme and simple syrup. Whisk very well or use a blending stick.

6. In a small sauté pan add oil and then shallots, sauté until soft.

7. On toast, spread the Brie cheese, top with warm shallots, then fava beans.

8. Brush well all the vegetables on the tray with the dressing.

9. Season with salt and pepper.

10. On a plate, place a portobello cap sliced or unsliced, followed by artichoke, sliced tomatoes, grape tomatoes, and asparagus.

11. Wrap onions with zucchini slices and place them on the plate. Garnish the plate with the carrot bacon and the fava bean toast.

12. Drizzle the plate with the Balsamic Reduction.

For a unique touch, I like to add a bit of my favorite sorbet with herbs such as pineapple sage.

5

Sandwiches

Sandwiches are as popular as ever—both standards and new combinations that emerge from the growing variety of breads and fillings available. The three elements of a great-tasting sandwich are bread, dressing, and filling.

Bread Use a high-quality bread that has a golden brown crust and great texture. Choose a bread that complements the flavor profile of the sandwich—for example, vanilla brioche with lobster salad—to enhance the lunch experience.

Dressing or Sandwich Spread A sandwich may be dressed in many ways beyond the traditional mayonnaise and mustard. A dill mayonnaise, for example, goes great with a salmon club, as does stone-ground mustard dressing. Always use the finest ingredients and be sure the dressing enhances the main items in the sandwich without overpowering them.

The Fillings Fillings can range from sliced meats or cold cuts to grilled items to salads such as shrimp or the classic tuna. They can be hot, cold, or even room temperature. Of course, fillings should be made with the freshest products available. Standards like turkey and roast beef should be purchased raw, then seasoned and roasted to moist perfection. It is important that main proteins that are grilled, such as chicken, shrimp, meats, or vegetables, are not overcooked, as the sandwich will be dry and not enjoyable for eating. The range of fillings is limited only by the imagination of the person preparing the sandwiches. Classic fillings can take on a seasonal twist. For example, in the fall, roasted apples and pears can be mixed in a traditional chicken salad along with a touch of pecan oil.

Traditional sandwiches can be renewed, as the Sports House Reuben, which has pastrami and corned beef with Munster cheese and a spiced sauce. Instead of a BLT, try the SBLT—the usual bacon, lettuce, and tomato, plus salmon.

Sandwiches are here to stay. They are favorites of club members and customers everywhere.

Lobster Club Sandwich

Lobster Burger with Foie Gras and
Yellow Tomato on Vanilla Brioche

SBLT (Salmon, Bacon, Lettuce,
and Tomato)

Sports House Reuben

Emiliana Panini

*Prosciutto, Fresh Mozzarella, Fried Eggplant,
and Tomato Sauce*

Sardinia Panini

*Tuna Salad, Roasted Onions, and Provolone
with Tomatoes*

Chicken and Pear Monte Cristo

Lobster Club Sandwich

SERVES: 4

1 qt Lobster Essence (see Chef's Pantry)

2 oz carrot, diced

2 oz onion, diced

2 oz celery, diced

1 bay leaf

Juice of 1 lemon

1 Tbsp Spice de Cosette

2 Maine lobster tails

1 vanilla bean

2 oz mayonnaise

1 vanilla brioche, baguette size

To taste, butter, unsalted, softened

1 Roma tomato

4 oz iceberg lettuce

4 slices bacon, cooked

1. Place the lobster stock in a 2-qt saucepan. Add the carrot, onion, celery, bay leaf, lemon juice, and Spice de Cosette, and bring to a strong simmer. Place the lobster tails in the stock and blanch for 3–5 minutes or until the lobster is fully cooked. Remove the lobster from the stock and place in ice water to stop the cooking process. After it has cooled, remove the meat from the shells. Slice the lobster meat into ¼-in. slices.

2. Split the vanilla bean and scrape the seeds into the mayonnaise. Mix thoroughly and reserve for service.

3. Slice the brioche into 12 slices, about ¼ in. thick. Spread softened butter on all of the slices and brown lightly in a nonstick skillet.

4. Slice 4 thin slices of tomato and reserve.

5. Cut the lettuce into pieces the same size as the brioche slices.

6. At time of service, spread a thin layer of vanilla mayonnaise on 1 brioche slice. Place 1 slice of the lobster tail on the bread. Place a second brioche slice on top of the lobster tail. Spread a small amount of mayonnaise on the second slice. Add 1 slice of the tomato, some lettuce, and a slice of bacon. Top with a third brioche slice. Secure with a toothpick or wooden skewer. Repeat to make 3 more sandwiches.

Lobster Burger with Foie Gras and Yellow Tomato on Vanilla Brioche

SERVES: 6

10 oz raw shrimp, peeled and deveined

6 oz sole

Juice of 1 lemon

4–5 oz heavy cream

Dash Tabasco Sauce

To taste, salt

To taste, ground white pepper

2 tsp Spice de Cosette

1 lb raw lobster meat (small dice from whole lobsters or diced raw tail meat; see Note)

1 Tbsp chopped dill

1 oz shallots, diced and sautéed

6 slices foie gras

12 enriched dollar-size buns

12 yellow tomato slices

To taste, extra-virgin olive oil

To taste, sea salt

1 oz frisée

To taste, vinaigrette

1. Place the shrimp and sole in a food processor and puree. Add the lemon juice, cream, Tabasco, salt, white pepper, and Spice de Cosette.

2. Remove the puree from the food processor and place in a bowl with the diced lobster meat. Add the dill and sautéed shallots, mix well, and let rest for at least 2 hours in the refrigerator.

3. Shape the mixture into 6 equal patties and grill 1–3 minutes on each side.

4. When the burgers are almost done, cook the foie gras to medium temperature in a heavy iron skillet on top of the grill.

5. Split the buns and place a slice of yellow tomato on the bottom of each. Place a lobster burger on top of each tomato slice and a slice of foie gras on top the tomato. Place some frisée on the foie gras and cover with the top half of the bun.

NOTE: Lobster meat can be difficult to remove from the shells. Plunging the whole lobsters into boiling water for 1–2 minutes makes the job easier. The lobster should not be fully cooked for this recipe.

SBLT (Salmon, Bacon, Lettuce, and Tomato)

SERVES: 6

12 slices fresh salmon, 2½ oz each

To taste, kosher salt

To taste, freshly ground black pepper

3 Tbsp olive oil

18 slices white bread, toasted

4 oz mayonnaise

¼ head iceberg lettuce

1 Beefsteak tomato, sliced

18 slices smoked bacon, cooked

2 Tbsp extra-virgin olive oil

1. Season the salmon with salt, pepper, and olive oil. Pan-sear 1–2 minutes on each side. The salmon should be firm and have a nice brown color. Let cool.

2. Lay out the bread slices and spread mayonnaise lightly on one side of each.

3. On 6 slices, place lettuce and tomato slices. Add 1½ bacon slices. Drizzle with extra-virgin olive oil.

4. Distribute the salmon over 6 more bread slices.

5. Place the remaining bacon on the remaining bread slices. Stack the sandwiches club-style, insert sandwich picks, cut in fours, and serve with pear tomato salad or potato chips.

Sports House Reuben

<small>SERVES: 4</small>

To taste, butter, unsalted, softened

8 slices rye bread

12 slices Swiss cheese

12 oz sauerkraut

1½ lb high-quality corned beef, thinly sliced

8 oz Chef Leonard's Special Sauce (see Chef's Pantry)

1. Spread a thin layer of softened butter on one side of each slice of the rye bread. Heat a nonstick skillet over medium heat. Place the rye bread butter-side down in the skillet and brown lightly. Remove the bread and place on a board, browned side down.

2. On each piece of bread, place 1½ slices Swiss cheese.

3. Divide the sauerkraut and corned beef evenly among the other 4 slices of the bread. Stack to form the sandwiches.

4. Place the sandwiches in a 300°F oven to warm through and melt the cheese, about 7 minutes. Serve with potato chips and a side of the Special Sauce.

ABOVE: *Emiliana Panini*

BELOW: *Sardinia Panini*

Emiliana Panini

SERVES: 4

1 eggplant, medium size

To taste, kosher salt

To taste, freshly ground black pepper

4 eggs

2 cups all-purpose flour

4 cups Italian bread crumbs

4 oz extra-virgin olive oil

8 slices ciabatta

12 oz fresh mozzarella

8 oz prosciutto, sliced thin

As needed, extra-virgin olive oil

1. Slice the eggplant into ¼-in. rounds. Season with salt and pepper.

2. Crack the eggs into a small mixing bowl and whisk lightly. Coat the eggplant lightly with flour, dip in the beaten eggs, remove from the eggs, and coat thoroughly with bread crumbs.

3. In a heavy-bottomed skillet, heat the olive oil over medium to high heat. Brown the breaded eggplant on both sides and drain on paper towels.

4. Place 4 slices of bread on a board and cover the slices with fried eggplant. Top each with 3 oz of the fresh mozzarella. Divide the prosciutto evenly among the sandwiches. Top with the remaining bread.

5. Drizzle each side of the sandwich with olive oil, place on a panini grill, and grill until lightly browned. Serve with a small side salad.

Sardinia Panini

2 oz extra-virgin olive oil

1 sweet onion, cut in ¼-in. slices

16 oz high-quality tuna packed in olive oil

To taste, kosher salt

To taste, freshly ground black pepper

4 Tbsp mayonnaise

8 slices ciabatta

8 slices aged provolone

12 petals Olive Oil Tomatoes (see Chef's Pantry)

As needed, extra-virgin olive oil

1. Heat a heavy-bottomed skillet over medium-high heat. Add 2 oz olive oil and brown the onion slices on both sides. Remove the onions from pan and drain on paper towels.

2. Drain the tuna and place in a small mixing bowl. Season with salt and pepper. Toss with enough mayonnaise to coat the tuna lightly.

3. Lay out 4 slices of the ciabatta. Divide the onions evenly among the slices. Place 2 slices of provolone on each piece of bread. Top with 4 oz tuna. Place 3 Olive Oil Tomatoes petals on top of the tuna. Cover with the remaining slices of bread.

4. Drizzle each side of sandwich with extra virgin olive oil. Place on panini grill and cook until golden brown.

Chicken and Pear Monte Cristo

3 cups port wine

1 cup fresh orange juice

1 cinnamon stick

¼ cup honey

1 star anise

2 pears

Four 6-oz chicken breasts, cleaned

To taste, kosher salt

To taste, freshly ground black pepper

To taste, olive oil

8 thick slices brioche

4 oz high-quality Brie

4 eggs

1 Tbsp granulated sugar

1 tsp potato starch

2 Tbsp milk

2 Tbsp butter, unsalted

As needed, confectioner's sugar

1. In a stainless-steel 2-qt saucepan, combine the port wine, orange juice, cinnamon stick, honey, and star anise. Peel, halve, and core the pears. Place the pear halves in the wine mixture and bring to a simmer over medium heat. Allow the pears to simmer gently until fork-tender. Cool the entire mixture over an ice bath. Remove the cooled pears and cut into ¼-in. vertical

slices. Reserve for service. Save the poaching liquid, as it can be used again or in other applications.

2. Season the chicken with salt and pepper. Gently rub with olive oil and grill until cooked through.

3. Place 4 bread slices on the workstation. Cut each chicken breast into 4 slices and place on a slice of bread.

4. Evenly divide the poached pears among the 4 sandwiches. Cut the Brie into 4 equal pieces and place 1 on each sandwich. Top with the remaining slices of bread.

5. In a medium mixing bowl, combine the eggs, sugar, potato starch, and milk. Whisk thoroughly to combine.

6. Preheat a large nonstick skillet over medium heat. Add the butter and allow it to melt until it turns foamy.

7. Dip the sandwiches in the egg batter and coat both sides thoroughly. Fry on each side for 2–3 minutes or until golden brown.

8. Remove the sandwiches from the pan and place on a cutting board. Cut in half and dust with confectioner's sugar. Place on warm plates and serve immediately.

6

Appetizers, Hors d'Oeuvre, Amuse-Bouches

The recipes featured in this chapter, no matter what name you give them, are the start of a reception or elegant dinner or the main feature of a cocktail party. They are what a chef may send with compliments to a table of guests before the meal.

At every stage of a meal or event, it is important to leave an impression on the guest. The appetizer course is a great opportunity to get guests talking about the food and its presentation and to interested them in the courses to come. It is a pleasure to observe the delighted reaction of guests when the service staff approaches with decorated and elegant trays of small bites of food. That delight is the experience one should have when eating those little bites traditionally known as *hors d'oeuvre*. I prefer to call them *appetizers* or *little plates* or *amuse-bouche*. I want my club members and their guests to look forward to the meal based on how wonderful the appetizer course was.

Much has changed in this category of food, both in presentation and the type of items served. That said, many people still love and ask for the traditional franks-in-a-blanket. Your job is to give them the best franks-in-a-blanket they ever had: a quality hotdog or petite hotdog, buttery, flaky puff pastry, and a high-quality mustard that shouts with flavor. Present it differently and make those franks-in-a-blanket new again.

The array of little bites of food is endless. This course is a grand one for showing off your culinary creativity. You can send out miniature versions of first plates, like a single seared scallop with pea coulis and truffle or an espresso cup filled with a rich and flavorful soup. The possibilities offer tremendous scope for the creative but sensible cooks who understand flavors.

I get ideas from books from all over the world—about the tapas of Spain, the dim sum of China—and I try to match flavor profiles that make exciting and tasty little bites of food. One approach is to cut down a lunch favorite to appetizer size, as I did with the lobster club sandwich. This chapter is full of flavorful, neat, practical items—and, most of all, great tasty food bites that will ensure a great start to any event.

MENU

The Chef's Canapés on a Stick

Melon and Prosciutto

Fig and Serrano Ham

Strawberry and Ricotta

Grilled Pineapple and Sage

Smoked Salmon and Cream Cheese

Trio of Crostini

Wild Mushroom

Olive Oil, Tomato, and Mozzarella

Seared Tuna and Red Pepper

Asparagus and Carrot Mousse on a Spoon

Tomato Tartar with Wine Jelly

Fruit Tartars with Caviar

Papaya Tartar

Strawberry Tartar

Avocado Tartar

Mango Tartar

Tomatoes Stuffed with Walnut Pesto

Sea Scallops with Pea Coulis

Soup Shots

Pistachio Soup

Moroccan Pumpkin Soup with Chickpeas

Avocado Soup with Salsa

Ginger Peach Soup

Cold Tomato Soup

Asparagus Soup

Velvet Chocolate Mousse with Spicy Baby Shrimp

Crispy Crab Fingers with Grand Marnier Orange Sections

Savory Cones with Potato and Truffle, Salade Niçoise, and Caesar Salad

The Chef's Canapés on a Stick

Melon and Prosciutto

SERVES: 6

1 ripe cantaloupe or other melon

6 thin slices prosciutto

1. Halve and seed the melon. With a large Parisian scoop, scoop out 6 balls of cantaloupe. Reserve the unused melon for later use.

2. Place 1 lollipop stick or wooden skewer in each piece of melon.

3. Holding by the skewer, wrap a slice of prosciutto around the melon and trim away extra meat with a small knife. Reserve the prosciutto trimmings for later use. Repeat for each skewered melon.

Fig and Serrano Ham

SERVES: 6

3 thin slices Serrano ham

3 brown Turkey figs

1. Lay out the ham slices. Using a small knife, cut each slice in half lengthwise to form 6 slices.

2. Cut each fig in half from top to bottom. Wrap each half in 1 slice of ham.

3. Place each wrapped fig on a lollipop stick or wooden skewer and serve.

Strawberry and Ricotta

SERVES: 6

6 strawberries, medium

3 oz fresh ricotta cheese

1. Wash strawberries gently under cold running water. Use a small knife to remove the stem from each strawberry. Cut a V-shaped incision in the tip of a strawberry. Turn the strawberry 90 degrees and cut another V-shaped incision. This should form an X on the tip of the strawberry. Incise each strawberry this way.

2. Place ½ oz ricotta into the incision on the tip of each strawberry. Place each filled strawberry on a lollipop stick or wooden skewer and serve.

Grilled Pineapple and Sage

SERVES: 6

1 pineapple

1 cup sugar

6 cups water

1 cup sage leaves, large

1. Using a serrated knife, remove all skin from the pineapple. Cut two 1-in. slices from the pineapple. Reserve the unused pineapple for later use. Grill the pineapple slices on both sides and place on a cutting board.

2. Using a 2-in. round cutter, punch out 6 rounds of pineapple, being careful not to include the core in the rounds.

Appetizers, Hors d'Oeuvre, Amuse-Bouches

3. In a small stainless-steel saucepan, combine the sugar, water, and scraps from the grilled pineapple. Bring this mixture to a boil, then remove from heat. Allow to cool for 10 minutes.

4. While the pineapple syrup is cooling, slice the sage leaves to into long, thin strips.

5. Wrap the outside of each round with sage and secure with a lollipop stick or wooden skewer.

6. Dip each pop into the syrup and serve.

Smoked Salmon and Cream Cheese

SERVES: 6

6 oz cream cheese

1 Tbsp fresh chives, chopped

6 thin slices smoked salmon, at least 4 in. in diameter

1. Combine cream cheese and chives. Mix thoroughly.

2. Divide the cream cheese mixture into 1-oz portions. Roll each portion in your hands to form small balls. Place a lollipop stick or wooden skewer in each ball. To make the cream cheese easier to handle, freeze the pops for 20 minutes or until firm.

3. Holding the stick, place 1 slice of smoked salmon over the cream cheese. Wrap tightly and trim away excess with a small knife. Reserve the trimmings for late use.

4. Allow the pops to thaw before serving.

Trio of Crostini

SERVES: 4

As needed, extra-virgin olive oil

10 oz assorted wild mushrooms, chopped

1 garlic clove, minced

1 shallot, small, minced

1 tsp finely chopped tarragon

To taste, kosher salt

To taste, cracked black pepper

2 Tbsp blended oil

8 oz ahi tuna, cleaned

1 baguette

To taste, sea salt

6 oz fresh mozzarella

12 petals Olive Oil Tomatoes (see Chef's Pantry)

3 basil leaves, chiffonade

To taste, crushed red pepper flakes

1. Preheat a sauté pan over high heat for 2 minutes. Add 2 Tbsp oil. Allow the oil to heat for about 1 minute. Add the mushrooms and sauté for 2 minutes. Add the chopped garlic and shallots. Continue to sauté for another 2 minutes or until the mushrooms are completely cooked; then remove from the heat and add the chopped tarragon. Season to taste with kosher salt and black pepper. Leave at room temperature and reserve for service.

2. Preheat a cast-iron pan over high heat. Season the tuna with kosher salt and black pepper. Add the blended oil to the pan and heat it until it just begins to smoke. Add the tuna and sear on all sides. The tuna should still be rare to medium rare at the end of the searing process. Remove the tuna from the pan and reserve at room temperature for service (no longer than 15 minutes).

3. Using a serrated knife, slice the baguette into ¼-in. slices. You will need 12 slices in all. Lay the slices on a baking sheet and drizzle with olive oil. Season lightly with kosher salt and pepper. Toast in a preheated 350°F oven for 8 minutes or until golden brown. Remove from oven and reserve for service.

4. At time of service, top 4 of the crostini with the mushroom mixture. Drizzle each with olive oil and season lightly with sea salt. Slice the fresh mozzarella into small pieces that fit on the crostini. Layer 2 tomato petals and 3 slices of the fresh mozzarella on 4 of the crostini. Sprinkle with the basil chiffonade and season lightly with olive oil, sea salt, and black pepper. Cut the tuna into 12 slices. Arrange 3 slices of the tuna on each of the 4 remaining crostini. Season with sea salt and crushed red pepper.

5. Place 1 of each crostini on each of 4 serving plates and serve immediately.

Appetizers, Hors d'Oeuvre, Amuse-Bouches

Asparagus and Carrot Mousse on a Spoon

SERVES: 8–12

ASPARAGUS MOUSSE

1 cup chopped trimmed asparagus

1 shallot, finely diced and sautéed in butter until tender

2 Tbsp thick mayonnaise

½ tsp fresh lime juice

Pinch cayenne pepper

6 Tbsp heavy cream

½ egg white

To taste, kosher salt

CARROT PUREE WITH GINGER

2 cups chopped carrots

½ cup clarified butter

4 Tbsp heavy cream, whipped to medium peaks

4 Tbsp crème fraîche

½ tsp finely minced fresh ginger

Pinch sea salt

ASPARAGUS MOUSSE

1. Cook the asparagus in salted boiling water until tender. Drain, place in a bowl of ice water to cool, remove, and dry well. Place into a processor with the shallot and puree until smooth. Pass the puree through a sieve.

2. Place the puree to a stainless-steel bowl and set it in a larger bowl of ice and water to chill for approximately 20 minutes. Remove the bowl and blend in the mayonnaise, lime juice, and cayenne. Cover and refrigerate.

3. Meanwhile, in a small bowl, whip the cream and set aside. In a separate bowl, beat the egg white with the salt until stiff peaks form.

4. Remove the chilled asparagus from the refrigerator and fold in the egg white and then the whipped cream. Season to taste. The mousse can be covered and set aside until serving time.

5. Make quenelles of the asparagus mousse and serve in party spoons. Garnish if desired.

CARROT PUREE WITH GINGER

1. Toss the carrots in the butter and roast in a 400°F oven, turning frequently, until tender and dry.

2. Place the roasted carrots in a food processor and puree. Pass the puree through a sieve.

3. Add the cream, crème fraîche, ginger, and salt. Shape into quenelles, then serve.

Tomato Tartar with Wine Jelly

SERVES: 6

1 cup muscat or white port

2 sheets sheet gelatin

3 Roma tomatoes

As needed, extra-virgin olive oil

To taste, kosher salt

To taste, freshly ground black pepper

2 oz Pecorino Romano, grated

1. In a small stainless-steel saucepan, bring the wine to a boil. Remove from heat.

2. Place the gelatin sheets in cold water for 1–2 minutes or until soft. Remove and squeeze out excess water. Place the gelatin in a small bowl and melt over a double boiler. Once melted, add to the wine and mix gently so as not to create bubbles.

3. Pour the wine mixture into a container large enough so the depth of the mixture is approximately ¼ in. Refrigerate until set, about 30 minutes.

4. In a 3-qt saucepan, bring 2 quarts of water to a rapid boil. Using a small knife, core the tomatoes and score a small *X* in the blossom ends. Submerge the tomatoes in boiling water for 15 seconds, remove, and plunge into an ice water bath to stop the cooking process.

5. Remove the tomatoes from the ice water and peel away the skin. Cut each tomato into quarters and remove the inside, leaving 12 clean petals in all.

6. Dice the tomato petals into ⅛-in. cubes. Place in a small bowl and season lightly with olive oil, salt, and pepper.

7. Remove the wine jelly from the refrigerator. Using a small knife, cut the wine jelly into ⅛-in. cubes. Add the wine jelly to the tomato tartar.

8. Place 2 oz of the tomato mixture on each of 6 spoons and sprinkle with Pecorino Romano cheese.

Fruit Tartars with Caviar

Papaya Tartar

SERVES: 6

1 cup finely diced papaya

2 tsp Chive Oil (see Chef's Pantry)

½ oz Osetra caviar

1. Mix papaya and Chive Oil in a bowl and marinate in refrigerator for 1 hour.

2. At time of service, divide the mixture among 6 spoons. Top each with a small amount of caviar.

Strawberry Tartar

SERVES: 6

1 cup finely diced strawberries

2 tsp Sweet and Sour Reduction (see Chef's Pantry)

½ oz Osetra caviar

1. Combine the strawberries and the Sweet and Sour Reduction in a bowl. Marinate in the refrigerator for 1 hour.

2. At time of service, divide the mixture among 6 spoons. Top each with a small amount of caviar.

Avocado Tartar

SERVES: 6

1 cup finely diced avocado

2 tsp Maple Vinegar Reduction (see Chef's Pantry)

½ oz Osetra caviar

1. Combine the avocado and Maple Vinegar Reduction in a bowl. Marinate in the refrigerator for 1 hour.

2. At time of service, divide the mixture among 6 spoons. Top each with a small amount of caviar.

Mango Tartar

SERVES: 6

1 cup finely diced mango

2 tsp Three-Herb Oil (see Chef's Pantry)

½ oz Osetra caviar

1. Combine the mango and Three-Herb Oil in a bowl. Marinate in the refrigerator for 1 hour.

2. At time of service, divide the mixture among 6 spoons. Top each with a small amount of caviar.

Tomatoes Stuffed with Walnut Pesto

SERVES: 6

6 cherry tomatoes, red or yellow

2 cups basil leaves, loosely packed

⅓ cup walnuts

2 garlic cloves

½ cup finely grated Parmigiano-Reggiano

½ cup extra-virgin olive oil

To taste, kosher salt

To taste, cracked black pepper

1. Bring 1 gal water to a rolling boil. Place the tomatoes in 2 qt heavily iced water for 20 seconds. Remove and place in the boiling water for 7–10 seconds. Remove and return to the ice water. Remove the tomatoes and peel off the skin. Cut the tomatoes in half. Gently remove the seeds and the meat from the inside the tomatoes. Reserve for service.

2. In a small food processor, place the basil, walnuts, garlic, and Parmigiano-Reggiano. Puree the mixture while slowly adding the olive oil to form a thick paste. Remove the paste from the food processor and season to taste with kosher salt and pepper.

3. Fill each tomato half with walnut pesto. Reassemble the stuffed tomatoes and season them lightly with kosher salt and pepper. Place each stuffed tomato on a fork and serve.

Appetizers, Hors d'Oeuvre, Amuse-Bouches

ABOVE: *Tomatoes Stuffed with Walnut Pesto*

BELOW: *Sea Scallops with Pea Coulis*

Sea Scallops with Pea Coulis

SERVES: 6

1 oz extra-virgin olive oil

3 oz butter, unsalted

¼ cup finely chopped shallots

2½ cups frozen petite peas or blanched fresh peas

½ cup Chicken Brodo (see Chef's Pantry)

3 tsp minced tarragon

3 Tbsp butter, unsalted, unsalted, cold

½ cup heavy cream

To taste, sea salt

To taste, freshly ground black pepper

1 tsp truffle oil

6 sea scallops

As needed, olive oil

6 slices white truffle

1. Heat a stainless-steel saucepan over medium heat. Add the olive oil and butter. Add the shallots and sauté 1 minute. Add the peas and sauté 2 minutes. Add the broth and bring to a simmer. Transfer mixture to a blender.

2. Add 1 tsp of the tarragon and the cold diced butter. Puree until smooth, about 3 minutes. Finish the puree with the heavy cream and season the mixture with sea salt, pepper, the truffle oil, and the remaining tarragon.

3. At time of service, heat a cast-iron skillet over high heat. Season the scallops with salt and pepper and sear in olive oil on both sides until golden brown.

4. To serve, place 1 oz pea coulis in the center of a plate. Place 1 scallop on the coulis and garnish with 1 slice white truffle.

Soup Shots

Pistachio Soup

SERVES: 4

1 Tbsp olive oil

1 shallot, chopped

2 leeks, white and light green only, rinsed well and chopped

1 garlic clove, crushed

2 Tbsp rice flour

6 cups Chicken Brodo (see Chef's Pantry)

1 cup pistachios, unsalted, ground

1 tsp kosher salt

4 tsp freshly ground black pepper

4 cups fresh orange juice

2 Tbsp fresh lime juice

4 cups whole unsalted pistachios, for garnish

1. Heat the olive oil over medium heat in a 4-qt heavy-bottomed sauce pot. Add the shallot and leeks and sauté 5 minutes, until translucent. Add the garlic and sauté for 3 minutes.

2. Add the rice flour, stirring constantly. Add the chicken broth and bring to a boil. Add the ground pistachios, salt, and pepper, and reduce heat to low. Cover and simmer 45 minutes, stirring occasionally.

3. Add the orange and lime juices and adjust the seasoning. Serve hot or cold, garnished with whole pistachios.

Moroccan Pumpkin Soup with Chickpeas

SERVES: 8–12

12 oz cooked chickpeas, drained

2 lbs pumpkin, butternut squash, or calabaza squash, peeled and cut in chunks

1 onion, peeled and quartered

2 lb stewing beef, cut in 2-in. chunks

2 tsp cinnamon, or to taste

2 cups Chicken Brodo (see Chef's Pantry)

2 Tbsp sugar, or to taste

1. In a 4-qt soup pot, combine the chickpeas, pumpkin, onion, and beef. Cover with water. Simmer, covered, 2 hours or until meat is tender.

2. Add the cinnamon, Chicken Brodo, and sugar. Blend, but do not puree, all ingredients in a food processor. Adjust seasoning. Reheat and serve. If the soup is too thick, add more water.

Avocado Soup with Salsa

SERVES: 4

SOUP

2 avocados, medium

2 cups Chicken Brodo (see Chef's Pantry)

1 cup half-and-half

2 tsp kosher salt

¼ cup fresh lime juice

2 tsp Tabasco Sauce

SALSA

¼ lb tomatillo, minced

¼ cup minced onion

1 garlic clove, small, minced

2 red bell peppers, roasted and peeled

1 Jalapeño, small

1 Tbsp minced cilantro

To taste, kosher salt

1. Blend the avocado flesh, brodo, half-and-half, salt, lime juice, and Tabasco until smooth. Chill thoroughly in the refrigerator.

2. At serving time, combine the salsa ingredients.

3. Ladle the soup into bowls and use a spoon to put a dollop of salsa on each.

The salsa is not merely a garnish but a delightful contrast in flavor and texture for this refreshing soup.

Ginger Peach Soup

SERVES: 4

1½ lb peaches

2 Tbsp + 1 tsp fresh lemon juice

1½ cups buttermilk

⅔ cup apple juice

2 tsp peeled and grated fresh ginger

1 tsp honey

1 scant tsp kosher salt

12–16 unsprayed rose petals or peach slices for garnish

1. Peel and pit the peaches, rubbing them with 2 Tbsp lemon juice or as needed to prevent discoloration.

2. Puree the peaches; then scrape them into a bowl and stir in remaining ingredients. Refrigerate until cold. Garnish each serving with unsprayed rose petals or peach slices.

Cold Tomato Soup

SERVES: 6

¼ cup olive oil

2 cups chopped onions

¾ cup chopped carrots

1 Tbsp minced garlic

1 tsp salt

1 tsp cayenne pepper

4 cups Chicken Brodo (see Chef's Pantry)

4 lbs tomatoes, peeled, seeded, and chopped

1. Heat the olive oil in a medium-sized heavy-bottomed saucepan over medium heat. Add the onions, carrots, and garlic; cook until softened, stirring occasionally, about 15 minutes. Mix in the salt and cayenne.

2. Add the stock and simmer for 30 minutes. Increase heat to high.

3. Add the tomatoes and cook until softened, about 10 minutes. Puree the soup. Transfer to a bowl; cover and refrigerate.

Asparagus Soup

SERVES: 4

3 Tbsp butter, unsalted

2 garlic cloves, minced

3 shallots, sliced

1 yellow onion, sliced

1 Idaho potato, peeled and sliced

5 cups Chicken Brodo (see Chef's Pantry) or vegetable broth

5 cups heavy cream

Pinch nutmeg

1 lb asparagus, trimmed, peeled, and cut into 1-in. pieces

1 cup English green peas

1. In a heavy-bottomed soup pot, melt 2 Tbsp of the butter over low heat until it foams. Add the garlic and shallots; cook until translucent. Add the onions; cook until translucent. Add the potato; cook for 2 minutes. Add the broth, cream, and nutmeg. Bring to a full boil.

2. Place the asparagus in a pasta basket and insert it into the boiling cream for 15 seconds. Immediately immerse the basket in ice water to stop the cooking process. Reserve the asparagus. Lower the heat and allow the soup to simmer.

3. Add the peas and simmer for 5 minutes. Remove the soup from heat. Place the reserved asparagus in the blender and pour the soup on top. Add the remaining 1 Tbsp butter, season with salt and pepper, and gently blend until smooth. Pour through a fine sieve. Adjust the seasoning with salt and pepper to taste.

Appetizers, Hors d'Oeuvre, Amuse-Bouches

Velvet Chocolate Mousse with Spicy Baby Shrimp

Serves: 8

MOUSSE

¼ cup heavy cream

1 Tbsp sugar

Pinch kosher salt

½ cup chopped extra-bitter chocolate

2 oz butter, unsalted

1 cup heavy cream, whipped to soft peaks

SPICY BABY SHRIMP

16 baby shrimp, 51/60 count

1 Tbsp Ariadna Chili Spice

To taste, kosher salt

2 oz olive oil

MOUSSE

1. In a stainless-steel saucepan, combine the cream, sugar, and salt. Bring to a boil over high heat, remove from heat, and whisk in the chocolate until smooth. Whisk in the butter until mixture is smooth once again. Cool the mixture to room temperature.

2. Fold in the whipped cream until evenly combined with the chocolate mixture. Chill the mousse in the refrigerator until set, about 1 hour.

SPICY BABY SHRIMP

1. In a small mixing bowl, combine the shrimp and the chili spice. Toss gently to evenly coat the shrimp. Season lightly with salt. Heat a sauté pan over medium heat. Add 2 oz olive oil and sauté the shrimp until fully cooked. Remove from heat and reserve at room temperature for service.

ASSEMBLY

1. Place the chocolate mousse in a piping bag. Pipe a small amount onto 8 spoons. Sprinkle the top of the mousse lightly with chili spice. Place 2 shrimp on each spoon. Serve immediately or hold in the refrigerator until time to serve.

Crispy Crab Fingers with Grand Marnier Orange Sections

SERVES: 6

1 navel orange

¼ cup Grand Marnier

1 Tbsp orange blossom honey

3 basil leaves, chiffonade

Pinch freshly ground black pepper

Six 1-oz pieces king crab meat

1 cup all-purpose flour

2 eggs, lightly beaten

1½ cups panko bread crumbs

To taste, kosher salt

1. Peel the orange, being certain to remove all the white pith. Using a small knife, segment the orange. Squeeze the juice from the remains of the orange and reserve for marinade.

2. Place the reserved orange juice, Marnier, and honey in a small stainless-steel saucepan and reduce by one-third over medium heat. Remove from heat and add the basil and black pepper. Place the mixture in a bowl and cool over an ice bath. Add the orange segments to the cooled mixture and allow to marinate for at least 1 hour.

3. Toss the crabmeat with the flour. Shake off excess flour and dip the crabmeat into the eggs, then the panko bread crumbs, coating evenly.

4. When ready to serve, deep-fry the crab until golden brown. Drain on paper towels and season lightly with salt. Place each crab finger on a fork and garnish with orange segments.

Appetizers, Hors d'Oeuvre, Amuse-Bouches

Savory Cones with Potato and Truffle, Salad Niçoise, and Caesar Salad

SERVES: 4

12 wonton wrappers

1 Yukon Gold potato, large, peeled

3 Tbsp kosher salt

3 oz heavy cream

2 oz butter, unsalted

1 oz truffle oil

To taste, kosher salt

To taste, cracked black pepper

1½ tsp minced garlic

3 white anchovy filets

2 Tbsp pasteurized egg yolks

2 Tbsp fresh lemon juice

2 Tbsp water

½ cup extra-virgin olive oil

¼ cup + 2 Tbsp finely grated Parmigiano-Reggiano

4 slices truffle

1 tsp chopped chives

4 romaine leaves, washed

4 oz frisée, washed and chopped

4 haricots verts, blanched, cut in half

1 quail egg, hard cooked

1 niçoise olive

2 oz potato, diced small, cooked

4 oz ahi tuna, diced small

1 Tbsp aged red wine vinegar

3 Tbsp extra-virgin olive oil

1. Preheat the oven to 350°F. Spray a 12-cone mold with nonstick spray. Wrap 1 wonton around each cone. Place the mold on a baking sheet and bake until the wonton wrappers are golden brown, 8–10 minutes. Remove from oven and allow to cool. Remove the wonton wrappers from the molds and reserve for service.

2. Dice the potato and place in a small saucepan. Cover with cold water and add 3 Tbsp salt. Bring to a simmer over medium heat. Cook until the potatoes are tender, about 10 minutes.

3. While the potatoes are cooking, heat the cream, butter, and truffle oil in a small pan. Drain the cooked potatoes and rice them in a small mixing bowl. Add the heated cream mixture and mix gently to incorporate. Season to taste with salt and pepper. Cover with plastic and reserve in a warm place for service.

4. To make the Caesar dressing, place the garlic, anchovy filets, and a pinch of salt and pepper in a small food processor and puree until smooth. Add the pasteurized yolks, lemon juice, and 2 Tbsp water. Process for 30 seconds. While the processor is running, slowly add the olive oil to form an emulsion. Remove the mixture from the processor and place in a small bowl. Stir in ¼ cup of the Parmigiano-Reggiano. Adjust the seasoning with salt and pepper if needed. Reserve for service.

5. At time of service, place the potato puree into a piping bag and fill 4 of the cones. Garnish these cones with sliced truffle and chopped chives.

6. Julienne the romaine leaves and toss them lightly with the Caesar dressing. Fill 4 of the cones with the dressed salad and top with the remaining Parmigiano-Reggiano.

7. Place 1 oz of the frisée in each of the remaining 4 cones. Add 2 pieces of haricots verts to each cone. Quarter the quail egg and place one quarter in each cone. Quarter the olive and place one piece into each cone. Top each with equal parts of the diced cooked potato and the raw tuna. In a small mixing bowl, mix the aged red wine vinegar along with salt and pepper. Lightly drizzle this on top of each niçoise cone. Serve immediately.

Appetizers, Hors d'Oeuvre, Amuse-Bouches

7

First Plates

The first plate, whether the beginning of a dinner or a special lunch, is the course that sets the tone for the rest of the meal. It is a wonderful opportunity to impress guests. A chef loves the challenge of creating a good first plate, one that makes the customers smile and leaves them wanting more.

The first plate can be a nice soup or a salad served before the main plate. I love when club members sit to dine and have a first plate, then a soup or salad, the main plate, and finish the meal with a nice pastry or cheese course. When I dine out, I like to try two or three first plates and then share a main plate so I can have my own tasting of smaller portions.

The menu of first plates should include vegetarian choices, seafood, combinations of the two, and small portions of meat, perhaps, but all items should complement the rest of the meal yet to come.

The first plate can be a scaled-down version of a main dish. It can be cold, warm, or hot. It can be a salad on a plate, such as our artichoke and roasted mushroom. It can be a surf-and-turf combination, such as seared sea scallop with braised short ribs. It can be as simple as oysters with mignonette sauce, as unassuming as a marinated avocado half filled with lump crabmeat, or as complex and rich as seared foie gras with apple cake and rhubarb.

Enjoy my selection of club favorites, which have started many a great meal.

MENU

Tomato Tartin, Frisée, Tomato Syrup,
and Basil Reduction

Baby Artichokes with Roasted Mushrooms,
Herbs, Radicchio, and Vinaigrette

Tender Veal Sliced Thin with Roasted Peaches,
Wilted Arugula, Aged Balsamic Vinegar,
and Parmigiano-Reggiano Dolce

Maui Shrimp Cocktail

Spiced Seared Tuna with Candied Fennel,
Grapefruit, and Red Onion Oil

Foie Gras with Rhubarb, Maple Apple Cake,
Apple Port Syrup, and Frisée

Pan-Seared Diver Scallop with Braised
Short Rib, Tomato Emulsion, and Basil Oil

Grilled Shrimp with Foie Gras Grits

Braised Artichoke with Petite Olive Oil
Tomatoes and Artichoke Chips

Tomato Tartin, Frisée, Tomato Syrup, and Basil Reduction

SERVES: 4

PESTO SAUCE

6 oz basil leaves

1 garlic clove, peeled

2 tsp pine nuts, lightly toasted

2 tsp grated parmesan cheese

½ cup extra-virgin olive oil

TOMATOES

10 heirloom tomatoes, peeled and cut into quarters

To taste, salt

To taste, freshly ground black pepper

2 tsp granulated sugar

4 Tbsp extra-virgin olive oil

CHEESE FILLING

2 Tbsp olive oil

9 oz fresh ricotta

2 tsp heavy cream

3 Tbsp Pesto Sauce

PASTRY

1 egg

2 tsp olive oil

4 puff pastry circles, 4-in. diameter

MELTED ONIONS

12 oz onions, thinly sliced

1 Tbsp olive oil

2 Tbsp butter, unsalted

1 Tbsp brown sugar

⅓ cup red wine

⅓ cup wine vinegar

1 tsp minced tarragon

To taste, salt

To taste, freshly ground black pepper

ASSEMBLY

4 bunches frisée

2 Tbsp Tomato Syrup (see Chef's Pantry)

2 Tbsp Basil Reduction (see Chef's Pantry)

PESTO SAUCE

1. Blanch basil leaves in boiling water.

2. Place the basil, garlic, pine nuts, parmesan, and ½ cup olive oil in a food processor. Blend well.

TOMATOES

1. Toss the tomato petals in the salt, pepper, sugar, and 4 Tbsp olive oil.

2. Line the bottoms of 4-in. tart pans with the tomatoes.

3. Bake at 300°F for 8 minutes; reserve.

CHEESE FILLING

1. Mix together 2 Tbsp olive oil, the ricotta, the cream, and 3 Tbsp pesto.

PASTRY

1. Mix egg and oil. Place disks (pastry circles) on a baking tray, brush lightly with the egg mixture, cover with a rack, and bake halfway through, about 7 minutes.

MELTED ONIONS

1. In a heavy-bottomed pan, sauté the onions with 1 Tbsp olive oil and the butter and sugar until caramelized, 7–10 minutes.

2. Add the wine and cook until it is almost evaporated. Add the vinegar and do the same.

3. Season with the tarragon, salt, and pepper.

ASSEMBLY

1. Distribute the cheese filling among the tart shells over the tomatoes; do the same with the onions. Place the pastry shell circles over the filled tart shells.

2. Bake at 350°F for 4–6 minutes or until the pastry is golden brown. Remove from the oven. Invert the tarts over a plate and place in the center. Remove the tart pan and the disk; you should have a nice tomato top.

3. Toss the frisée in Tomato Syrup and Basil Reduction and place in the center of the tomatoes. Drizzle the plate with more syrup and reduction. Serve hot.

Baby Artichokes with Roasted Mushrooms, Herbs, Radicchio, and Vinaigrette

SERVES: 6

Juice of 2 lemons

20 artichokes

5 cups + 2 Tbsp olive oil

12 garlic cloves

1 tsp crushed red pepper

2 cups Chicken Brodo (see Chef's Pantry)

2 cups white wine

1 Roma tomato

1 Tbsp sugar

1 Tbsp butter, unsalted

2 garlic cloves, finely minced

2 Tbsp finely minced shallots

1 cup high-quality balsamic vinegar

1 oz honey

1 Tbsp minced basil

18 oz assorted wild mushrooms

To taste, kosher salt

To taste, cracked black pepper

1 Tbsp finely chopped thyme

1 head radicchio

6 flatbreads, 1 in. by 4 in.

1. Combine 1 gal cold water with the lemon juice. Remove the tough outer leaves from 18 of the artichokes and peel the stems with a peeler. Trim about ½ in. off the top of each artichoke. Keep the artichokes in the lemon water while you are cleaning the rest to prevent them from turning brown.

2. In a heavy-bottomed stockpot, place 2 cups of the olive oil, 12 cloves garlic, and the crushed red pepper. Set over medium heat and cook until the garlic just begins to turn brown. Add the drained trimmed artichokes, the brodo, and the white wine. Cover, bring to a simmer, and simmer slowly until the artichokes are tender, 45–50 minutes. Remove the artichokes from the liquid and reserve for service.

3. Slice the tomato from top to bottom into ⅛-in. slices. Lay the slices on a Silpat set on a baking sheet. Combine the sugar with a heavy pinch of salt and pepper. Sprinkle this mixture over the tomato slices. Preheat the oven to 200°F and dry the tomato slices in it for about 1 hour or until firm but tender. Reserve for service.

4. In a small pan, heat the butter and 1 Tbsp olive oil. Add the minced garlic and shallots. Cook until tender and allow to cool.

5. In a medium mixing bowl, combine the balsamic vinegar, honey, basil, and cooked garlic and shallots. Whisking constantly, slowly add 3 cups of the olive oil. Season the vinaigrette with salt and pepper to taste. Reserve for service.

6. Set a cast-iron skillet in a preheated 400°F oven for 5 minutes. While the pan is heating, cut the mushrooms into quarters. Toss lightly with the remaining 1 Tbsp olive oil, salt, and pepper. Remove the hot pan from the oven and put the mushrooms in it. Return the pan to the oven and roast the mushrooms, stirring occasionally, until they are golden brown and tender, about 5 minutes. Remove the mushrooms from the oven and toss with the fresh thyme. Adjust the seasoning with salt and pepper if needed. Reserve at room temperature for service.

7. Using a slicing machine, thinly slice the 2 remaining artichokes. Deep fry the artichoke slices in hot oil until crispy. Drain on paper towels and season with salt and pepper.

8. Using a sharp knife, cut the radicchio into thin strips and reserve for service.

9. At time of service, place 3 cooked artichokes on each service plate. Drizzle lightly with vinaigrette, salt, and pepper. Top with fried artichokes. Break the flatbreads in half and set one half on each plate. Toss the radicchio with the remaining vinaigrette and place an equal amount on each flatbread. Top with the remaining flatbread halves and 1 dried tomato slice. Divide the mushroom mixture evenly among the plates. Serve at room temperature.

Tender Veal Sliced Thin with Roasted Peaches, Wilted Arugula, Aged Balsamic Vinegar, and Parmigiano-Reggiano Dolce

SERVES: 6

One 2–3-lb veal loin

2 Tbsp brown sugar

2 oz butter, unsalted

1 vanilla bean, split

2 cloves

½ cup peach juice

3 peaches

To taste, sea salt

To taste, cracked black pepper

To taste, extra-virgin olive oil

12 oz arugula, clean and picked

As needed, 12-year-old balsamic vinegar

30 curls Parmigiano-Reggiano Dolce

12 flatbreads, 1 in. by 4 in.

1. Using a small knife, remove all fat and sinew from the veal loin. Roll the loin tightly in plastic wrap to form a cylinder and place into freezer for at least 4 hours.

2. In a stainless-steel saucepan, combine the brown sugar, butter, vanilla bean, cloves, and peach juice. Bring to a boil over medium heat and allow to simmer for 3 minutes.

3. Place the peaches on a wire rack set over a baking sheet. Bake in a preheated 375°F oven, basting with juice every 5 minutes, until the skin begins to brown, about 10 minutes. Remove the peaches from the oven and allow to cool. Carefully skin the cooled peaches. Cut each peach in half and remove the pit. Reserve for service.

4. At time of service, lay out 6 serving plates. Using a slicing machine, slice the veal very thin. Arrange the slices to cover the bottom of each plate. Lightly season the veal with salt, pepper, and olive oil. Place one peach half in the center of each plate.

5. In a mixing bowl, toss the arugula lightly with olive oil and vinegar. Divide the arugula into 6 equal portions and place 1 portion in each peach. Drizzle vinegar lightly around the peaches.

6. Garnish each plate with Parmigiano-Reggiano curls and flatbreads.

Maui Shrimp Cocktail

SERVES: 4

SHRIMP

2 cups Giancarlo's Brodo (see Chef's Pantry)

1 celery stalk, chopped

2 cups coconut milk

1 Tbsp peeled and thinly sliced fresh ginger

2 Tbsp light soy sauce

½ cup small pineapple dice with core and skin

16 jumbo shrimp, shells on

COCONUT COCKTAIL SAUCE

½ cup chili sauce

¾ cup ketchup

Juice of 1 lime

2 Tbsp Frank's Red Hot

2 Tbsp sesame oil

2 oz horseradish

4 Tbsp shredded fresh coconut

½ cup cream of coconut

2 oz soy sauce

½ cup minced sweet pineapple

1 Tbsp finely chopped parsley

1 Tbsp finely chopped sage

SHRIMP

1. Place the brodo, celery, coconut milk, ginger, soy sauce, and pineapple in a large saucepan and bring to a boil. Let simmer for 10 minutes.

2. Add the shrimp to the liquid. Remove when the liquid returns to the boil and the shrimp are just cooked. Cool the shrimp, then remove the shells and veins.

COCONUT COCKTAIL SAUCE

1. Combine all the ingredients in a bowl and mix well. Refrigerate until ready to use.

ASSEMBLY

1. Serve the shrimp with the coconut cocktail sauce.

Strain the broth and refrigerate or freeze to use again for more shrimp or as a seafood marinade.

Spiced Seared Tuna with Candied Fennel, Grapefruit, and Red Onion Oil

SERVES: 4

TUNA

1 lb sashimi-quality tuna belly

2 Tbsp Spice de Cosette

2 tsp sea salt

1 tsp crushed black peppercorns

4 Tbsp grapeseed oil

CANDIED FENNEL

1 bulb fennel

1 Tbsp lime zest

1 tsp orange zest

2 star anise

½ cup simple syrup

GRAPEFRUIT

1 Ruby Red grapefruit

1 white grapefruit

RED ONION OIL

4 red onions, peeled and thinly sliced

1½ cups grapeseed oil

FENNEL COOKIE

1 bulb fennel, trimmed and thinly sliced

½ cup simple syrup

TUNA

1. Trim the tuna and remove any veins and skin.

2. Combine the spice, salt, and peppercorns. Coat all sides of the tuna well with spice mixture.

3. In a hot cast-iron pan, heat the oil. Sear tuna on both sides. Remove the tuna from the pan and let sit at room temperature.

CANDIED FENNEL

1. Trim all leaves and stem from the fennel. Remove the outer layer. Separate the remaining layers and slice them. Place the fennel slices in a pan with the zests and star anise.

2. Cover the fennel slices with simple syrup and cook until the fennel is just tender and syrup forms. Remove the fennel pieces to a Silpat and let dry.

GRAPEFRUIT

1. Remove the skin and white pith from the grapefruits and separate the segments. After the segments are removed, squeeze the juice from the remains of the grapefruit and store the segments in this juice.

RED ONION OIL

1. Put the onion slices in a stainless-steel saucepan, cover them with oil, and bring to a boil. Simmer slowly until the onions are soft, 3–5 minutes.

2. Place in a high-speed blender, puree for 1–2 minutes or until smooth, and then strain through a chinois. Refrigerate the strained oil.

FENNEL COOKIE

1. Brush the fennel slices with simple syrup, place on a Silpat, and dry in a 160°F oven, 6–8 hours.

ASSEMBLY

1. Slice the tuna loin, sprinkle with sea salt, and plate. Place grapefruit sections on each plate and spoon some grapefruit juice over them. Season the sections with pepper and top with slices of candied fennel. Place a few drops of fresh minced red onion on the plate, top with onion oil, and garnish the plate with a fennel cookie.

2. Finish with salt, pepper, and minced red onion softened in onion oil for 3–5 minutes.

Foie Gras with Rhubarb

Serves: 4

FOIE GRAS

1 lobe foie gras, grade A

To taste, kosher salt

To taste, freshly ground black pepper

MAPLE APPLE TOWER

3 gelatin sheets

4 red apples

1 cup apple cider

¼ cup sugar

2 cups apple cider

1 Tbsp maple syrup

1 tsp minced sage

JAM

3 stalks rhubarb

1½ cups orange juice

4 Tbsp sugar

2 Tbsp raisins

1 tsp orange zest

½ Tbsp gelatin

CHIPS

¼ cup sugar

1 cup water

2 apples

ASSEMBLY

1 tsp butter, unsalted

3 Tbsp Demi de Cosette (see Chef's Pantry)

1 tsp Dried Orange Zest (see Chef's Pantry)

4 bunches frisée

FOIE GRAS

1. Soak the foie gras in salted water for 2 hours.

2. Pat dry with a clean towel and carefully remove veins. Clean and trim into a lobe for slicing, saving the trimmings for other uses.

3. Slice 4 slices from the lobe, score them, and refrigerate until cooking time.

MAPLE APPLE TOWER

1. Soak the gelatin sheets in water to soften.

2. Peel and core the apples; place the seeds, peels, and trimmings in a pot. (Reserve the apples.) Add 1 cup apple cider and sugar to the pot and bring to a boil. Reduce heat and simmer until the liquid reaches a syrupy consistency. Reserve apple syrup for service.

3. Cut the reserved apples into 8 pieces each. In a saucepan, cover the apple pieces with 2 cups cider and cook until they are soft but still slightly firm. Strain the juice and save for other uses. Mash the hot apple pieces in a bowl with a fork. Squeeze the water from the gelatin sheets and add it to the mashed apple with the maple syrup and sage. Mix well, then mold in tall cylinder molds, about 3 in. high.

JAM

1. Cut the rhubarb into 1-in. pieces.

2. Place the rhubarb in a heavy-bottomed saucepan with the orange juice, sugar, raisins, zest, and gelatin. Bring to a boil, reduce heat, and simmer until the rhubarb is cooked through and the mixture thickens slightly.

CHIPS

1. Whisk together the sugar and water until the sugar is dissolved.

2. Slice the apples thinly on a mandoline or with a sharp knife. Dip the slices in the sugar water and place on a Silpat. Dry the apples in a 160°F oven until crisp, about 1 hour. To make a ring for the frisée, shingle the slices together, but do not completely dry out.

ASSEMBLY

1. Season the slices of foie gras with salt. Heat the butter in a sauté pan over medium heat. Brown the foie gras on both sides, remove from pan, and reserve.

2. In the same sauté pan, add the Demi de Cosette and mix with a spoon.

3. On each plate, place an apple tower topped with zest, rhubarb jam, and frisée. Place a foie gras slice on the jam, spoon some of the demi and foie gras fat mixture on each slice of foie gras, and drizzle the plate with apple syrup.

Pan-Seared Diver Scallop with Braised Short Rib, Tomato Emulsion, and Basil Oil

SERVES: 6

BASIL OIL

4 cups kosher salt

3 cups basil, tightly packed

1 cup olive oil

DRIED TOMATOES

1 Roma tomato

1 tbsp sugar

Pinch kosher salt

Pinch freshly ground black pepper

SHORT RIBS

6 meaty short ribs, 4–6 in. in length

To taste, sea salt

To taste, cracked black pepper

3 Tbsp olive oil

3 Tbsp butter, unsalted

1 onion, large, chopped

2 carrots, medium, chopped

½ cup chopped portobellos

3 celery stalks, chopped

½ cup chopped fennel

½ cup tomato paste

2 cups dry red wine

½ cup aged red wine vinegar

1 qt Beef Brodo (see Chef's Pantry)

2 cups veal stock

2 bouquets garni

3 garlic cloves, sliced

¼ cup carrot brunoise

¼ cup onion brunoise

¼ cup celery brunoise

2 tbsp all-purpose flour

½ cup peeled, seeded, and diced Roma tomatoes

½ cup tomato sauce

TOMATO EMULSION

2 eggs, soft-boiled

1 garlic clove, minced

½ cup roasted tomatoes, peeled and seeded

2 tsp tomato paste

3 tbsp balsamic vinegar

½ cup extra-virgin olive oil

2 leaves basil

4–8 tbsp Giancarlo's Brodo (see Chef's Pantry)

ASSEMBLY

1 Tbsp oil, blended

6 diver scallops

BASIL OIL

1. Bring 2 gal water and the 4 cups kosher salt to a rapid boil. Place the 3 cups basil leaves in a strainer and dip into the boiling water for 10 seconds. Remove directly to heavily iced water to stop the cooking process. Squeeze the basil dry.

2. Place half the basil in a high-speed blender. Add ½ cup olive oil and puree at medium speed for 2 minutes. Add the rest of the basil and another ½ cup oil and puree for 2 more minutes.

3. Place the oil in a strainer lined with a coffee filter. Allow to drain for 2 hours. Discard the filter and its contents. Place the basil oil in a squeeze bottle and reserve for service.

DRIED TOMATOES

1. Combine the sugar, salt, and pepper. Slice the tomato from top to bottom into ⅛-in. slices. Place the slices on a Silpat set on a baking sheet. Sprinkle with the sugar mixture.

2. Dry the tomato slices in a 200°F oven for about 1 hour. Remove the tomatoes from the oven when they are firm but tender. Reserve for service.

SHORT RIBS

1. Preheat the oven to 450°F. Trim the ribs, if needed, and pat dry. Sprinkle with salt and pepper. Place the ribs on a sheet pan with a roasting rack. Sear in the oven for 12–15 minutes to remove fat and brown. Reserve.

2. Heat a 6-qt heavy-bottomed braising pan over medium heat. Add 2 Tbsp olive oil and 2 Tbsp butter. Add the chopped onions, carrots, mushrooms, celery, and fennel. Cook until light brown. Add tomato paste and cook for 2 minutes. Deglaze with the wine and vinegar. Continue to cook until almost all the liquid is reduced.

3. Place the ribs in the pan along with the brodo, veal stock, and bouquets garni. Cover the pot tightly. Gently cook the ribs in a 275°F oven until they are tender, 3–4 hours.

4. Remove the pan from the oven. Reserve the ribs. Strain the liquid through a fine sieve into a saucepan. Bring to a simmer and allow to cook for 20 minutes. Remove from heat and reserve.

5. In a clean saucepan, heat 1 Tbsp butter and 1 Tbsp olive oil. Sauté the sliced garlic and the brunoise vegetables until tender. Add the flour, mix well, and cook the flour for 2 minutes. Add the diced tomatoes, tomato sauce, and reserved broth from the ribs. Bring to a boil and simmer for 30 minutes. Season with salt and pepper to taste. Reserve for service.

TOMATO EMULSION

1. Place the eggs in a blender with the minced garlic, roasted tomatoes, tomato paste, and balsamic vinegar. Blend on high speed while slowly adding the olive oil. At the last moment, add the basil.

2. Strain through a fine sieve, adjust the consistency with the brodo, and season with salt and pepper. Reserve for service.

ASSEMBLY

1. At time of service, heat a seasoned cast-iron pan over high heat. Add the oil and allow to heat until it just begins to smoke. Season the scallops with salt and pepper. Sear on both sides until golden brown.

2. Slice the meaty part of each rib into 3 slices. Reheat gently in the sauce. Place 3 slices on each of 6 heated serving plates. Spoon a little sauce over the meat.

3. Place 1 scallop on top of the ribs. Drizzle with basil oil and tomato emulsion. Garnish with dried tomato and sea salt. Serve immediately.

First Plates

Grilled Shrimp
with Foie Gras Grits

SERVES: 4

3½ cups quick-cooking grits

2 qt Chicken Brodo (see Chef's Pantry)

1 qt milk

½ cup + 1 tsp butter, unsalted

1 Tbsp olive oil

12 jumbo shrimp

4 oz morel mushrooms

4 oz fava beans, cleaned

1 lb foie gras, diced

To taste, kosher salt

To taste, cracked black pepper

1. In a medium saucepan, combine the grits, broth, milk, and ½ cup butter. Place over medium-low heat and bring to a simmer, stirring often. Allow to simmer until all the liquid is absorbed. If grits are grainy and not fully cooked, add more chicken broth and simmer for a few more minutes.

2. In a medium sauté pan, melt 1 tsp butter and 1 Tbsp olive oil. Add the shrimp and sauté over medium heat until fully cooked. Remove the shrimp and add the morels and fava beans. Cook until tender. Remove from the pan and reserve.

3. Discard the fat from the pan and return the pan to the heat. Add the foie gras and sauté until evenly browned. Return the favas and morels to the pan. Heat gently for 1 minute. Add this mixture, including the fat, to the grits and stir gently to combine. Season to taste with salt and pepper.

4. Divide the grits evenly among 4 heated serving dishes. Top each dish with 3 shrimp. Serve immediately.

Braised Artichoke with Petite Olive Oil Tomatoes and Artichoke Chips

SERVES: 6

BRAISED ARTICHOKES

6 Roma artichokes with stem

4 large shallots, finely sliced

4 Tbsp grapeseed oil

2 carrots, medium, finely sliced

1 garlic clove, finely sliced

6 white button mushrooms, thinly sliced

2 celery stalks, peeled and sliced

2 Tbsp tomato paste

1 cup pinot grigio wine

As needed, Chicken Brodo (see Chef's Pantry)

1 tsp thyme

1 tsp finely chopped chocolate mint leaves

2–3 oz clarified butter

To taste, salt

To taste, freshly ground black pepper

To taste, grated parmesan

PETITE OLIVE OIL TOMATOES

36 cherry tomatoes with stems, lightly blanched and peeled

3 garlic cloves, thinly sliced

4 Tbsp extra-virgin olive oil

2 tsp bar sugar

6 large basil leaves

1 tsp kosher salt

1 tsp crushed red pepper flakes

As needed, extra-virgin olive oil

ASSEMBLY

Braised Artichokes

To taste, tomato dressing

To taste, Tomato Syrup (see Chef's Pantry)

To taste, balsamic vinegar

BRAISED ARTICHOKES

1. Peel the artichoke stems and trim about 1 in. from the base. Cut a thin slice off the top and pluck the outer leaves until you reach the tender lighter green leaves. Reserve the artichokes in acidulated water.

2. In a heavy-bottomed stainless-steel braising pan, sweat the shallots in the oil. Add the carrots, garlic, and mushrooms. Cook until

3. Remove the artichokes from the acidulated water and dry well. Melt the butter in a stainless-steel sauté pan and fry the artichokes until the outer leaves are lightly brown. Transfer to the broth. Simmer until the artichokes are tender, 20–40 minutes. Add broth if needed during the cooking process. Remove the artichokes from the broth and let cool.

ARTICHOKE CHIPS

1. Remove a few leaves from each of the cooled artichokes. Season them with salt and deep-fry until crisp.

PETITE OLIVE OIL TOMATOES

1. Place the tomatoes in a bowl; gently toss with the garlic, olive oil, sugar, basil, and salt. Spread the tomatoes evenly in a small stainless-steel baking pan. Cover with olive oil.

2. Place the tomatoes in a 140°F oven for 6–8 hours. Carefully remove the tomatoes from the oil. Save the oil to make dressing and refrigerate.

ASSEMBLY

1. Place an artichoke in the middle of each plate, stem up.

2. Garnish with 6 tomatoes, Tomato Dressing, Tomato Syrup, and balsamic vinegar, if desired.

tender, then add the celery and cook 1–2 minutes more. Add the tomato paste, cook 1 more minute, and then deglaze the pan with the wine. Add the broth, thyme, and chocolate mint. Bring to a low simmer.

8

Seafood

I have mentioned using fresh, high-quality ingredients many times, but when it comes to seafood, only the highest quality will truly create an extraordinary culinary experience.

The time the fish is caught, how it is handled, and the temperature at which it is maintained are all steps that matter to preparing and serving high-quality seafood. Private clubs as well as hotels and restaurants cultivate relationships with top fishmongers in order to obtain the best fish.

The same connections should be made by the home consumer. Look for a private fish market or excellent supermarket with a busy fish department, which indicates quick turnover of product. Make sure the seafood is held at a minimum of 36°F and maximum of 38°F, presented in a very clean setting on clean trays, and topped with ice bags as well as being handled by a knowledgeable and skilled staff. Seafood fileted, proportioned, or cut to your specification is often the best bet for home usage and even some professional kitchens.

The primary ingredient for success in preparing seafood, whether shellfish, round fish, or flatfish, is not to overcook it. Perfectly cooked seafood is moist, flaky, and a delight to the palate.

This chapter encompasses fish and shellfish teamed with terrific, unusual flavor profiles. These preparations, along with clean and contemporary presentations, make for splendid dining experiences. You can substitute other favorite fish in many of these recipes; for example, the recipe for pan-seared sea bass with lobster mashed potatoes can be also prepared with grouper, snapper, or skate wing.

Fresh seafood, cooked perfectly with simplicity and elegance, is a true gift to the diner.

MENU

Pan-Seared Sea Bass with
Lobster Mashed Potatoes,
Favas, and Citrus Butter Sauce

Grilled Sea Bass on a Bed of
Seasonal Vegetables, Asparagus
Cream, and Artichoke Hearts
with Tomato and Onion Jam

Pan-Roasted Grouper,
Caramelized Onion and
Potato Tart, Tomato Confit,
Bay Spiced Shrimp, and
Asparagus Emulsion

Roasted Zucchini-Wrapped
American Grouper with
Potato Disk, Artichokes,
Shrimp, Tomatoes, and
Red Pepper Sauce

Pan-Roasted Alaskan Salmon
with Choucroute and
Mustard Cream

Grilled Salmon Filets with
a Sweet Corn, Fava Bean, and
Pea Relish with Corn Cream

Sea Scallop on Potato Cake
with White Truffle Hollandaise
and Foie Gras Bits

Seared Sea Scallops with
Clam Chowder Sauce,
Mushroom Essence,
and Watercress Jus

Grilled Spiced Shrimp with
Pulled Braised Pork Spring
Roll, Asian Vegetables,
Chili Oil, and Mint
Foamy Sauce

Cosette's Pot of Poached
Shrimp in Olive Oil Broth
with Tomatoes, Spring Peas,
and Artichokes

Pan-Seared Sea Bass with Lobster Mashed Potatoes, Favas, and Citrus Butter Sauce

SERVES: 4

LOBSTER MASHED POTATOES

1½ lb Yukon Gold potatoes

As needed, kosher salt

½ cup heavy cream

½ cup milk

8 ozs butter, unsalted

As needed, sea salt

As needed, cracked black pepper

1 tsp chopped thyme

8 oz picked lobster meat, diced

CITRUS BUTTER SAUCE

¼ cup dry white wine

2 Tbsp fresh lime juice

2 Tbsp fresh orange juice

2 Tbsp diced red onion

1 bay leaf

½ tsp black peppercorns

¼ cup heavy cream

10 oz butter, unsalted, diced and cold

1 tsp finely chopped tarragon

To taste, sea salt

SEA BASS

As needed, olive oil

Four 6-oz portions sea bass

To taste, kosher salt

To taste, white pepper

FAVAS

2 Tbsp olive oil

12 oz fava beans, clean

To taste, kosher salt

To taste, freshly ground black pepper

LOBSTER MASHED POTATOES

1. Wash the potatoes well under cold water. Do not peel.

2. Place the potatoes in a large stainless-steel soup pot and cover with cold water by 2 in. Add 1 Tbsp kosher salt for every 4 cups water. Place over medium heat and bring to a simmer. Continue cooking until the potatoes are tender, about 15–20 minutes.

3. Drain the potatoes immediately and place on a towel to cool slightly and dry.

4. In a saucepan, combine the cream and milk, bring to a boil, and reserve.

5. Peel the potatoes while they are still hot. Cut them into pieces and rice them twice into a heavy-bottomed sauce pot. Set the pot over low heat and slowly add 6 oz of the butter while stirring gently with a wooden spoon, mixing well until the butter is incorporated and the potatoes are fluffy. Slowly add the cream mixture while stirring the potatoes gently. Season with sea salt, pepper, and reserve.

6. In a small sauté pan, add the remaining 2 oz butter, the thyme, and the lobster meat. Heat until the butter is melted and the lobster is evenly coated with butter.

7. Fold the lobster into the potatoes. Adjust the consistency, if needed, with more hot cream. Reserve the potatoes in a warm place until service.

CITRUS BUTTER SAUCE

1. In a medium stainless-steel saucepan, combine the wine, lime juice, orange juice, red onion, bay leaf, and peppercorns. Bring to a boil over medium heat and simmer until reduced by half.

2. Add the heavy cream and return to a boil. Simmer until the liquid is reduced by half.

3. Reduce the heat to low and whisk in the butter 1 Tbsp at a time, adding each new piece before the previous one is completely incorporated. Remove the pan from the heat periodically to prevent the sauce from getting too hot and breaking. The sauce should be thick enough to coat the back of a spoon. Strain the sauce through a fine strainer and into a clean container.

4. Add the tarragon and season to taste with sea salt. Cover and keep in a warm place until service.

SEA BASS

1. Heat a nonstick skillet over medium-high heat for 3 minutes. Add 2 Tbsp olive oil and allow to heat for 2 minutes.

2. Season the sea bass filets with salt and pepper. Place the fish in the hot pan and sear on all sides until golden brown.

3. Move the fish to a preheated 350°F oven. Cook until it is firm and cooked through, about 10 minutes.

FAVAS

1. While the fish is cooking, preheat a sauté pan over medium heat for 2 minutes. Add the 2 Tbsp olive oil and allow to heat for 2 more minutes. Add the favas and sauté for 3–5 minutes or until tender. Season to taste with salt and pepper.

ASSEMBLY

1. At time of service, preheat 4 dinner plates. Place 2 quenelles of the lobster mashed potatoes on each plate. Divide the favas evenly among the plates. Place 1 piece of sea bass on the favas. Drizzle lightly with the citrus butter sauce and serve immediately.

Grilled Sea Bass on a Bed of Seasonal Vegetables, Asparagus Cream, and Artichoke Hearts with Tomato and Onion Jam

SERVES: 4

TOMATO AND ONION JAM

2 lb ripe tomatoes, peeled and seeded

As needed, kosher salt

As needed, freshly ground black pepper

2 Tbsp granulated sugar

1 sweet onion, small, julienne

3 Tbsp aged red wine vinegar

3 Tbsp brown sugar

1 Tbsp basil, chiffonade

ASPARAGUS CREAM

24 asparagus spears, medium, trimmed

As needed, butter, unsalted

2 Tbsp sliced shallots

1 garlic clove, sliced

1½ cups heavy cream

VEGETABLES

8 baby carrots

SEA BASS

Four 6-oz portions sea bass filets

As needed, olive oil

BABY ARTICHOKES COOKED IN A VACUUM BAG

2 lemons

3 limes

8 baby artichokes (about 4 in. tall)

3 oz butter, unsalted, diced

2 tsp sea salt

¼ cup extra-virgin olive oil

¼ cup wine

4 parsley sprigs

3 thyme sprigs

ASSEMBLY

2 oz butter, unsalted

2 oz olive oil

To taste, kosher salt

To taste, freshly black pepper

TOMATO AND ONION JAM

1. Puree the tomatoes in a food processor. Place the puree in a stainless-steel saucepan and set over medium heat. Stir in 2 tsp kosher salt and the granulated sugar. Bring to a boil over medium heat and cook, uncovered, until the tomato is reduced by one-third, about 30 minutes.

2. While the tomato puree is cooking, caramelize the onion julienne in a sauté pan over medium heat until golden brown. Reserve.

3. Add to the tomato reduction the caramelized onions, vinegar, a pinch of black pepper, and the brown sugar. Continue to cook until the jam is very thick and holds it shape when mounded onto a large spoon, about 30 minutes.

4. Remove the jam from the heat and stir in the basil. Adjust the seasoning with kosher salt and black pepper. Allow the mixture to cool. It is best to do this the day before and allow the mixture to set in the refrigerator overnight to marry the flavors.

ASPARAGUS CREAM

1. Using a knife, cut 12 of the asparagus into small pieces. Melt 2 oz butter in a small saucepan and add the shallots and garlic. Cook over medium heat until the shallots are translucent.

2. Add the chopped asparagus and sauté for 2 minutes. Add 1 cup of the cream and bring to a simmer over medium heat. Continue to cook until the asparagus are tender.

3. Place the mixture in a blender and puree for 2 minutes. Add the remainder of the cream if necessary to produce a lighter consistency. Strain the mixture through a sieve and adjust the seasoning with kosher salt and pepper. Reserve in a warm place for service.

VEGETABLES

1. Bring 1 gal water plus 1 cup kosher salt to a rapid boil over high heat. Add the carrots and cook until al dente. Remove the carrots and shock in an ice bath to stop the cooking process. Reserve for service.

2. Return the water to a rapid boil and add the remaining asparagus. Cook for 3 minutes or until the asparagus is tender. Remove the asparagus and shock in an ice bath to stop the cooking process. Reserve for service.

SEA BASS

1. At time of service, heat a nonstick sauté pan over high heat for 3 minutes. Add 2 Tbsp olive oil and allow the oil to heat for 2 minutes.

2. Season the sea bass filets with kosher salt and pepper. Sear the fish in the hot oil on both sides until golden brown. Finish cooking in a preheated 350°F oven until the fish is firm and cooked through, 8–10 minutes.

BABY ARTICHOKES COOKED IN A VACUUM BAG

1. Cut the 2 lemons and 3 limes in half and squeeze the juice into a large bowl filled with cold water. Drop the squeezed lemon and lime halves into water.

2. Set a bowl of acid water next to your work area.

3. Start with 1 artichoke at a time; remove the top few layers of dark green leaves, exposing the tender yellow leaves below.

4. With a sharp paring knife, pare away the tough, outer layer around the base of the artichoke, then trim off the tip of the artichoke slightly to flatten the top, cut artichoke in half.

5. Drop each half into the bowl of acid water, as they are trimmed.

6. When all artichokes are cleaned, remove the artichokes and place into a FoodSaver or Cryovac bag.

7. Add remaining items, then seal the bag by vacuum method.

8. Bring to a simmer a 4-qt pot filled with water. Add the bag of artichokes and cook for 45–50 minutes or until artichokes are tender.

ASSEMBLY

1. While the fish is cooking, heat 2 oz butter and 2 oz olive oil in a large sauté pan. Add the blanched carrots and the artichokes. Cook for 2 minutes, then add the asparagus and continue to cook for 2 more minutes or until the vegetables are thoroughly heated. Season to taste with kosher salt and pepper.

2. Heat 4 dinner plates. Divide the carrots and artichokes evenly among them.

3. Place 1 piece of fish on each plate of vegetables. Drizzle lightly with asparagus cream and garnish with a quenelle of the tomato and onion jam. Serve immediately.

Pan-Roasted Grouper, Caramelized Onion and Potato Tart, Tomato Confit, Bay Spiced Shrimp, and Asparagus Emulsion

SERVES: 4

PAN-ROASTED GROUPER

Four 6-oz portions grouper, skin removed

To taste, sea salt

To taste, freshly ground black pepper

3 oz extra-virgin olive oil

4 thyme sprigs, picked

2 tsp Spice de Cosette

Juice of 2 limes

1 Tbsp honey

4 oz white wine

2 oz butter, unsalted, diced

1 lemon

CARAMELIZED ONION AND POTATO TART

2 Tbsp butter, unsalted

3 Tbsp olive oil

3 tsp sugar

3 onions, medium, julienne

2 oz white wine

4 high-quality frozen or fresh puff pastry sheets, 3-in. by 5-in.

1 lb Yukon Gold potatoes, large

½ tsp freshly ground black pepper

1 Tbsp chopped parsley

To taste, sea salt

1 Tbsp kosher salt

2 tsp truffle oil

2 tsp thyme

1 tsp sea salt

BAY SPICED SHRIMP

4 jumbo shrimp, peeled and deveined

2 Tbsp olive oil

1 Tbsp Spice de Cosette

ASSEMBLY

As needed, Tomato Confit (see Chef's Pantry)

8 Butter-Poached Asparagus Spears (see Chef's Pantry)

As needed, Asparagus Emulsion (see Chef's Pantry)

As needed, Tomato Syrup (see Chef's Pantry)

PAN-ROASTED GROUPER

1. Pat filets dry. Mix salt and pepper and the olive oil, thyme, Spice de Cosette, lime juice, and honey in a bowl. Add the filets and toss to coat well. Cover and let sit for 20–30 minutes.

2. Bring to medium-high heat a seasoned cast-iron skillet or heavy bottomed nonstick sauté. Place the coated filets in the pan skin side up and cook for 3–4 minutes or until nicely browned. Turn over and cook 2–3 minutes more or until browned.

3. Remove the filets to a baking dish and deglaze the pan with the wine. Top the fish with the butter and a squeeze of lemon juice. Place in a 350°F oven for 4–5 minutes or until the fish is flaky and just cooked through.

CARAMELIZED ONION AND POTATO TART

1. Heat a sauté pan over medium-high heat. Add the butter and olive oil. When the butter is melted, add the sugar and the onions. Cook, tossing every 2–3 minutes, until the onions are brown and caramelized.

2. Deglaze the pan with wine and cook until dry, 1–2 minutes. Reserve and allow to cool.

3. On a greased or parchment-lined tray, place squares of puff pastry. Dock the pastry with a fork, then cover with parchment paper and 2 baking trays to weigh them down. Bake in a 350°F oven until light brown. Let cool.

4. Brush the cooled pastry with the melted butter. Divide the onions among the pastry sheets and spread out.

5. Toss the potato slices with the remaining butter. Season lightly with salt and pepper. Place the potato slices evenly over the onion tarts. Bake the tarts at 350°F for 5–7 minutes or until the pastry is golden brown.

BAY SPICED SHRIMP

1. Toss the shrimp with the oil and spice. Grill until cooked through.

ASSEMBLY

1. Place a tart on each of 4 plates and top with fish. Place 2 pieces of Tomato Confit on each piece of fish and top with 1 shrimp. Garnish with 2 Butter-Poached Asparagus Spears and Asparagus Emulsion. Squeeze some Tomato Syrup on the plate.

Roasted Zucchini-Wrapped American Grouper with Potato Disk, Artichokes, Shrimp, Tomatoes, and Red Pepper Sauce

SERVES: 4

GROUPER

Juice of 2 limes

3 Tbsp extra-virgin olive oil

2 tsp honey

As needed, sea salt

Four 7-oz portions American snapper, trimmed

To taste, freshly ground black pepper

6 leaves fresh sage, chopped fine

16 long, thin zucchini slices

As needed, clarified butter

SHRIMP, ARTICHOKE, AND TOMATO SALAD

12 shrimp, peeled and deveined

¼ cup olive oil

1 Tbsp fresh lemon juice

6 artichokes, cooked and halved

1 cup grape tomatoes or small cherry tomatoes

2 oz Chef Leonard's Basic Vinaigrette (see Chef's Pantry)

8 sprigs fresh parsley

POTATO DISK

3 baked potatoes

4 Tbsp clarified butter

To taste, sea salt

RED PEPPER SAUCE

2 cups chopped roasted red bell pepper

½ cup Giancarlo's Brodo (see Chef's Pantry)

½ Tbsp chopped fresh sage

¼ tsp kosher salt

¼ tsp red pepper flakes

1 Tbsp high-quality tomato paste

3 Tbsp aged balsamic vinegar

2 tsp honey

GROUPER

1. Mix the lime juice, olive oil, honey, and 1 tsp sea salt. Marinate the snapper in the mixture for 20 minutes. Sear the fish in a hot pan for 2 minutes on each side. Cool.

2. Season the cooled fish with pepper and sage. Wrap the fish pieces with zucchini slices, brush with clarified butter, season with salt and pepper, and bake at 350°F for 12–15 minutes.

SHRIMP, ARTICHOKE, AND TOMATO SALAD

1. Toss the shrimp with the olive oil and lemon juice.

2. In a hot sauté pan, cook the shrimp for 30 seconds. Add the artichokes and cook for 1 minute. Add the tomatoes and sauté 1 more minute.

3. Add the vinaigrette and parsley, toss well, and remove from stove.

POTATO DISK

1. Peel the potatoes and slice them into ½-in. disks.

2. Sauté in the clarified butter until golden brown. Season with salt. Reserve for service.

RED PEPPER SAUCE

1. Simmer the bell peppers and brodo in a stainless-steel saucepan for 15 minutes. Add the sage, salt, pepper flakes, tomato paste, vinegar, and honey; simmer another 10 minutes.

2. Place the mixture in a high-speed blender. Blend until smooth, then strain.

3. If needed, return the sauce to the stove and reduce to desired consistency.

ASSEMBLY

1. Place 3–4 potato disks in the middle of each plate. Distribute the salad around the potatoes. Place the snapper on top of the potatoes. Spoon the sauce around plate.

Pan-Roasted Alaskan Salmon with Choucroute and Mustard Cream

SERVES: 4

SALMON

Four 6-oz portions center-cut salmon

To taste, kosher salt

To taste, freshly ground black Tellicherry pepper

¾ cup honey

½ cup extra-virgin olive oil

Juice of 2 limes

Juice of 1 lemon

2 Tbsp minced tarragon

CHOUCROUTE

5 pieces smoked bacon, matchbook cut

1 Tbsp peanut oil

1 onion, small, medium dice

2 cloves garlic, sliced thin

2 cups very thinly sliced savoy cabbage

½ cup apple cider vinegar

1 tsp caraway seeds

½ cup white wine

1 cup blanched sliced new potatoes or fingerlings

2 carrots, blanched, bias cut

1 cup Giancarlo's Brodo (see Chef's Pantry)

1 Tbsp chopped parsley

To taste, kosher salt

To taste, freshly ground black pepper

2 Tbsp butter, unsalted

MUSTARD CREAM

1 shallot, minced

½ cup dry white wine

1 tsp mustard seed

4 oz butter, unsalted, cold and diced

½ cup heavy cream, warm

2 tsp lemon-infused honey

2 Tbsp Dijon mustard

To taste, sea salt

SALMON

1. Season each salmon filet with salt and pepper.

2. Mix the honey, olive oil, lime juice, lemon juice, and tarragon. Coat the filets with the marinade. Let sit for 20–30 minutes.

3. Pan-sear the filets until golden brown, 2–3 minutes per side. Finish in a 400°F oven until just cooked in the center.

CHOUCROUTE

1. Render the bacon in the oil until crisp. Add the onion and garlic; cook until soft.

2. Add the cabbage and vinegar; cook for 7 minutes.

3. Add the caraway seeds. Deglaze the pan with the wine.

4. Add the potatoes, carrots, and brodo. Simmer until the vegetables and potatoes are tender.

5. Season with parsley, salt, and pepper. Add the butter and adjust seasonings. Hold to serve hot.

MUSTARD CREAM

1. Place the shallot, wine, and mustard seeds in a saucepan. Bring to a boil and simmer until the wine is almost evaporated.

2. Whisk in the butter, a little at a time. Add the cream, honey, and Dijon mustard. Simmer for 2–3 minutes, strain twice, and season with salt.

Grilled Salmon Filets with a Sweet Corn, Fava Bean, and Pea Relish with Corn Cream

SERVES: 4

SALMON

3 Tbsp extra-virgin olive oil

Juice of 2 limes

7 thyme sprigs

To taste, kosher salt

To taste, freshly ground black pepper

Four 6-oz portions salmon filet

CORN CREAM

3 ears corn

½ cup heavy cream

2 Tbsp honey

RELISH

5 oz smoked bacon, diced

1 oz butter, unsalted

1 shallot, minced

6 oz shelled fava beans

4 Tbsp champagne vinegar

1 Tbsp sugar

1 Tbsp chopped parsley

4 oz peas, blanched

To taste, kosher salt

To taste, freshly ground black pepper

ASSEMBLY

1 cup Mashed Potatoes (see Chef's Pantry)

8 pieces lavash or thinly sliced toast

SALMON

1. Combine the olive oil, lime juice, thyme, salt, and pepper. Marinate the salmon filets in this mixture for 20 minutes.

2. Grill the salmon to desired doneness.

CORN CREAM

1. Place the ears of corn on a roasting rack and roast at 400°F for 10 minutes or until browned. Allow to cool. With a small knife, remove the corn kernels.

2. Place the cornhusks, half of the roasted corn kernels, the cream, and the honey in a saucepan. Bring to boil and let simmer for 8–10 minutes.

3. Remove the husks and discard. Puree the corn mixture in a blender, strain, season with salt and pepper, and reserve.

RELISH

1. Sauté the bacon until brown. Add the butter, the remaining corn, the shallots, and the fava beans; sauté 2–3 minutes.

2. Add the vinegar, sugar, and parsley to the pan and simmer 2–3 minutes. Add the peas and cook until warmed through. Season with salt and pepper.

ASSEMBLY

1. Spread the mashed potatoes on 4 pieces of toast. Place 1 salmon filet on top of each.

2. Place the relish on the other 4 slices of toast. Top with corn cream.

Sea Scallop on Potato Cake with White Truffle Hollandaise and Foie Gras Bits

SERVES: 4

TRUFFLE HOLLANDAISE

3 egg yolks

4 oz vinegar

1 tsp truffle paste

½ Tbsp black truffle oil

4 oz clarified butter

1–2 Tbsp lemon juice

1 tsp thyme

To taste, salt

To taste, freshly ground black pepper

POTATO CAKES

4 cups mashed Potatoes (see Chef's Pantry)

2 eggs, beaten

1 cup all-purpose flour

To taste, sea salt

2 pinches nutmeg

1 tsp chopped chives

1 cup Potato Buds

½ cup clarified butter

SCALLOPS

8 fresh dry-pack sea scallops

2 Tbsp olive oil

1 tsp Spice de Cosette

FOIE GRAS BITS

4 slices grade A foie gras

ASSEMBLY

12 Butter-Poached Asparagus Spears (see Chef's Pantry)

As needed, truffle slices

As needed, asparagus tips

TRUFFLE HOLLANDAISE

Follow the procedure for Hollandaise Sauce (see Chef's Pantry).

POTATO CAKES

1. In a medium mixing bowl, combine the mashed potatoes, egg, flour, salt, nutmeg, and chives. Mix well.

2. Using a 3-in. ring mold, form 8 potato cakes. Dredge the cakes in the Potato Buds and allow to stand for 15 minutes in the refrigerator.

3. Heat clarified butter as needed in a large frying pan over low heat. Place the potato cakes in the pan. Turn them over when the bottom is browned, 3–5 minutes. Brown the other side, about 3 minutes. Reserve and keep warm.

SCALLOPS

1. Toss the scallops in the olive oil and seasoning. Allow to stand for 10 minutes.

2. Sauté the scallops in a hot pan, 1–2 minutes on each side. Reserve and keep warm.

FOIE GRAS BITS

1. Place the foie gras slices in a cold refrigerator or freezer for 10 minutes. Cut them to a medium dice.

2. In a sauté pan, sauté the diced fois gras until nicely brown. Spoon onto a napkin. Reserve the fat.

ASSEMBLY

1. Place 2 potato cakes in the center of each plate. Set 1 scallop on top of each.

2. Spoon hollandaise over each scallop. Garnish with truffle slices and asparagus tips, if desired.

3. Lay 2 butter-poached asparagus spears on each plate and equally divide the foie gras bits over them. Drizzle more sauce or a touch of the foie gras drippings.

Seared Sea Scallops with Clam Chowder Sauce, Mushroom Essence, and Watercress Jus

Serves: 4

WATERCRESS JUS

2 cups watercress leaves, tightly packed

1 cup Giancarlo's Brodo (see Chef's Pantry)

To taste, kosher salt

To taste, cracked black pepper

MUSHROOM ESSENCE

⅔ cup dried porcini

½ cup dried morels

6 cups Giancarlo's Brodo, 4 cups warm, 2 cups cold (see Chef's Pantry)

½ cup fresh shiitakes, diced

½ cup fresh portobellos, diced

2 shallots, peeled and chopped

6 black peppercorns

1 blade mace

8 tarragon leaves

1 bay leaf, small

CLAM CHOWDER SAUCE

3 slices smoked bacon, chopped small

6 oz butter, unsalted

1 garlic clove, sliced thin

½ cup diced celery

½ cup diced onion

2 oz all-purpose flour

3 cups high-quality clam broth

1½ cups heavy cream

2 cups diced Idaho potatoes

To taste, Tabasco Sauce

1 oz Anise honey

2 Tbsp finely chopped thyme

ASSEMBLY

3 Tbsp olive oil

12 sea scallops

8 oz fresh clam meat

WATERCRESS JUS

1. Bring 1 gal water and 1 cup kosher salt to a rapid boil over high heat. Place the watercress in the boiling water for 10 seconds and then remove immediately to an ice bath to stop the cooking process. Squeeze the watercress dry and place in a blender. Add ½ cup of the brodo and puree for 2 minutes or until smooth. Add more of the brodo as needed. Remove the jus from the blender and season to taste with kosher salt and black pepper. Reserve at room temperature for service.

MUSHROOM ESSENCE

1. Combine the dried mushrooms in a bowl with the warm brodo. Set a small plate on top to keep the mushrooms submerged. Cover and allow to sit for 1 hour.

2. Remove the mushrooms from the liquid and squeeze out as much liquid as possible. Return this liquid to the soaking liquid.

3. Chop the mushrooms thoroughly.

4. In a medium saucepan, combine the soaked mushrooms, fresh mushrooms, shallot, peppercorns, mace, tarragon, bay leaf, and cold brodo. Bring to a simmer over medium heat. Simmer for 10 minutes.

5. Strain the liquid from the dried mushrooms through a fine sieve twice. Add the strained liquid to the saucepan and return to a simmer over medium heat. Continue to simmer for an additional 20 minutes. Strain well into a clean saucepan.

6. Bring this liquid back to a simmer over medium heat. Continue to simmer until the liquid has reduced to 1 cup. Remove from heat and season to taste with kosher salt. Reserve for service.

CLAM CHOWDER SAUCE

1. In a 2-qt saucepot, render the bacon over low heat with 2 oz of the butter. Add the garlic, celery, and onions. Cook until tender.

2. Add the flour and continue to cook for 2 minutes, stirring constantly.

3. Add the clam broth and stir until smooth. Bring to a light simmer and continue to cook, stirring occasionally, until the flour is cooked out.

4. Stir in the cream and potatoes. Simmer gently until the potatoes are almost cooked through.

5. Add the Tabasco Sauce, anise honey, and thyme. Adjust the seasoning with salt and pepper. Reserve for service.

ASSEMBLY

1. At time of service, preheat a cast-iron skillet over medium-high heat for 5 minutes. Add 3 Tbsp olive oil and allow to heat for 2 minutes.

2. Season the scallops with salt and pepper. Sear on both sides until golden brown, 1–2 minutes each side.

3. Bring the chowder sauce back to a simmer. Add the clam meat and the remaining cold butter.

4. Place 3 scallops on each of 4 heated dinner plates. Spoon the clam chowder sauce over the scallops. Drizzle lightly with the mushroom essence and the watercress jus. Serve immediately.

Grilled Spiced Shrimp with Pulled Braised Pork Spring Roll, Asian Vegetables, Chili Oil, and Mint Foamy Sauce

SERVES: 4

20 jumbo shrimp, clean and deveined

2 Tbsp Spice de Cosette

½ cup grapeseed oil

2 lb pork shoulder

4 garlic cloves

½ cup sliced onion

As needed, Chicken Brodo (see Chef's Pantry)

½ cup dry sherry

⅓ cup dark soy sauce

2 crystals Chinese yellow rock sugar

3 star anise

3 cloves

1 cinnamon stick

6 dried chiles, small

3 pieces dried tangerine peel

2 thick slices fresh ginger

As needed, kosher salt

To taste, cracked black pepper

½ head savoy cabbage, shaved thin

1 carrot, grated

1 onion, diced small

2 garlic cloves, minced

1 cup olive oil

Eight 8-in. rice paper wrappers

1 cup mint, tightly packed

2 cups heavy cream

3 oz olive oil

2 cups vegetable oil

1. Place the shrimp in a medium mixing bowl and add the Spice de Cosette. Toss gently and allow to marinate until service.

2. Heat a heavy-bottomed braising pan over high heat for 5 minutes. Add the grapeseed oil and allow to heat for an additional 3 minutes. Place the pork in the hot oil and sear on all sides until evenly browned.

3. Add the garlic cloves and sliced onions and brown slightly. Add to the pot enough brodo to cover the pork. Add the sherry wine and bring to a boil. Lower the heat to a slow simmer and partially cover. Cook for 50 minutes.

4. Add the soy sauce, Chinese rock sugar, star anise, cloves, cinnamon stick, 2 of the dried chiles, tangerine peel, ginger, and scallion to the pork and continue to simmer for another 2½–3 hours, or until the pork is very tender.

5. Remove the pork from the liquid and allow to cool slightly. Strain the liquid and reduce to a syrup over medium heat.

6. While the liquid is reducing, shred the pork using two forks. Add the syrup to the shredded pork and toss gently. Season the

pork mixture with kosher salt and pepper to taste. Add the cabbage, carrots, onion, and garlic to the pork. Adjust the seasoning with salt and pepper if needed and reserve.

7. Grind the remaining chiles to a fine dust in a coffee grinder and place the ground peppers in a small saucepan. Add 1 cup olive oil and set over a low flame. Heat the oil slowly for 5 minutes. Remove from the heat and cover. Allow the oil to sit at room temperature for 24 hours. Strain through a coffee filter and reserve for service in a squeeze bottle.

8. Gently submerge 1 rice paper wrapper in warm water in a shallow pan or dish, then rest the wrapper over the edge of a colander for 1 minute to soften.

9. Spoon 2–3 Tbsp of the pork and vegetable mixture onto the softened wrapper. Roll one side of the wrapper over the filling, tuck in the top and bottom ends, and continue rolling. Place seam side down on a plate and cover with a damp towel. Continue filling and rolling wraps until all wraps are filled. Reserve covered for service.

10. Bring 1 gal water and 1 cup kosher salt to a boil over high heat. Place the mint leaves in the boiling water for 10 seconds. Remove immediately to an ice bath to stop the cooking process. Squeeze the mint dry and chop roughly.

11. Combine the cream and the blanched mint in a small saucepan. Heat gently over medium heat and allow to simmer for 5 minutes. Place the mixture in a high-speed blender and puree on high for 2 minutes. Strain through a fine sieve. Place the liquid in a foam gun with 2 charges of CO_2. Reserve for service.

12. Heat a large sauté pan over medium heat for 5 minutes. Add the olive oil and allow to heat for 2 minutes. Add the marinated shrimp and cook until cooked through. Reserve in a warm place.

13. At time of service, heat the vegetable oil in a large saucepan over medium heat until it reaches 350°F. Fry the spring rolls in the hot vegetable oil a few at a time until golden brown and heated through.

14. Place 2 spring rolls in the center of each of 4 heated dinner plates. Divide the shrimp evenly among the four plates. Top the shrimp with the mint foam and drizzle with the chile oil. Serve immediately.

Cosette's Pot of Poached Shrimp in Olive Oil Broth with Tomatoes, Spring Peas, and Artichokes

SERVES: 4

16 jumbo shrimp, shell on

¼ cup chopped carrots

¼ cup chopped celery

¼ cup chopped leeks

¼ cup chopped onion

4 oz extra-virgin olive oil, preferably Tuscan

2 oz dry white wine

3 cups light shrimp stock

1 bouquet garni

1 bay leaf

1 sprig thyme

2 sprigs Italian parsley

1 tsp black peppercorns

1 tsp mustard seeds

1 lemon, cut in half

8 oz spring peas, shelled

8 artichokes, cut in half

24 red grape tomatoes, peeled

1 tsp chopped thyme

To taste, sea salt

To taste, freshly ground black pepper

2 Tbsp best-quality extra-virgin olive oil

1. Remove the shells from the shrimp and reserve them for the broth. Devein the shrimp and rinse them gently under cold running water. Reserve the shrimp in the refrigerator until needed.

2. Place the shrimp shells in a small roasting pan and roast in a preheated 350°F oven until they are bright red.

3. Place the roasted shells into a small stockpot and add the carrots, celery, leeks, onion, olive oil, wine, stock, and bouquet garni. Bring to a simmer over medium heat and allow to simmer gently for 20 minutes. Strain the broth through cheesecloth into another small stockpot.

4. Place the bay leaf, thyme sprig, parsley, peppercorns, mustard seeds, and lemon in cheesecloth to form a sachet. Add the sachet to the strained broth and return to a simmer over medium heat.

5. Add the shrimp and gently poach them until just cooked, 2–3 minutes. Remove and reserve in a warm place until service.

6. Remove the sachet from the broth and return the liquid to a simmer. Add the spring peas and artichokes and simmer gently until the peas are tender, about 1 minute. Add the tomatoes and simmer 1 more minute.

7. Heat 4 serving bowls and divide the vegetables equally among them. Place 4 shrimp in each bowl.

8. Add the fresh thyme to the broth and bring to a simmer. Add butter and blend with a blender stick for 2 minutes. Adjust the seasoning with salt and pepper. Place the olive oil in a small squeeze bottle. Pour 4 oz broth into each bowl drizzle the extra virgin olive oil into each bowl and serve immediately.

9

Beef

Meat, especially red meat, is the traditional soul of club cuisine. From the days of beef Wellington, tournedoes Rossini, and other favorites, it is a member favorite. Before club cuisine began exploring new roads, for many club members a good steak or a prime rib of beef was their best bet. For golf clubs, no outing is complete without the grills being fired up and filled with large, well-seasoned steaks. Even though the cuisine has changed steaks remain a favorite, as do the infamous prime rib nights.

In my kitchens, we use a natural beef that we age for 14 to 21 days. We do our own butchering to the cuts required on the menu or for a special event. The meat is seasoned with a special steak seasoning just before cooking and coated with butter, olive oil, or a beef glaze prior to roasting in a hot oven. Many grilled or pan-seared steak dishes are also featured; these give the meat a nice crust that seals in the juices.

We also feature weekly butcher specials—oversized cuts that are simply grilled and finished with a drizzle of Tuscan extra-virgin olive oil. I tend to like meat with some body and texture. There is no doubt that fillet mignon is a club favorite, but for me, a great dry-aged New York sirloin or rib-eye wins every time. I hope you try my version of the classic Rossini, usually made with fillet mignon but in this case a mignon of prime dry-aged New York sirloin.

They say beef is back; I do not believe it ever left.

MENU

Natural Beef New York Sirloin
Steak Pan-Seared in a Cast-Iron
Pan, Swiss Chard, Potato and
Bean Chili, and Roasted Shallot Jus

New York Sirloin with Cèpe,
Chestnut, and Chanterelle Stew,
Garlic Jus, and Potato Puree

Petite Fillet Mignon Char-Grilled,
Potato Cake, Truffle Yukon Potato
Sauce, Beets, Roasted Onion,
and Garlic

Pièce de Boeuf Rossini

*Sliced Prime Beef with Madeira Sauce, Truffles,
and Foie Gras, Potatoes Anna, and Spinach*

Roast of Beef Tenderloin with
Crispy Bacon, Potato Cake,
Red Carrots, and Barley Jus

Fillet of Beef Roasted in Coffee
Beans with a Velvet Chile Sauce

Natural Beef New York Sirloin Steak Pan-Seared in a Cast-Iron Pan, Swiss Chard, Potato and Bean Chili, and Roasted Shallot Jus

SERVES: 4

STEAKS

2 cloves garlic

3 lb center-cut sirloin steaks, trimmed, cut into 4 portions

2 Tbsp extra-virgin olive oil

1 tsp sea salt

POTATO AND BEAN CHILI

1 lb Idaho potatoes, peeled and diced small

1 onion, large, small dice

1 red pepper, large, diced

⅓ cup dried morels

2 Tbsp walnut oil

4 Tbsp olive oil

¼ cup tomato paste

1 garlic clove, large, sliced thin

2–3 Tbsp Ariadna Chili Spice

½ cup Chianti

1 cup peeled, diced roma tomatoes

1 cup white beans, cooked

2 cups Giancarlo's Brodo (see Chef's Pantry)

1 Tbsp fresh pluches oregano

½ tsp red pepper flakes

2 tsp Chipotle sauce

4 Tbsp extra-virgin olive oil

To taste, kosher salt

To taste, freshly ground black pepper

ASSEMBLY

As needed, Swiss chard or spinach, sautéed

STEAKS

1. Cut the garlic cloves in half. Rub the garlic over the steaks on both sides. Rub the steaks next with olive oil. Sprinkle with salt.

2. Heat a cast-iron skillet on medium-high heat. Pan-sear the steaks 3–4 minutes per side, then finish to desired doneness.

POTATO AND BEAN CHILI

1. Sauté the potatoes, onion, red pepper, and morels in the walnut and olive oils for 4 minutes. Add the tomato paste, garlic, and chili spice; cook 1 minute more. Add the red wine to deglaze the pan.

2. Add tomatoes, beans, and brodo. Bring to a boil, reduce to a simmer, and cook for 30 minutes or until the potatoes are almost tender and the mixture is thickened.

3. Add the oregano, pepper flakes, and chipotle sauce, and olive oil. Adjust the seasoning with salt and pepper.

ASSEMBLY

1. Serve the steaks with sautéed Swiss chard or spinach.

New York Sirloin with Cèpe, Chestnut, and Chanterelle Stew, Garlic Jus, and Potato Puree

SERVES: 4

STEAKS

2 Tbsp ChefNique Master Steak Seasoning

3 Tbsp olive oil

2 Tbsp fresh lime juice

3–4 lb center-cut New York sirloin of natural beef, cut in 4 portions

4 Tbsp clarified butter

As needed, Cashew Salt (see Chef's Pantry)

CÈPE, CHESTNUT, AND CHANTERELLE STEW

3 oz butter, unsalted

2 Tbsp olive oil

1 shallot, finely diced

1½ lbs cèpes

1½ lbs chanterelles

2 Tbsp all-purpose flour

2 Tbsp tomato paste

1 cup dry red wine

3 cups mushroom broth

1 cup chestnuts, roasted, peeled, cut in half

1¼ cup heavy cream

2 Tbsp butter, unsalted, cold, diced

To taste, tarragon, chopped

To taste, kosher salt

ASSEMBLY

Mashed Potatoes, Simply the Best (see Chef's Pantry)

As needed, Garlic Jus (see Chef's Pantry)

STEAK

1. Mix steak seasoning, olive oil, and lime juice well; let sit for 10 minutes. Rub all over steaks on both sides.

2. Melt the butter in a cast-iron skillet and brown the steaks well on both sides.

3. Place the steak in a 375°F oven until it reaches the desired doneness. Remove steak to cake rack and let rest for 3–5 minutes.

4. Place the steak on a plate; leave whole or slice. Lightly sprinkle with Cashew Salt.

CÈPE, CHESTNUT, AND CHANTERELLE STEW

1. Melt the butter and oil in a heavy-bottomed soup pot over medium heat. Sauté the shallots, cèpes, and chanterelles until tender.

2. Add the flour and tomato paste. Cook, stirring often, for 5 minutes. Deglaze with red wine and stir until the wine is almost evaporated.

3. Add the broth and chestnuts. Simmer for 20–30 minutes or until the mushrooms are cooked and the sauce is thickened.

4. Add the cream. Stir in the butter. Season to taste with tarragon and salt.

ASSEMBLY

1. Top the steak with the mushroom mixture.

2. Serve with the potatoes and garlic jus.

Petite Fillet Mignon Char-Grilled, Potato Cake, Truffle Yukon Potato Sauce, Beets, Roasted Onion, and Garlic

SERVES: 4

STEAK

Four 6-oz fillets mignon

To taste, salt

To taste, freshly ground black pepper

As needed, grapeseed oil

TRUFFLE YUKON POTATO SAUCE

1 Yukon Gold potato, peeled and diced

2 tsp arrowroot

2 tsp Chicken Brodo, cold (see Chef's Pantry)

⅔ cup Chicken Brodo, hot (see Chef's Pantry)

2 Tbsp butter, unsalted

1 tsp truffle slices

1 tsp truffle oil

To taste, salt

To taste, freshly ground black pepper

ROASTED BEETS AND ONIONS

20 baby beets

2 Tbsp olive oil

2 Tbsp fresh lime juice

4 Tbsp extra-virgin olive oil

2 Tbsp brown sugar

Pinch kosher salt

Pinch white pepper

8 garlic cloves, peeled

12 cipolline onions, peeled

5 Tbsp butter, unsalted, diced

½ cup Giancarlo's Brodo (see Chef's Pantry)

2 tsp chopped tarragon

To taste, sea salt

POTATO CAKE

3 Yukon Gold potatoes, large

3 Tbsp butter, unsalted

2 Tbsp extra-virgin olive oil

To taste, kosher salt

To taste, white truffle oil

2 eggs, medium-boiled and diced

⅓ cup clarified butter

ASSEMBLY

3 oz Demi de Edward Christopher (see Chef's Pantry), hot

As needed, Fried Onions (see Chef's Pantry)

STEAK

1. Season both sides of the fillets with salt and pepper. Rub well with oil.

2. Place the fillets on the grill at a 45-degree angle to establish nice grill marks. Cook to desired doneness. Remove the steaks from the grill and let rest 5 minutes before serving.

TRUFFLE YUKON POTATO SAUCE

1. Boil the potatoes in lightly salted water until tender. Strain and place in a blender.

2. Mix the arrowroot with the cold brodo. Whisk this mixture into the hot brodo.

3. Add half the brodo mixture to the potatoes and puree completely. Add the remaining brodo and puree, but do not overmix.

4. Remove the puree from blender to a stainless-steel pan. Adjust consistency with more brodo if needed. Whisk in the butter, truffle slices, and oil. Season to taste with salt and pepper. Place in a squeeze bottle and reserve.

ROASTED BEETS AND ONIONS

1. Rub the beets with the olive oil. Roast in a 375°F oven until the beets are just tender. Peel the beets and reserve.

2. In a bowl, whisk together the lime juice, olive oil, sugar, salt, and pepper. Toss this marinade with the garlic and onions.

3. In a small roasting pan, place the garlic, onions, and marinade. Add 3 Tbsp of the butter. Roast at 350°F, turning as needed, until light brown and tender, about 10–15 minutes depending on your oven. If needed, add some brodo to avoid drying out the onions or burning the pan.

4. Add the beets and the remaining butter. Roast at 375°F for 3–5 minutes. Season with tarragon and salt.

POTATO CAKE

1. In salted water, cook the whole potatoes until tender. Drain well. Peel while still hot.

2. In a stainless-steel bowl, mash the potatoes with a fork or masher. Gently mash in the butter and olive oil. Season with salt and truffle oil. Fold in the diced eggs.

3. Divide the potato mixture equally among 4 stainless-steel ring molds and let cool.

4. In a nonstick pan, sauté the potato cakes in the clarified butter until brown on both sides.

ASSEMBLY

1. Place 1 potato cake in the center of each plate. Top with 1 fillet. Spoon hot demi on the fillet.

2. Spoon roasted beets and onions around the fillet. Garnish the fillet with Fried Onions.

3. Squeeze potato sauce around the fillet and vegetables.

Pièce de Boeuf Rossini

SERVES: 4

BEEF

3 tsp sea salt

Four 6-oz mignons of prime New York sirloin

3 Tbsp clarified butter

FOIE GRAS

4 slices of grade A foie gras, about ½ in. thick and 2–3 in. in diameter

8 slices truffle

½ cup Madeira wine

POTATOES

2 Yukon Gold potatoes, large

To taste, kosher salt

½ cup clarified butter

SAUCE

2 carrots, diced

1 onion, small, diced

2 Tbsp grapeseed oil

1 tsp butter, unsalted

½ cup chopped mushrooms

2 Tbsp butter, unsalted

3 Tbsp tomato paste

½ cup Madeira

1 cup Beef Brodo (see Chef's Pantry)

½ cup Demi de Edward Christopher (see Chef's Pantry)

2 Tbsp butter, unsalted, diced and cold

1 Tbsp minced truffle slices

1–2 Tbsp truffle liquor

To taste, salt

SPINACH

2 Tbsp olive oil

1 garlic clove, sliced thin

1 large bunch fresh baby spinach, washed and stemmed

2–3 Tbsp Giancarlo's Brodo (see Chef's Pantry)

To taste, kosher salt

To taste, freshly ground black pepper

ASSEMBLY

4 fried bread croutons, 3 in. square, for garnish

BEEF

1. Rub the salt on the beef just prior to cooking.

2. In a heavy-bottomed pan, heat the butter and sear the beef until rich brown on both sides.

3. Place the beef on a rack in a roasting pan. Finish cooking in a 350°F oven until desired doneness. Let the beef rest on the rack for 3–5 minutes before serving.

FOIE GRAS

1. Marinate the foie gras and truffle slices in the wine for 10 minutes. Pat the foie gras dry and season with salt.

2. Sauté the foie gras until cooked and browned on both sides; reserve.

3. Drain the truffles; reserve.

POTATOES

1. Peel the potatoes and slice very thin. Place in the clarified butter and season with a little kosher salt.

2. In 3–4-in. pans, layer the buttered potatoes in a circle.

3. Cook the potatoes over medium heat until golden brown. Turn over the potatoes and brown the other side.

4. Remove the potato disks from the pans and place on paper towel.

SAUCE

1. In a saucepan, sauté the carrots and onions in the oil and 1 tsp butter until light brown. Add the mushrooms and 2 Tbsp butter; cook 2–3 minutes.

2. Add the tomato paste and mix well over on low heat. Deglaze the pan with the wine, then raise the heat to medium. Add the brodo and cook for 15 minutes.

3. Strain the sauce and place in a small saucepan. Add the demi and reduce to desired consistency.

4. Finish the sauce with the cold diced butter, truffles, and truffle liquor. Season with salt.

SPINACH

1. In a large skillet, heat the oil and sauté the garlic for 1 minute. Add the spinach and sauté, stirring occasionally, until the leaves are wilted and bright green. Add the brodo, salt, and pepper; sauté for 1 more minute.

ASSEMBLY

1. Place 1 crouton on each plate and place 1 fillet on top.

2. Place the foie gras on the beef and top with 1 potato disk.

3. Place spinach on the plate, garnish with 2 oz sauce, and serve.

Roast of Beef Tenderloin with Crispy Bacon, Potato Cake, Red Carrots, and Barley Jus

SERVES: 4

BACON

2 Tbsp grapeseed oil

12 oz slab fresh bacon

½ cup white wine

½ cup Giancarlo's Brodo (see Chef's Pantry)

1 tsp peppercorns

2 star anise

4 cloves

2 shallots, diced

½ cup diced apple

BEEF

2–3 Tbsp olive oil

Four 8-oz pieces of center-cut beef tenderloin

To taste, sea salt

½ cup demi-glace

GLAZED RED CARROTS

3 cups peeled and cut red carrots or whole peeled
    baby red carrots

½ cup Giancarlo's Brodo (see Chef's Pantry)

⅓ cup Riesling

½ vanilla bean

2 Tbsp high-quality butter, unsalted

1 Tbsp fresh lime juice

1 Tbsp granulated sugar

2 Tbsp brown sugar

1 tsp candied ginger

ASSEMBLY

4 Potato Cakes (see page 142)

As needed, Barley Jus (see Chef's Pantry)

As needed, Fried Onions (see Chef's Pantry)

BACON

1. In a sauté pan, heat the oil and brown the bacon slab on both sides until golden brown.

2. Preheat the oven to 240°F. Place the bacon in a roasting pan with the wine, stock, peppercorns, star anise, cloves, shallots, and apple. Cover tightly with foil and roast for 45 minutes.

3. Increase the oven temperature to 375°F. Remove the foil and cook for another 15 minutes.

4. Chill the bacon and cut it into 1- or 2-in. pieces. Deep fry or roast the bacon pieces until crisp.

BEEF

1. Preheat the oven to 400°F. Heat a cast-iron pan and add oil.

2. Season the tenderloins with salt. In the hot pan, brown them on all sides until nicely browned.

3. Place the tenderloins on a rack in a roasting pan and roast in the oven for 3–4 minutes.

4. Brush the demi-glace on the meat, then finish roasting until desired doneness.

5. Let the meat rest on the rack 3–5 minutes before slicing.

GLAZED RED CARROTS

1. Cook the carrots, brodo, wine, vanilla bean, and butter in a large skillet over medium heat for 10–12 minutes or until the liquid is evaporated.

2. Reduce heat to medium-low. Stir in the lime juice, sugars, and ginger. Cook for 5 minutes, stirring occasionally, or until carrots are glazed. Remove the vanilla bean and toss carrots with candied ginger.

ASSEMBLY

1. Place 1 Potato Cake on each plate and garnish with Fried Onions. Slice the tenderloins into 3 or 4 slices each and place around the cake. Place carrots on plate, spoon barley jus around the plate, and distribute the crisp bacon pieces.

Fillet of Beef Roasted in Coffee Beans with a Velvet Chile Sauce

Serves: 4

2 Tbsp olive oil

1 Tbsp pureed roasted garlic

½ cup diced onion

3 oz ancho chiles, chopped

1 oz tomato paste

½ cup strong coffee

½ cup roasted red peppers

½ cup Chicken Brodo (see Chef's Pantry)

1 Tbsp chili powder

2 Tbsp high-quality cocoa powder

1 cup Veal Demi-Glace (see Chef's Pantry)

2 Tbsp butter, unsalted, cold and diced

To taste, salt

To taste, freshly ground black pepper

4 Tbsp grapeseed oil

2 Tbsp butter, unsalted

Four 5-oz center-cut fillet mignon steaks

1 cup ground high-quality coffee

1. Heat the olive oil in a heavy-bottomed sauté pan and sauté the garlic, onions, and chiles. Add the tomato paste and cook for 1–2 minutes. Add the coffee, deglaze, and simmer 2–3 minutes.

2. Add the red peppers, broth, chili powder, and cocoa powder, and simmer for 25 minutes.

3. Place the mixture in a blender or food processor and blend until smooth.

4. Fold in 1 cup hot Veal Demi-Glace. Stir in the butter. Adjust seasonings and consistency, if needed.

5. In a stainless-steel heavy bottomed sauté pan, heat the grapeseed oil and butter. Coat the steaks well with the ground coffee. Sauté the steaks over medium heat until a light brown crust forms, 2–3 minutes per side. Do not overbrown, as the coffee will become bitter.

6. Place the browned meat on a rack in a 350°F oven and roast to desired doneness.

7. Let the meat rest 1–2 minutes, plate, and coat with chili sauce.

Chef's Note: For safety, be careful not to overfill the blender with hot food, and be sure to build up blending speed slowly.

Chef's Note: Serve this dish with rice and beans for a real treat.

10

Beyond Beef

This chapter is one of my favorites. Beef and seafood are always popular with club members and guests, but it is the challenge of creating exciting dishes with chicken, veal, lamb, and other meats, tempting the diner to forget about beef and seafood, that excites me.

My first fine dining experience at an expensive restaurant with a top chef was New York City's Lutèce. The chef at the time was Andre Soultner, and he was famous for, believe it or not, roasted chicken. Until I experienced Chef Soultner's roasted chicken, I did not truly understand the art and the skill needed to do something so simple so well.

A similar example is one of the club's most popular dishes: veal Milanese. While this is a simple piece of fried breaded meat served with a salad, it is only when sound cooking principles are properly applied that this simple piece of meat becomes a customer favorite. Many procedures combine to make this dish great: the pounding of the meat, the seasoning, the breading procedure. For the pan-frying (it should not be put in a Frialator), clarified butter should be used. The pan must be hot enough to brown the veal and the crumbs such that the veal is not greasy and yet not so hot that the crumbs burn or the breading is cooked before the meat is done. The care and attention given to every stage of preparation and cooking transform a dish into a memorable experience.

The dishes in this chapter also offer flavor profiles that harmonize and complement the main item. Read, study, and cook beyond beef; experience all the larger world has to offer.

MENU

French Breast of Chicken with Artichoke, Olive Oil Tomatoes, Peas, Roasted Garlic Emulsion, and Risotto Cake

French Breast of Chicken with Spring Asparagus Three Ways on Parmesan Risotto

Braised Veal Cheeks with Maple-Glazed Veal Loin, Candied Apple, Polenta, and Root Vegetables

Veal Milanese

Breaded Veal Cutlet Pan-Fried with a Salad of Arugula and Tomatoes

Pan-Seared Duck Breast Infused with Cinnamon, Savory Cobbler of Maple-Braised Duck, Sweet Potatoes, Pecans, Brussels Sprouts, and Cranberry Jus

Broiled Pork Rib-Eye, Roasted Cipolline, Roasted Potato, Swiss Chard, and Sage Potato Butter

Roast Loin of Colorado Lamb over a Warm Salad of Fingerling Potatoes, Artichokes, and Grape Tomatoes with a Light Garlic Jus

Sautéed Lamb with Eggplant and Orange Relish and Cardamom Caramel Sauce

French Breast
of Chicken with
Artichoke, Olive Oil
Tomatoes, Peas, Roasted
Garlic Emulsion,
and Risotto Cake

SERVES: 4

CHICKEN

4 French breasts of chicken

2 Tbsp olive oil

1 tsp chopped parsley

½ tsp chopped thyme

To taste, salt

To taste, milled peppercorns

As needed, Olive Oil Tomatoes (see Chef's Pantry)

ROASTED GARLIC EMULSION

1 cup garlic cloves

As needed, Giancarlo's Brodo (see Chef's Pantry)

2 Tbsp honey

1 oz butter, unsalted

⅓ cup white wine

2 shallots, minced

1½ cups heavy cream

4–6 Tbsp butter, unsalted, cold

To taste, salt

To taste, freshly ground black pepper

2 Tbsp extra-virgin olive oil

RISOTTO CAKES*

3 Tbsp butter, unsalted

1 Tbsp olive oil

1 leek, thinly sliced and diced

1 cup raw short-grain Italian rice (Vialone Nano)

2½ cups Chicken Brodo, hot (see Chef's Pantry)

2 Tbsp chopped basil

2 Tbsp chopped parsley

¾ cup shredded Asiago cheese

4 Tbsp whole butter, unsalted

4 Tbsp cream

To taste, kosher salt

To taste, freshly ground black pepper

As needed, clarified butter

ASSEMBLY

8 artichoke halves, prepared as in Grilled Sea Bass
    recipe (see page 116)

¼ cup petite peas

2 Tbsp whole butter, unsalted

To taste, kosher salt

½ tsp minced fresh mint leaves

*Make the risotto cakes at least 3 hours or up
to 1 day before preparing the rest of this dish.

CHICKEN

1. Place the chicken in a bowl with the olive
   oil, parsley, thyme, salt, and pepper. Toss to
   season evenly.

2. Chicken can be roasted or grilled to your
   liking. I prefer placing the chicken on a
   rack over a pan and roasting for 6 minutes
   at 425°F, then another 8–12 minutes at

325°F, until the chicken is just done and the juice runs clear. Keep the chicken warm.

ROASTED GARLIC EMULSION

1. Place the garlic in a small pan. Cover to three-quarters depth with the brodo. Add the honey and butter. Bring to a gentle simmer and cook until the garlic cloves are tender, 10–12 minutes. Remove garlic cloves and reserve the broth.

2. In a saucepan, simmer the wine and shallots until reduced to about 1 oz.

3. Add the garlic cloves to the wine reduction. Add the cream and 2 oz of the reserved broth. Simmer until the liquid is reduced in half.

4. Puree the mixture with a hand blender while slowly adding the cold butter. Do not allow the emulsion to break.

5. Strain the emulsion and season with salt, pepper, and the olive oil.

RISOTTO CAKE

1. Place the butter and oil in a heavy-bottomed pan. Add the leek and cook until soft.

2. Add the rice and cook 1–2 minutes. Add half of the brodo, bring to a simmer, and cook slowly until all of the liquid is absorbed.

3. Add the remaining brodo and cook until it is absorbed and the rice is tender but still slightly firm.

4. Fold in the basil, parsley, Asiago, butter, and cream. Season with salt and pepper. Spread the mixture on a small pan 1 to 1½ in. in height. Cool in the refrigerator overnight.

5. Cut the chilled rice mixture into the desired shapes. Pan-fry the cakes in clarified butter until golden brown on each side.

ASSEMBLY

1. In a saucepan, take the artichoke halves, peas, butter, and mint along with the remaining reserved broth and cook for 2–3 minutes until items are hot.

2. Place the risotto cake in the middle of the plate. Top with the chicken breast. Around the plate, distribute the peas, artichokes, and tomatoes. Lace the emulsion over the items on the plate from a squeeze bottle, or place spots of sauce around the plate.

French Breast of Chicken with Spring Asparagus Three Ways on Parmesan Risotto

SERVES: 4

CHICKEN

4 french breasts of chicken

To taste, kosher salt

To taste, freshly ground black pepper

¼ cup clarified butter

3 Tbsp whole butter, unsalted

2 shallots

6 oz mushrooms

½ cup white wine

2 oz butter, unsalted

4–6 Tbsp Chicken Jus (see Chef's Pantry)

1 tsp chopped tarragon

2 tsp chopped parsley

To taste, salt

To taste, freshly ground black pepper

PARMESAN RISOTTO

3 Tbsp butter, unsalted

1 Tbsp olive oil

3 shallots, finely diced

1 cup raw short-grain Italian rice (Vialone Nano)

½ cup white wine

1½–2 cups Chicken Brodo, hot (see Chef's Pantry)

¾ cup grated high-quality Parmigiano-Reggiano

5 Tbsp high-quality butter, unsalted, cold and diced

To taste, salt

To taste, freshly ground black pepper

ASPARAGUS COULIS

1 lb asparagus, cleaned, ends cut off, and chopped

2 shallots, diced

6 Tbsp butter, unsalted

2 Tbsp all-purpose flour

1 cup Giancarlo's Brodo (see Chef's Pantry)

1½ cups cream, hot

6 Tbsp butter, unsalted, diced

To taste, kosher salt

½ teaspoon ground white pepper

3 Tbsp high-quality extra-virgin olive oil

ASSEMBLY

24 Butter-Poached Asparagus Spears (see Chef's Pantry)

4 parmesan cookies

8 asparagus ribbons

12 grape or cherry tomatoes, red and yellow peeled and sautéed

As needed, Tomato Syrup (see Chef's Pantry)

CHICKEN

1. Season the chicken to taste with salt and pepper.

2. Place the clarified butter in a sauté pan over high heat. Add the chicken to the pan. Cook until golden brown on both sides, about 4 minutes per side; then reserve on a small rack.

3. Add the butter and chopped shallots to the pan and sauté. Add the mushrooms and cook for another 2 minutes. Before the mushrooms begin to color, add the white wine. Reduce by the liquid by half and simmer for 1 minute.

4. Add the jus, tarragon, and parsley to the sauce. Return the chicken to the pan and cook gently, glazing the chicken with the jus for 2–3 minutes. Reserve.

PARMESAN RISOTTO

1. Heat the butter in a heavy-bottomed ovenproof casserole. Add the olive oil to the pan and sauté the shallots for 2 minutes. Add the rice and stir for 1 minute. Add the white wine and cook until it is absorbed.

2. Pour half of the hot brodo into the rice. Stir and cook over low heat until it is completely absorbed and the rice is al dente. Add the remaining brodo and stir continuously until it is absorbed. All of the brodo should be absorbed in about 15 minutes.

3. Stir in the parmesan and butter; adjust seasoning.

4. To make parmesan cookies, grate parmesan on a Silpat and bake for 4–6 minutes at 325°F until crisp.

ASPARAGUS COULIS

1. In a skillet over medium heat, cook the asparagus with the shallots and butter, salted lightly, for 3 minutes. Add the flour. Continue to stir over low heat another 2 minutes.

2. Add the brodo. Bring to a boil, stirring constantly, and simmer until the asparagus is tender, about 6 minutes.

3. In a blender, puree the asparagus with the cooking liquid until smooth, slowly start adding the cream until the desired consistency is reached.

4. Strain the puree twice with a chinois into a stainless-steel pan. Whisk in the butter and season to taste with salt and the white pepper. Drizzle in oil and stir slightly.

5. To make asparagus ribbons, take a peeler and shave strips of asparagus lengthwise. The ribbons can be used as they are or lightly sautéed in butter for about 30 seconds.

ASSEMBLY

1. Place 6 asparagus spears in the center of each plate. Set a ring mold on the asparagus and fill it with risotto.

2. Remove the ring mold. Top the risotto with a parmesan cookie and then a chicken breast.

3. Place 3 tomatoes around the chicken, sauce with 3 puddles of the coulis and the Tomato Syrup, and garnish with asparagus ribbons.

Braised Veal Cheeks with Maple-Glazed Veal Loin, Candied Apple, Polenta, and Root Vegetables

SERVES: 4

VEAL CHEEKS

10–12 pieces veal cheeks

1 oz clarified butter

½ cup flour, seasoned

To taste, salt

To taste, freshly ground black pepper

4 oz onions, small dice

3 oz carrots, small dice

2 oz celery, small dice

4 oz morels, quartered

1 oz garlic, sliced thin

2 oz shallots, minced

4 Roma tomatoes, peeled and seeded

1 sachet (rosemary, thyme, bay leaf, peppercorn, parsley stems)

½ cup California chardonnay

6 cups fortified veal stock

POLENTA

1 cup milk

½ cup Giancarlo's Brodo (see Chef's Pantry)

½ tsp chopped basil

¼ tsp chopped thyme

3 Tbsps butter, unsalted

¾ cup yellow cornmeal

To taste, salt

To taste, freshly ground black pepper

½ cup grated parmesan

2 Tbsp butter, unsalted, cold

1 Tbsp extra-virgin olive oil

VEAL LOIN

2 cups apple cider

6 oz maple syrup

1 apple, chopped

4 cloves

1 cinnamon stick

3 oz butter, unsalted

Four 6-oz veal tenders or mignons cut from the loin

To taste, salt

To taste, freshly ground black pepper

4 Tbsp olive oil

ROOT VEGETABLES

1 cup apple cider

¼ cup maple syrup

½ cup white port wine

4 Tbsp high-quality butter, unsalted, cold

½ cup peeled, cut, and shaped turnip

½ cup peeled, cut, and shaped parsnip

½ cup roll-cut carrots

½ cup medium diced sweet potatoe

½ cup paysanne-cut rutabaga

4 Tbsp butter, unsalted, cold and diced

To taste, salt

To taste, freshly ground black pepper

CANDIED APPLE

Eight ⅛-in. slices apple
As needed, simple syrup

VEAL CHEEKS

1. Clean the veal cheeks by removing excess fat and connective tissue from the surface of the meat. Heat the butter over medium-high heat. Dredge the cheeks in the seasoned flour and then place in the hot butter. Brown both sides well and season with salt and pepper.

2. After a fond begins to form on the surface of the brazier, add the onions, carrots, celery, and morels. Continue cooking until the vegetables are well browned. Add the garlic, shallots, and tomatoes.

3. When the tomatoes, garlic, and shallots are cooked out, add the sachet and the wine and reduce until the liquid is almost like syrup. Add the veal stock and bring the liquid up to a simmer. Braise the cheeks for about 2½ hours at 350°F. Remove the cheeks from the pot and place on a oven tray.

4. Glaze them by brushing them with some of the reduced braising liquid at 350°F for about 5 minutes. Let the liquid form a nice coating on the cheeks.

5. Reduce the leftover braising liquid to sauce consistency. Adjust the taste. Remove the sachet. Do not drain the sauce.

POLENTA

1. In a heavy-bottomed saucepan, bring the milk, brodo, basil, thyme, and butter to a boil. Slowly add the cornmeal while stirring continuously with a wooden spoon.

2. When all the cornmeal is incorporated, stir over low heat for 10–12 minutes until the polenta is smooth and starts to thicken. Season with salt and pepper. Fold in the parmesan, butter, and olive oil.

VEAL LOIN

1. In a stainless-steel saucepan, simmer the cider, syrup, chopped apple, clove, cinnamon, and butter until the liquid is reduced to a syrup. Strain well into a stainless-steel pan.

2. Season the tenderloins with salt and pepper and pan-sear them in the oil until brown on all sides.

3. Place the meat on a baking rack in a roasting pan. Brush with the syrup and roast in a 350°F oven until done to medium, 8–10 minutes, basting with the syrup at least 3 times. Remove the meat from the oven. Brush with the syrup once more.

ROOT VEGETABLES

1. In a stainless-steel saucepan, boil the cider, maple syrup and wine until reduced by one-half, about 30 minutes. Whisk in the butter.

2. Preheat the oven to 425°F.

3. Peel all of the vegetables and cut them into ½-in. pieces of different shapes.

4. Fill a 4-qt pot with water and add 2 Tbsp salt. Blanch all vegetables in the salted water for 5 minutes. Drain well.

5. Toss the vegetables in the cider mixture. Place in a roasting pan with the butter.

6. Roast in the 425°F oven 20–30 minutes, stirring occasionally, until vegetables are tender and golden. Season with salt and pepper.

CANDIED APPLE

1. Dip the apple slices in the syrup and place them on a Silpat.

2. Dry in a 160°F oven until crisp, about 2 hours. These can be made the night before or in advance and stored in an airtight container lined with a Silpat.

ASSEMBLY

1. Fill ramekins or small service pots two-thirds full of polenta. Top with cheeks and sauce and place on the plates.

2. Cut the loin into 2 or 3 pieces, shingle them on the plates, and drizzle with sauce from the cheeks.

3. Spoon on the vegetables. Garnish each plate with 2 candied apple slices.

Veal Milanese

SEASONED FLOUR

1 cup all-purpose flour

½ cup grated parmesan

2 tsp freshly ground black pepper

1 tsp chopped sage

VEAL

Four 10–12-oz Frenched veal chops

3 eggs

2 Tbsp extra-virgin olive oil

1 tsp salt

2 tsp chopped parsley

2 cups panko bread crumbs

As needed, duck fat

SALAD

4 cups cleaned and picked arugula

*12 petals Olive Oil Tomatoes (see Chef's Pantry) or
    olive oil cherry tomatoes*

To taste, kosher salt

To taste, freshly ground black pepper

6 Tbsp extra-virgin olive oil

2 Tbsp high-quality balsamic vinegar

SEASONED FLOUR

1. In a bowl, whisk together the flour, parmesan, pepper, and sage until blended.

VEAL

1. Pound out the veal chops to about ¼-in. thick, leaving in the bone. Use 1 cup of the seasoned flour to coat the veal.

2. Beat the eggs with the olive oil, salt, and parsley. Dredge veal in the egg mixture, then coat with bread crumbs. Chill the breaded veal for 1 hour.

3. In a cast-iron skillet, heat enough duck fat to cover the pan to a depth of ¼ in. Pan-fry the veal over medium-high heat until both sides are golden brown. Set the veal on paper towels to absorb excess fat.

SALAD

1. Toss together the arugula, tomatoes, salt, pepper, olive oil, and vinegar.

Pan-Seared Duck Breast Infused with Cinnamon, Savory Cobbler of Maple-Braised Duck, Sweet Potatoes, Pecans, Brussels Sprouts, and Cranberry Jus

SERVES: 4

3 oz sea salt

3 oz brown sugar

4 duck legs with thighs, cleaned

1 cup granulated sugar

To taste, cracked black pepper

1 cinnamon stick

1 cup kosher salt

2 Tbsp Cinnamon Honey (see Chef's Pantry)

4 duck breasts, cleaned

4 oz vegetable oil or duck fat

2 carrots, medium dice

2 onions, large, medium dice

2 celery stalks, peeled and diced

3 Bosc pears, ripe, peeled and diced

4 oz tomato paste

2 cups merlot

10 juniper berries, lightly crushed

1 bouquet garni

4 cloves

1 oz orange zest

1 cinnamon stick, crushed

6 black peppercorns

1 cup veal stock

1–2 cups Demi de Edward Christopher (see Chef's Pantry) or another demi-glace

2 lb sweet potatoes

Pinch salt

1 cup evaporated milk

2 eggs

2 Tbsp butter, unsalted, melted

To taste, kosher salt

To taste, freshly ground black pepper

1 cup crushed cornflakes

½ cup chopped pecans

2 Tbsp brown sugar

As needed, butter, unsalted

3 cups duck stock

1 bay leaf

1 cup dried cranberries

12 oz Brussels sprouts, cleaned and cut in half

2 slices bacon, diced small

As needed, Chicken Brodo (see Chef's Pantry)

1. Combine the sea salt with the brown sugar. Place the duck legs in a shallow dish and coat with the salt mixture. Set the duck legs in the refrigerator for 24 hours.

2. Combine the granulated sugar, pepper, and the cinnamon stick in a coffee grinder and grind for 20 seconds. Place in a mixing bowl and add the kosher salt and cinnamon honey. Mix well.

3. Sprinkle half of the cinnamon mixture over the bottom of a bowl. Place the duck breasts skin side down in the pan. Sprinkle the remaining mixture over the breasts. Allow to sit for 2 hours, turning once after 1 hour. Remove the breasts from the cure, rinse gently, and pat dry. Reserve.

4. Gently wash the cured duck legs, pat dry, and reserve.

5. In a heavy cast-iron skillet, heat the vegetable oil over medium heat. Add the duck legs and cook on all sides until the skin is crisp. Remove and reserve the legs. Drain and reserve the fat.

6. In a heavy-bottomed braising pan, heat 4 Tbsp of the reserved duck fat over medium heat. Add the carrots, onions, celery, and pears and sauté until lightly brown. Add the tomato paste and cook, stirring constantly, 4–5 minutes. Add the merlot to deglaze the pan; simmer until the liquid is reduced by half.

7. Add the duck legs, juniper berries, bouquet garni, cloves, zest, crushed cinnamon stick, peppercorns, and veal stock. Add demi until it fills one-third of the pan. Cover tightly and place in a preheated 325°F oven. Cook until tender, 1–2 hours. Remove the duck legs from the liquid; cool. Strain the liquid and reserve.

8. Remove the meat from the cooled duck legs and reserve.

9. Peel the sweet potatoes, place in a saucepan, and cover with cold water by 2 in. Add a big pinch of salt and bring to a simmer over medium heat. Simmer until tender. Drain the potatoes and rice into a mixing bowl.

10. In a mixing bowl, whip the evaporated milk and the eggs to combine.

11. Add 2 Tbsp melted butter and the egg mixture to the sweet potato puree. Mix gently until combined well. Season to taste with kosher salt and pepper. Reserve.

12. In a medium mixing bowl, combine the corn flakes, pecans, and 2 Tbsp brown sugar. Mix well and reserve.

13. Divide 4 oz sweet potato mixture among 4 ovenproof ramekins. Add to each 2 oz duck leg meat and 1 oz braising liquid. Cover each with another 1 oz sweet potato mixture. Top completely with the corn flake mixture. Reserve the cobblers.

14. In a small saucepan, bring the duck stock, the bay leaf, and the dried cranberries to a simmer and cook for 10 minutes. Strain into a clean saucepan. Return to a simmer and reduce by half. Reserve.

15. Bring 1 gal heavily salted water to a rapid boil. Add the Brussels sprouts and cook until tender, 3–5 minutes. Plunge the sprouts into an ice bath to stop the cooking process. Pat dry and reserve.

16. Score the skin side of the duck breasts in a crisscross pattern. Place skin side down in a cast-iron skillet. Cook slowly over very low heat for about 1 hour or until the skin becomes thin and crisp.

17. While the duck is rendering, render the bacon in another cast-iron skillet. When the bacon is almost crisp, add the Brussels sprouts along with a little brodo. Season with salt and pepper to taste. Continue to cook the sprouts, adding brodo as needed, until they are tender and glazed.

18. Once the skin on the duck is crisp, turn over the breasts, and raise the heat slightly. Cook for 2 minutes or to the desired doneness. Allow to rest in a warm place.

19. At time of service, place the cobblers into a preheated 375°F oven for 10 minutes or until heated through.

20. Return the cranberry jus to a simmer and whisk in 2 Tbsp cold butter. Adjust seasoning if necessary.

21. Slice the duck breasts into 5 pieces each and place on heated dinner plates. Place 1 cobbler onto each plate. Divide the Brussels sprouts evenly among the plates. Dress the duck breasts with the cranberry jus and serve immediately.

Broiled Pork Rib-Eye, Roasted Cipolline, Roasted Potato, Swiss Chard, and Sage Potato Butter

SERVES: 4

PORK RIB-EYE

Four 12-oz pork rib-eye steak chops

3 Tbsp olive oil

2 tsp kosher salt

1 tsp crushed red pepper

ONIONS

2 Tbsp butter, unsalted

16–20 cipolline onions, blanched and peeled

1 garlic clove, peeled and cut in half

½ cup authentic balsamic vinegar di Modena

4 Tbsp sugar

2 Tbsp butter, unsalted, cold and diced

SWISS CHARD

2 Tbsp olive oil

2 Tbsp butter, unsalted

1 tsp brown sugar

1 bunch red Swiss chard, rinsed and chopped

¼ cup diced kalamata olives

¼ cup diced apples

½ teaspoon coarse sea salt

⅓ cup apple juice

To taste, freshly ground black pepper

2 Tbsp butter, unsalted

ROASTED POTATOES

4 Yukon Gold potatoes, medium, peeled and squared off

2 Tbsp butter, unsalted, melted

1 Tbsp honey

1 tsp dry mustard

Pinch salt

Pinch freshly ground black pepper

ASSEMBLY

As needed, Sage Potato Butter (see Chef's Pantry)

As needed, fried sage leaves

PORK RIB-EYE

1. Rub the steaks with the olive oil, then season with salt and red pepper.

2. Broil on medium-high heat to desired doneness.

ONIONS

1. Melt the butter in a heavy-bottomed pan. Add the onions and garlic. Add the vinegar and cook at high heat for 3–4 minutes.

2. Toss in the sugar and butter. Place in a 375°F oven and roast until the onions are tender and vinegar is evaporated.

SWISS CHARD

1. In a cast-iron skillet, heat the olive oil, add the butter and sugar, and cook for 1 minute.

2. Stir in the chard, olives, and apples. Cook until the chard is slightly wilted, about 3 minutes. Stir in the salt. Continue cooking until chard is wilted, about 2 minutes more.

3. Add the apple juice. Season with pepper, add the butter, and cook 1–2 minutes more.

ROASTED POTATOES

1. Boil the potatoes in salted water until tender but still firm, about 20 minutes. Drain well and dry.

2. In a small saucepan, melt the butter over low heat. Whisk in the honey, mustard, salt and pepper.

3. In a small bowl, toss the potatoes with the seasoned butter. Place the potatoes in a small roasting pan and roast in a preheated 375°F oven, turning until brown on all sides, 20–25 minutes.

ASSEMBLY

1. Place 1 potato on each plate. Divide the chard among the plates, then lean the pork over the potato. Top with the roasted onions.

2. Drizzle each plate with Sage Potato Butter and garnish with fried sage leaves.

Roast Loin of Colorado Lamb over a Warm Salad of Fingerling Potatoes, Artichokes, and Grape Tomatoes with a Light Garlic Jus

SERVES: 4

12 oz fingerling potatoes

As needed, kosher salt

10 garlic cloves

¼ cup olive oil

1 qt lamb stock

To taste, kosher salt

To taste, cracked black pepper

3 Tbsp olive oil

Four 6-oz portions boneless lamb loins, cleaned

2 oz olive oil

1 shallot, minced

1 garlic clove, minced

6 artichokes halves, prepared as in Grilled Sea Bass recipe (see page 116)

20 grape tomatoes, peeled

1 tsp chopped thyme

1 tsp chopped Italian parsley

As needed, Garlic Jus (see Chef's Pantry)

4 Tbsp butter, unsalted, diced and very cold

1. Wash the potatoes well under cold running water. Place into a medium saucepan and cover with cold water by 2 in. Add 1 Tbsp kosher salt for every quart of water. Bring to a simmer over medium heat and cook 20–25 minutes until the potatoes are tender. Remove the potatoes from the water immediately and cool them in the refrigerator. Cut in half and reserve.

2. Place the garlic cloves in a 2-qt saucepan, add ¼ cup olive oil, and set over medium-low heat. Gently cook the garlic, stirring often, until it is golden brown and tender.

3. Add the lamb stock to the saucepan and simmer for 20 minutes. Puree the sauce with a blending stick and season to taste with kosher salt and black pepper. Reserve.

4. Heat a cast-iron skillet over high heat for 3 minutes. Add 3 Tbsp olive oil and allow to heat for an additional 2 minutes.

5. While the pan is heating, season the lamb with kosher salt and black pepper. Add to the hot oil and sear on both sides until golden brown. Place in a preheated 350°F oven and cook to desired temperature. Remove from the oven and allow to rest for 5 minutes before serving.

6. At time of service, heat a medium skillet over medium heat. Add 2 oz olive oil and allow to heat for an additional 2 minutes. Add the potatoes and sauté until golden brown.

7. Add the minced shallots, minced garlic, and artichokes and sauté for 2 minutes or until are warmed through. Add the tomatoes and sauté for 1 additional minute. Add the thyme and parsley and season with kosher salt and black pepper to taste. Reserve in a warm place.

8. At time of service, bring the Garlic Jus to a simmer and whisk in the cold diced butter. Adjust the seasoning if necessary.

9. Place an equal amount of the potato mixture in the center of each of 4 heated dinner plates. Slice each lamb steak into 2 pieces and place on the salad. Spoon the Garlic Jus over the lamb and serve immediately.

Sautéed Lamb with Eggplant and Orange Relish and Cardamom Caramel Sauce

SERVES: 4

EGGPLANT AND ORANGE RELISH

2 oranges

½ cup eggplant, diced, salted, and pressed for 2 hours

⅛ cup raisins

½ Tbsp ground cardamom

Pinch ground cumin

⅛ cup brown sugar

⅛ cup granulated sugar

POTATOES

4 Yukon Gold potatoes, large

¼ cup kosher salt

CARDAMOM CARAMEL SAUCE

1 cup granulated sugar

2 Tbsp cardamom seeds

1 Tbsp coriander seeds

6 Tbsp water

2 tsp cream of tartar

⅔ cup heavy cream

9 Tbsp butter, unsalted, diced, and very cold

ASSEMBLY

As needed, extra-virgin olive oil

As needed, kosher salt

As needed, freshly ground black pepper

Four 5-oz portions boneless lamb loin

1 garlic clove, sliced thin

2 shallots, diced small

1 lb spinach, cleaned and stems removed

EGGPLANT AND ORANGE RELISH

1. Finely zest the oranges, taking care not to gather the pith. Place the zest in a bowl. Cut the skin and pith from the oranges. Remove the segments, saving all of the juice. Reserve.

2. In a heavy-bottomed saucepan, add the eggplant, raisins, reserved orange juice, zest, ground cardamom, cumin, brown sugar, and granulated sugar. Simmer over medium heat until the juice is reduced and thick.

3. Add the orange segments and remove the pan from the stove. Stir gently to combine. Transfer the relish to a container and refrigerate until service.

POTATOES

1. Wash the potatoes well under cold running water. Place them in a medium stockpot and cover with 2 in. cold water. Add ¼ cup kosher salt. Bring to a simmer over medium heat and cook until the potatoes are tender. Remove from the water immediately and place on a linen towel. Allow to cool for 10 minutes.

2. Peel the cooled potatoes, slice them into ¼-in. slices, and reserve for service.

CARDAMOM CARAMEL SAUCE

1. In a stainless-steel heavy-bottomed saucepan, combine 1 cup granulated sugar and the cardamom seeds, coriander seeds, water, and cream of tartar. Place over medium heat and cook, stirring, until the sugar is dissolved.

2. Raise the heat to medium-high and cook without stirring until the syrup turns light golden brown, swirling the pan occasionally.

3. Remove from the heat, gradually add the heavy cream, and whisk until smooth. Add the butter and whisk until melted and incorporated. Strain the sauce through a fine sieve and reserve in a warm place until service.

ASSEMBLY

1. At time of service, toss the potato slices in olive oil and season with kosher salt and pepper. Place on a baking sheet and bake in a preheated 400°F oven until golden brown, 15–20 minutes.

2. Preheat a cast-iron skillet over medium heat for 4 minutes. Add 2 oz olive oil and allow to heat for an additional 2 minutes. Season the lamb with kosher salt and pepper. Place the lamb in the hot pan and sear on each side for 2 minutes. Remove the lamb and reserve in a warm place.

3. Heat a sauté pan over medium heat. Add 1 Tbsp olive oil along with the garlic and shallots. Cook until the shallots are translucent and the garlic is tender. Add the spinach and sauté until cooked, about 2 minutes. Season to taste with kosher salt and pepper. Reserve in a warm place.

4. Place 6 slices of the roasted potatoes in a half-moon shape in the center of each of 4 heated dinner plates. Divide the spinach into 4 equal portions and place in the opening of the half-moon. Place the lamb on top of the potatoes and spinach. Place 1 Tbsp eggplant relish on top of the lamb. Drizzle the caramel sauce over the lamb and around the plate. Serve immediately.

11

Pasta, Beans, and Rice

Pasta, beans, and rice are staples of many cuisines. They are also customer favorites and offer a great deal to the creation of hearty and flavorful dishes. The elegance of such dishes would surprise people who historically cooked these items to fill stomachs cheaply and because they could not afford meats and fish. Today these staples still extend flesh foods. Needless to say, a 6-ounce piece of meat or a chicken feeds many more people when paired with pasta, beans, or rice.

In this chapter, we transform these three comfort foods into elegant dishes such as Gnocchi with Lobster, Truffle Macaroni Gratin, Spaghetti with Chestnut Sauce, and Crab Bean Cassoulet.

These dishes feature great seasonal flavor profiles. The Bean Ravioli had the chefs licking the pan after the photo shoot. Risotto rises to new levels with the addition of vanilla and lobster or veal bacon and shrimp. Enjoy this chapter and see new success in serving pasta, beans, or rice.

Gnocchi with Lobster, Peas,
and Pumpkin with Sage Butter

Signature Truffle Macaroni Gratin

Penne Pasta with Asparagus, Peas,
Morels, Favas, and Tomato Broth

Spaghetti with Chestnut Sauce,
Truffle Cream, Prosciutto, and Cèpes

Lobster Pumpkin Risotto

Veal Bacon Risotto

Bean Ravioli with a Sauce of Sausage,
Escarole, and Beans

Crab Bean Cassoulet

Gnocchi with Lobster, Peas, and Pumpkin with Sage Butter

Serves: 4

GNOCCHI

1 lb fresh ricotta, strained

⅓ cup grated Parmigiano-Reggiano

1 tsp kosher salt

1 egg, slightly beaten

1 cup all-purpose flour

GARNISH

Two 1½ lb Maine lobsters

½ cup fresh shucked peas

1 cup diced pumpkin

1 Tbsp clarified butter

2 Tbsp brown sugar

1 tsp sea salt

SAGE BUTTER

½ cup clarified butter

10 sage leaves

¼ cup Giancarlo's Brodo (see Chef's Pantry)

¼ cup extra-virgin olive oil

ASSEMBLY

To taste, salt

To taste, freshly ground black pepper

2 Tbsp butter, unsalted, diced

As needed, Vanilla Oil (see Chef's Pantry)

8 Fried Sage Leaves (see Chef's Pantry)

GNOCCHI

1. Place the ricotta, Parmigiano-Reggiano, salt, egg, and flour in a bowl and mix by hand slowly until all items are incorporated. Do not overmix.

2. Roll a piece of the dough into a cylinder about ½ in. Cut the cylinder into small pieces and roll each in your hand to the desired shape. Place on a pan lined with paper; freeze. Move frozen gnocchi to zippered plastic bags and keep frozen until ready to cook.

GARNISH

1. Cook the lobsters in boiling water for 4 minutes, then shock them in ice water.

2. Remove the meat from the lobsters. Slice the tail into slices, cut the knuckle and claw meat into medium-size pieces, and reserve.

3. Blanch peas in boiling salted water and then shock in ice water to stop cooking. Reserve.

4. In a bowl, toss the diced pumpkin with the butter, brown sugar, and salt. Place the pumpkin in a roasting pan and cook in a 350°F oven, turning occasionally, until tender, 5–7 minutes.

SAGE BUTTER

1. In a pan, heat the butter. Add the sage, simmer 1 minute, and add the brodo and olive oil. Bring to a light boil, mix with a blender stick, and season to taste.

Pasta, Beans, and Rice

1. Bring a pot of salted water to boil and add the gnocchi. When all gnocchi rise to the top, carefully remove them to a bowl with a spider or slotted spoon and toss gently with 2–3 Tbsp of the sage butter.

2. In a sauté pan, heat 1 Tbsp of the butter and sauté the lobster lightly until just cooked. Add the pumpkin and cook 30 more seconds. Add the peas and the remaining 1 Tbsp butter. Remove from the heat; toss. In a bowl, gently add the garnish to the pasta with some more of the sage butter; season with salt and pepper. Place in 4 bowls or 4 roasted pumpkins, lace with more sauce if desired, and top with the Vanilla Oil and 2 Fried Sage Leaves.

Signature Truffle Macaroni Gratin

Serves: 4

1 cup whole milk

1 Tbsp truffle slices

1 Tbsp butter, unsalted

1 Tbsp truffle oil

2 Tbsp all-purpose flour

To taste, sea salt

To taste, ground white pepper

To taste, freshly grated nutmeg

½ cup heavy cream

½ lb dried macaroni

¼ cup grated Pecorino Romano

To taste, kosher salt

To taste, ground white pepper

2 cups panko crumbs

1 egg, cooked hard, chopped fine

4 Tbsp extra-virgin olive oil

1. In a medium saucepan, combine the milk and truffle slices. Warm the milk over high heat until bubbles form around the edge of the pan. Remove from the heat and let steep for 10 minutes. Strain the milk; reserve the truffle slices and milk separately.

2. In another small saucepan, combine the butter and the truffle oil and place over a low flame. When the butter is melted, whisk in the flour and cook, stirring constantly to avoid browning, for 1 minute.

3. Remove the roux from the heat and gradually whisk in the reserved milk, stirring constantly until the sauce is completely smooth. Season with a large pinch of sea salt and a generous grating of white pepper and nutmeg.

4. Return the pan to low heat and cook the sauce, stirring constantly, until it thickens, about 5 minutes. Remove from the heat and let cool slightly. Stir in the heavy cream.

5. Bring 1 gal heavily salted water to a rapid boil. Add the macaroni and cook until al dente. Drain the macaroni and place in a mixing bowl.

6. Add the white sauce to the pasta along with the reserved truffle slices and the grated cheese; toss to coat. Adjust the seasoning with kosher salt and white pepper if necessary. Divide the mixture among 4 gratin dishes.

7. In a mixing bowl, combine the panko crumbs, chopped egg, and olive oil. Cover each gratin dish with an even layer of crumb mixture.

8. At time of service, place the gratins into a preheated 400°F oven. Bake until heated through and golden brown on top, 6-7 minutes. Allow to sit for 5 minutes before serving.

Penne Pasta with Asparagus, Peas, Morels, Favas, and Tomato Broth

SERVES: 6

1 lb dried penne pasta

2 Tbsp olive oil

12 spears asparagus, trimmed

5 oz shelled peas

5 oz fava beans, cleaned

4 Tbsp olive oil

4 garlic cloves

1 onion, small, chopped fine

5 Tbsp Italian tomato paste

¼ cup red wine

6 leaves basil, chiffonade

1 tsp chopped parsley

1 cup tomato water

1 cup Chicken Brodo (see Chef's Pantry)

5 oz morels

3 Tbsp butter, unsalted, diced

2 Tbsp extra-virgin olive oil

To taste, salt

To taste, freshly ground black pepper

4 vine-ripened tomatoes, core removed

1. Bring 1 gal heavily salted water to a rapid boil over high heat. Add the dried pasta and stir so the pasta does not stick together. Continue cooking, stirring often, until the pasta is al dente.

2. Drain the pasta and toss lightly with 2 Tbsp olive oil. Lay out on a half-sheet pan and place in the refrigerator to cool.

3. In a small saucepan, bring 1 qt heavily salted water to a boil, then keep at a simmer.

4. Blanch the asparagus spears, the peas, and the favas until al dente. Reserve.

5. In a saucepan, add oil, then the garlic and onions. Cook for 2–3 minutes.

6. Add the tomato paste and cook another minute, then deglaze with the wine.

7. Add the herbs, tomato water, and brodo with the morel mushrooms and bring to a boil; simmer for 3 minutes.

8. Add the butter and oil, and season with salt and pepper, if needed.

9. Cut 2–3 cores from the tomatoes with a ¾-in. by 2-in. cutter (or any cutter you may have).

10. In a stainless-steel 4-qt braising pan, place the broth, pasta, favas, and peas. Cook for 2 minutes or until pasta is hot.

11. Mix all items for the dressing and toss with the tomato cores and the asparagus.

12. Place the pasta in bowls. Garnish with the tomatoes and 2 asparagus spears each.

Spaghetti with Chestnut Sauce, Truffle Cream, Prosciutto, and Cèpes

SERVES: 4

1 thyme sprig, small

4 parsley sprigs

1 bay leaf

4 Tbsp butter, unsalted

1 onion, finely chopped

⅜ cup sherry

2 Tbsp all-purpose flour

1½ cups Chicken Brodo (see Chef's Pantry)

8 oz chestnuts, peeled

To taste, kosher salt

To taste, cracked black pepper

3 cups heavy cream

1 tsp truffle oil

1 lb dried spaghetti

As needed, olive oil

8 oz cèpes

8 oz prosciutto, diced small

1 Tbsp truffle slices

1. Using butcher's twine, tie together the thyme, parsley, and bay leaf; reserve.

2. In a skillet, melt three-quarters of the butter over medium heat. Add the onion and sauté for 5 minutes. Add the carrot and sauté for 5 minutes more, stirring occasionally.

3. Carefully pour in the sherry and simmer over high heat for 5 minutes. Stir in the flour and mix well.

4. Add the chicken broth and tied herbs. Stir until the flour is incorporated and the mixture is free of lumps. Bring to a simmer and simmer for 20 minutes.

5. Coarsely chop the chestnuts and add them to the pan. Simmer for an additional 10 minutes. Remove the tied herbs and discard.

6. Puree the sauce with a blending stick and strain through a fine sieve. Season to taste with kosher salt and pepper. Reserve for service.

7. In a small saucepan, combine the heavy cream and truffle oil. Place over medium heat and reduce by half. Season with kosher salt and pepper. Reserve for service.

8. Bring 1 gal heavily salt water to a rapid boil. Add the spaghetti and stir so the pasta does not stick together. Continue to cook, stirring occasionally, until the pasta is al dente. Drain the pasta and toss with 1 Tbsp olive oil. Reserve for service.

9. At time of service, heat 1 Tbsp olive oil in a skillet. Add the cèpes and sauté until golden brown and tender. Add the prosciutto and cook for 1 minute more. Add the chestnut sauce and bring to a simmer.

10. In a separate saucepan, bring the truffle cream to a simmer and add truffle slices.

11. Add the cooked pasta to the chestnut sauce. Toss lightly to coat the pasta evenly.

12. Divide the pasta evenly among 4 heated pasta bowls. Drizzle the truffle cream over the pasta and serve immediately.

Pasta, Beans, and Rice

Lobster Pumpkin Risotto

SERVES: 4–6

1 cup peeled and diced pumpkin or butternut squash

2 oz butter, unsalted

3 oz olive oil

1 diced shallot

½ cup diced pancetta

2 cups Vialone Nano rice

1 cup white wine

2 cups fish stock

6 cups Lobster Broth (see Chef's Pantry)

*3 cups chicken stock or Chicken Brodo
    (see Chef's Pantry)*

6 oz butter, unsalted

2 cups cooked fresh lobster meat chunks

¼ cup heavy cream

½ cup petite peas

GARNISH

2 cooked lobster tails sliced for garnish

1. Cook the pumpkin cubes in boiling water until al dente, 2–3 minutes.

2. In a 2-qt saucepan, heat the butter and oil. Add shallots, pancetta, and pumpkin; cook until light brown.

3. Add the rice and cook 2–3 minutes

4. Deglaze the pan with wine and simmer 2–3 minutes. Add half of the Lobster Broth. Cook until the liquid is absorbed.

5. Add the remaining stock and cook until liquid is just absorbed.

6. Fold in the butter along with the remaining items.

7. To finish to order: about 4 oz base, 4 oz stock, parmesan, cream, peas, and 2 oz lobster meat.

ASSEMBLY

1. Divide onto 6 plates and garnish with sliced lobster tail. Serve with grated Reggiano, if desired.

Veal Bacon Risotto

SERVES: 4

1 Tbsp olive oil

4 oz veal bacon, diced small

1 lb carnoli rice

¼ cup white wine

1½–2 qt chicken stock

1 cup fresh peas

1 tsp chopped parsley

1 tsp chopped thyme

¼ cup grated Parmigiano-Reggiano

¼ cup heavy cream

4 Tbsp butter, unsalted

To taste, kosher salt

To taste, cracked black pepper

2 Tbsp olive oil

20 jumbo shrimp

1. In a large, heavy-bottomed saucepan, heat 1 Tbsp olive oil over medium-low heat. Add the bacon and shallots. Cook, stirring occasionally, until the bacon begins to become crisp.

2. Add the rice and stir to coat it with the fat. Continue to cook for 2 minutes.

3. Deglaze the pan with the wine and cook, stirring constantly, until the wine is absorbed.

4. Over medium heat, add a total of 6 cups chicken stock 2 cups at a time, stirring often (about 20–30 minutes). Be sure that each addition of stock is fully absorbed before adding the next. If needed, add additional stock. Rice should be creamy and slightly firm to the bite.

5. Remove from the stove and add the peas, parsley, thyme, cheese, cream, and butter. Season with salt and pepper to taste.

6. A few minutes before the risotto is finished, heat 2 Tbsp olive in a sauté pan over medium heat. Add the shrimp and the Spice de Cosette and sauté until the shrimp are fully cooked.

7. Divide the risotto among 4 nice bowls or plates and top each with 5 cooked shrimp. Serve immediately.

TOP: *Lobster Pumpkin Risotto*

BOTTOM: *Veal Bacon Risotto*

Bean Ravioli with a Sauce of Sausage, Escarole, and Beans

SERVES: 4

1 lb all-purpose flour

1 lb "00" flour

16 eggs

1 Tbsp extra-virgin olive oil

Pinch kosher salt

1 Tbsp olive oil

1 shallot, minced

1 Tbsp chopped thyme

4 cups cooked white beans

⅛ cup grated Parmigiano-Reggiano

To taste, kosher salt

To taste, cracked black pepper

1 lb sweet Italian sausage

3 Tbsp olive oil

5 garlic cloves, sliced thin

1 onion, large, chopped

⅓ cup chopped parsley

½ tsp red pepper flakes

2 cups Beef Brodo (see Chef's Pantry)

1 cup escarole, cleaned and chopped

1 tsp chopped sage

1. Sift together the flours. Place in a mound on a cutting board. Make a well in the middle of the flour.

2. Crack the eggs into a medium mixing bowl. Add the olive oil and a pinch of salt. Beat lightly with a whisk. Pour the egg mixture into the well in the center of the flour. Slowly combine the egg and flour.

3. After the flour and the egg mixture are thoroughly combined, knead the dough for an additional 10 minutes. The dough should be moist to the touch, but not sticky. Add more flour or a little cold water as needed to achieve the proper feel. Wrap the dough in plastic and allow to rest at room temperature for at least 2 hours.

4. Heat a small saucepan over medium-low heat. Add 1 Tbsp olive oil and allow to heat for 2 minutes. Add the minced shallot and garlic and cook until the shallots are translucent and the garlic is tender. Add the thyme and cook for 1 minute. Remove from the heat and reserve.

5. Place 2 cups of the beans in a food processor. Add the cooked shallot and garlic mixture and puree until smooth. Transfer the puree to a small mixing bowl.

6. Add 1 cup of the cooked beans and the grated cheese to the puree. Combine well and season with kosher salt and pepper to taste. Reserve for service.

7. Remove the casing from the sausage and crumble the meat into bite-size pieces. Heat a 3-qt saucepan over medium heat. Add 3 Tbsp olive oil and cook the sausage, stirring often, until browned.

8. Add the sliced garlic, onion, ¼ cup of the chopped parsley, and the red pepper flakes. Cook, stirring frequently, until the onion is limp.

9. Add the broth, escarole, and sage. Bring to a boil, then reduce to a simmer and cook 10-12 minutes Add the remaining 1 cup beans and cook until warmed through. Season to taste with kosher salt and pepper. Skim off and discard any excess fat and reserve for service.

10. To make the ravioli, roll the pasta dough into thin sheets, about 1/16 in. thick.

11. Lay 1 sheet on a flat work surface and brush lightly with cold water. Drop 1-oz mounds of the bean puree filling onto the pasta sheet, spacing the mounds far enough to allow room to cut the ravioli. Lay another sheet of pasta over the filling mounds. Press gently around the mounds, being careful to remove all air from around the filling.

12. Using a knife or pastry wheel, cut the ravioli into the desired shapes. Depending on size, each serving should include 3–5 ravioli. Dust the ravioli lightly with flour. Cover with plastic and reserve for service.

13. At time of service, bring 1 gal heavily salted water to a rapid boil. Place the ravioli in the water and cook until the filling is heated through and the pasta is cooked, 3–5 minutes.

14. While the ravioli are cooking, reheat the sauce. Adjust the seasoning if necessary.

15. Remove the ravioli and drain well. Divide them evenly among 4 heated serving vessels. Spoon the sauce over and serve immediately with grated cheese on the side.

Pasta, Beans, and Rice

Crab Bean Cassoulet

SERVES: 4

½ lb dried red beans

½ lb dried white beans

2 carrots, cut in half

1 vanilla bean, split

6 cups Crab Broth (see Chef's Pantry)

4 tsp butter, unsalted

1 onion, medium, chopped

¼ cup molasses

2 cups tomato puree

1 tsp sea salt

¼ tsp dry mustard

⅛ tsp red pepper flakes

1 Tbsp Worcestershire sauce

9 Tbsp butter, unsalted

1 cup seasoned dry bread crumbs

12 oz picked crabmeat

½ cup pancetta

1. Soak the beans in water overnight. Drain the beans; then cook them over slow heat with the carrots, vanilla, and Crab Broth for 1–2 hours or until almost tender. Drain the beans, saving the broth. Remove the carrots and vanilla bean.

2. In a heavy-bottomed pan, heat the butter and sauté the onion until soft. Add the molasses and tomato puree, simmer 2–3 minutes, and mix well. Add 3 cups of the reserved Crab Broth. Add salt, mustard, red pepper flakes, and Worcestershire sauce. Add the drained beans, cover, and cook on low for 1 hour.

3. In a sauté pan over low heat, melt 1 Tbsp of the butter and sauté the bread crumbs, stirring constantly for 1 minute or until lightly browned.

4. Adjust the seasoning of the bean mixture. Fold in the crabmeat and the remaining 8 Tbsp butter. Place in small ovenproof casserole dishes and top with sautéed bread crumbs. Bake in a 375°F oven for 8–12 minutes.

12

Pastry

There is always room for dessert. No matter how hard a chef works and how many courses are served, the dessert course impresses and dazzles, placing the pastry chef at the focal point of the evening. A great dessert that is masterful in presentation, flavors, and creative imagination always pleases club members and guests.

My pastry team creates exciting displays of sugar, chocolate, and gum paste along with stunning decorated cakes. I work with this team to develop flavor profiles, looking at pastry the same way I do savory dishes. Harmony of texture, seasonal flavor, fruits, and spices—delight in every bite—is what we strive for. Hot and cold yield especially flavorful combinations, such as warm roasted fruits topped with fresh vanilla bean ice cream.

The desserts featured in this chapter all offer a tasting of flavors on the plate and a combination of texture and temperature. My favorite is the Pineapple Pot, not because I created it from that old standby, Baked Alaska, but because it encompasses my favorite flavors and philosophy of food. Picture a layer of sponge cake, vanilla bean ice cream, roasted pineapple in brown sugar, more cake, pineapple sorbet, more cake, more ice cream, and then a layer of streusel topped with fluffy meringue and baked in the oven. What else is there to say besides Wow!

A Study of Pears

Pear and Pistachio Mousse, Pear Soup, Pear Ricotta Fritters

Elements of Spring Taste

*Lemon Mousse, Blueberry Compote, Raspberry Soup,
Vanilla Sorbet*

The New Peach Melba

Pineapple Pot

Chocolate

*Milk Chocolate Chip Ice Cream, Milk Chocolate Crème
Brûlée, Chocolate Genoise, Banana Chocolate Praline Mousse*

Infused Fruits

Simply Sinful

*Vanilla Bean Crème Brûlée, Chocolate Truffle,
and Cheesecake Pop*

A Study of Pears

SERVES: 4

PEAR AND PISTACHIO MOUSSE

5 sheets gelatin

2 cups heavy cream

½ cup egg yolks

½ cup confectioner's sugar

¼ cup pureed pears

¼ cup pistachio paste

¼ cup ground pistachios

PEAR SOUP

3 pears, peeled, cored, and diced

1 vanilla bean

½ cup granulated sugar

As needed, sparkling water

½ tsp honey

1 Tbsp butter, unsalted

1 Tbsp Poire Williams

PEAR RICOTTA FRITTERS

½ cup diced pears

¼ cup egg whites

1½ cups ricotta

1 cup semolina

½ cup cake flour

¾ cup granulated sugar

1½ Tbsp baking powder

½ tsp salt

As needed, confectioner's sugar

TUILES

¼ cup all-purpose flour

¼ cup granulated sugar

¼ cup egg whites

¼ cup butter, melted

RASPBERRY COULIS

½ cup raspberries

¼ cup granulated sugar

2 Tbsp fresh lemon juice

1 vanilla bean

PEAR AND PISTACHIO MOUSSE

1. Bloom the gelatin in cold water until the sheets are soft. Drain the water.

2. In a mixing bowl and using the whisk attachment, whip the heavy cream to soft peaks. Transfer the cream to another bowl and set aside.

3. In the same mixer with the whisk attachment, whip the yolks and the confectioner's sugar until thick ribbons form. Add the pear puree, pistachio paste, and ground pistachios.

4. Heat the gelatin until hot over a double boiler, and then pour into the mixer while it is still running. Fold in the whipped cream. Quickly pour into prepared molds of your choice. (The new silicone molds work great and are available in many shapes.) Freeze until set.

PEAR SOUP

1. Place the pears in a saucepan with the vanilla bean and sugar. Add sparkling water until

the pears are just covered. Simmer over medium heat until the pears are tender.

2. Puree the pear mixture to a fine consistency. Fold in the honey, butter, and liqueur. Strain and place in the refrigerator to cool.

PEAR RICOTTA FRITTERS

1. In a bowl, combine the pears, egg whites, ricotta, semolina, cake flour, sugar, baking powder, and salt. Use a small ice cream scoop or a spoon to shape fritters and drop them into a 324°F fryer. Fry for about 3 minutes.

2. Remove the fritters from the fryer and dust with powdered sugar.

TUILES

1. In a mixer, combine the flour, sugar, and egg whites. Slowly stream in the melted butter until the batter is smooth and shiny.

2. Using an offset spatula, spread the batter onto a tuile template of your choice. Bake at 350°F until the batter loses its shine. Remove from the oven and let cool.

3. Bake again at 325°F until light golden in color. While they are still warm, delicately bend the tuiles around a spoon handle to create the desired spiral shape.

RASPBERRY COULIS

1. Place the raspberries, sugar, lemon juice, and vanilla bean in a saucepan with about ¼ cup water. Simmer until the sauce reduces to syrup consistency. Strain and cool.

ASSEMBLY

1. On a long plate, serve the soup in an espresso cup, placing the mousse in the center and topping with the tuile. Pour some of the coulis on the plate and place a fritter over it.

Elements of Spring Taste

SERVES: 4

LEMON MOUSSE

¼ cup + 1 Tbsp water

¾ cup granulated sugar

½ cup egg yolks

½ cup fresh lemon juice

Zest of 1 lemon

3 cups heavy cream, whipped to soft peaks

BLUEBERRY COMPOTE

1 cup blueberries

½ cup granulated sugar

As needed, water

½ lemon

1 cinnamon stick

RASPBERRY SOUP

2 cups raspberries

¾ cup granulated sugar

1 vanilla bean, split

3 Tbsp butter, unsalted, cold

VANILLA SORBET

2 cups granulated sugar

1 cup water

1 vanilla bean, split and scraped

Juice of ½ lemon

PHYLLO NESTS

2 sheets phyllo dough

½ cup butter, unsalted, melted

½ cup granulated sugar

2 Tbsp ground cinnamon

LEMON MOUSSE

1. In a heavy-bottomed saucepan, combine the water and sugar. Bring to a boil over medium heat. Be sure to wash down sides of the pan with a brush. Continue to cook the sugar mixture until it reaches 220°F on a candy thermometer.

2. While the sugar is cooking, whip the egg yolks until light and fluffy.

3. After the sugar has reached the appropriate temperature, carefully stream the syrup into the egg yolks while whipping constantly. Continue to whip the mixture until it has cooled, then add the lemon juice and lemon zest. Fold in the whipped cream.

4. Pour the mousse into the desired molds and place in the refrigerator until set.

BLUEBERRY COMPOTE

1. Place the blueberries, sugar, water, lemon, and cinnamon stick in a heavy-bottomed saucepan and cook over medium heat until the mixture reduces to a thick consistency; then strain. Allow to cool and reserve for service.

RASPBERRY SOUP

1. Place the raspberries, sugar, and vanilla bean in a stainless-steel saucepan. Cook over medium heat and simmer for 20 minutes. Remove vanilla bean and place mixture in blender, puree on high speed, adding butter. Strain twice.

VANILLA SORBET

1. Place all ingredients except the vanilla bean in a heavy saucepan.

2. Split and scrape the seeds from the vanilla bean into the mixture. Dice the bean. Add the bean to the cream, along with the star anise.

3. Bring the mixture to a slow boil.

4. Strain through a fine sieve, and cool.

5. Freeze to a soft stage in an ice cream maker, and store.

PHYLLO NESTS

1. Cut 2 sheets of the phyllo pastry into squares measuring about 3 in. by 3 in. Cover the squares with a damp paper towel until ready to use.

2. Combine the sugar and cinnamon in a bowl.

3. *Lightly* brush 1 phyllo one square with melted butter. Sprinkle with cinnamon sugar. Bunch the square into a mini muffin tin mold. Repeat with remaining squares.

4. Bake the phyllo in the tin at 400°F for about 2 minutes or until golden brown.

The New Peach Melba

SERVES: 4

ROASTED PEACHES

1 cup brown sugar

¼ cup peach liqueur

2 Tbsp fresh orange juice

1 vanilla bean

1 cinnamon stick

2 peaches

2 Tbsp honey

MERINGUE DISKS

¼ cup egg whites

2 Tbsp granulated sugar

Pinch cream of tartar

VANILLA ICE CREAM

1½ cups milk

¾ cup cream

½ cup granulated sugar

1 vanilla bean, split and scraped

6 egg yolks

ASSEMBLY

As needed, Raspberry Coulis (see Chef's Pantry)

Phyllo Nests (see preceding recipe)

ROASTED PEACHES

1. In a deep roasting pan, combine the brown sugar, peach liqueur, and orange juice until it is incorporated as a smear. Add the vanilla bean and cinnamon stick to the pan. Place the peaches in the liquid whole and drizzle with honey.

2. Cover the pan with foil and place in a 300°F oven until the peaches are soft and the skin is wrinkled and browning.

3. Cool. Slice the peaches in half and remove the cores. Strain the liquid through a fine mesh sieve and reserve.

MERINGUE DISKS

1. Over a double boiler, whisk the egg whites, sugar, and cream of tartar until warm and the sugar is dissolved. With the whisk attachment of an electric mixer, whip until stiff peaks form. Place in a pastry bag fitted with a round tip.

2. Cover a sheet pan with parchment paper. Starting at the center and spiraling outward, pipe the egg white mixture onto the parchment to form a disk.

3. Form a second, smaller disk in the middle of the big disk.

4. Bake the disks at 225°F until slightly off-white in color and stiff enough to lift off the paper.

VANILLA ICE CREAM

1. In a saucepan, heat the milk, cream, ¼ cup of the sugar and the vanilla bean with scrapings to a boil.

2. Whisk the yolks and the remaining ¼ cup sugar together in a bowl.

3. Stir some the hot milk mixture into the yolks and pour the resulting mixture back into the hot milk. Constantly stir over low heat until the mixture coats the back of a spoon, 4–5 minutes. Cool on an ice bath. Strain and store in the refrigerator until well chilled.

4. Freeze in an ice cream maker according to the manufacturer's instructions.

Pineapple Pot

STREUSEL

1 cup all-purpose flour

1 cup oats

½ cup granulated sugar

½ cup brown sugar

2 Tbsp ground cinnamon

¼ cup ground nuts (optional)

8 Tbsp butter, unsalted, diced

VANILLA SPONGE CAKE

1 cup cake flour

¼ cup cornstarch

10 eggs

1½ cups granulated sugar

6 Tbsp butter, unsalted, melted

ROASTED PINEAPPLE

2 Tbsp butter, unsalted

2 cups diced pineapple

¼ cup brown sugar

1½ Tbsp ground cinnamon

PINEAPPLE SORBET

1 pineapple, peeled and cubed

¾ cup sugar

½ cup water

MERINGUE

½ cup egg whites

¼ cup granulated sugar

Pinch cream of tartar

STREUSEL

1. Combine the flour, oats, sugar, brown sugar, cinnamon, and nuts.

2. Add the butter until the streusel forms. Reserve.

VANILLA SPONGE CAKE

1. Sift the flour and cornstarch together.

2. Whisk the eggs and sugar in a mixing bowl over a double boiler until the mixture reaches 110°F. Place the bowl on a mixer and whip until the mixture triples in volume.

3. Add the dry ingredients, then the butter.

4. Spread the batter onto a greased pan and bake at 375°F until the top of the cake is golden and bounces back to the touch.

5. When the cake is cooled, cut out pieces using a round cookie cutter the size of the pot you will build your pineapple dessert in. Slice the rounds to about ½ in. thick.

ROASTED PINEAPPLE

1. Heat a sauté pan and melt the butter in it. Add the diced pineapple, sauté, and add the brown sugar and cinnamon. Cook until nicely browned and coated.

2. Add 1 cup of the reserved streusel to the pan. Remove from the heat; let cool.

PINEAPPLE SORBET

1. Puree the pineapple and ¼ cup of the sugar in a food processor until the mixture is smooth.

2. Boil the remaining ½ cup sugar and the water. Cool.

3. Combine ¾ cup of the pineapple puree with the sugar syrup. Strain through a sieve and let cool. Freeze in an ice cream maker according to the manufacturer's instructions.

MERINGUE

1. Over a double boiler, whisk the egg whites, sugar, and cream of tartar until the mixture is warm and the sugar is dissolved. Using the whisk attachment of an electric mixer, whip the mixture until stiff peaks form.

2. Place the meringue in a pastry bag with a star tip.

ASSEMBLY

1. Place a circle of the sponge cake on the bottom of the pot. Layer with pineapple sorbet. Let freeze for a few minutes.

2. Layer with vanilla ice cream. Top with pineapple puree.

3. Pipe the meringue to cover the top to the edges. Bake in a 425°F oven until the meringue browns.

Chocolate

FRESH FRUIT

¼ cup blueberries

¼ cup quartered strawberries

¼ cup raspberries

2 Tbsp corn syrup

MILK CHOCOLATE CHIP ICE CREAM

¾ cup heavy cream

¼ cup milk

¼ cup granulated sugar

2 oz milk chocolate, melted

3 egg yolks

1 oz dark chocolate, chopped

MILK CHOCOLATE CRÈME BRÛLÉE

1½ cups heavy cream

½ cup, plus extra for garnish, granulated sugar

Seeds from ½ vanilla bean

4 oz milk chocolate

½ cup egg yolks

CHOCOLATE GENOISE

¾ cup granulated sugar

5 eggs

½ cup cake flour, sifted

3 Tbsp cornstarch

1½ Tbsp cocoa powder

BANANA CHOCOLATE PRALINE MOUSSE

4 eggs, separated

½ cup granulated sugar

¼ cup praline paste

3 oz milk chocolate, melted

¼ cup banana puree

2¼ cups heavy cream

FRESH FRUITS

1. In a small mixing bowl, combine the blueberries, strawberries, raspberries, and corn syrup. Mix gently and reserve for service.

MILK CHOCOLATE CHIP ICE CREAM

1. In a heavy-bottomed saucepan, combine the cream, milk, and sugar. Bring to a boil over medium heat. Remove from the heat and add the melted chocolate.

2. In a medium mixing bowl, gently whip the egg yolks while adding 1 cup of the hot cream mixture.

3. Whisking constantly, pour the egg yolk mixture into the cream mixture. Set the pan over a medium flame and heat gently for 2 minutes, stirring constantly.

4. Strain the mixture through a fine sieve and cool over an ice bath.

5. Place the cooled mixture in an ice cream machine and freeze according to the manufacturer's directions. Remove from the machine and fold in the chopped chocolate pieces. Reserve in the freezer until service.

MILK CHOCOLATE CRÈME BRÛLÉE

1. Preheat the oven to 310°F.

2. In a heavy-bottomed saucepan, combine the cream, ½ cup sugar, the vanilla bean seeds, and the milk chocolate. Bring to a boil over medium heat, then remove from heat.

3. In a medium mixing bowl, gently whip the egg yolks. Slowly add 1 cup of the hot cream mixture, whisking constantly.

4. Stirring constantly, add the egg yolk mixture to the cream mixture. Divide evenly among espresso cups.

5. Place the espresso cups in a shallow baking dish. Set the dish in the preheated oven and add enough warm water to come halfway up the sides of the cups. Bake until set, 25–40 minutes.

6. Remove the custards from the baking dish and cool in the refrigerator.

CHOCOLATE GENOISE

1. Combine the sugar and eggs in a mixing bowl. Heat until warm over a double boiler, stirring constantly. Move the bowl to an electric mixer and, using the whisk attachment, whip on high speed for 8 minutes.

2. Remove from the mixer and fold in the flour, cornstarch, and cocoa powder.

3. Pour the batter into a greased and lined sheet pan. Spread it evenly over the pan. Bake in a preheated 300°F oven for 12–14 minutes. Remove from oven; leave the genoise in the sheet pan to cool.

BANANA CHOCOLATE PRALINE MOUSSE

1. In a medium mixing bowl, combine the egg yolks and ¼ cup of the sugar. Whip until light and fluffy.

2. In a separate mixing bowl, combine the praline paste, melted chocolate, banana puree, and ¼ cup of the cream. Set aside.

3. In medium mixing bowl, whip the egg whites with remaining ¼ cup sugar until the mixture forms medium peaks.

4. Combine the egg yolk mixture with the praline paste mixture.

5. Whip the remaining 2 cups cream to soft peaks. Fold into the praline mixture.

6. Line a terrine mold with a layer of the chocolate genoise and fill the terrine with the banana chocolate praline mousse. Cover the mousse with another layer of genoise. Freeze the terrine for 2 hours or until set.

ASSEMBLY

1. Cover the crème brûlée with a thin layer of granulated sugar. Caramelize the sugar using a propane torch. Be careful not to burn the sugar.

2. Place 1 crème brûlée on each dessert plate.

3. Remove the terrine from the freezer and slice into 4 even slices. Place 1 slice on each plate.

4. Divide the marinated fruits among the plates.

5. Add 1 scoop of the chocolate chip ice cream to each plate just before service.

Infused Fruits

SERVES: 4

VANILLA BEAN ICE CREAM

¾ cup heavy cream

¼ cup milk

¼ cup granulated sugar

1 vanilla bean, split

3 egg yolks

LINZER COOKIES

1¼ cups butter, unsalted

1 cup granulated sugar

1 Tbsp ground cinnamon

1 egg, jumbo

2¾ cups cake flour

½ cup hazelnut flour

1 tsp baking powder

½ cup crushed pecans

BERRIES AND SYRUP

2 Tbsp granulated sugar

1 Tbsp water

3 cloves

1 cup quartered strawberries

1 cup blueberries

1 cup blackberries

1 vanilla bean, split

VANILLA BEAN ICE CREAM

1. In a heavy-bottomed saucepan, combine the cream, milk, sugar, and vanilla bean. Bring to a boil over medium heat, then remove from flame.

2. In a small mixing bowl, lightly beat the egg yolks. While whisking, add 3 oz of the cream mixture to heat the yolks slightly. Add the egg yolk mixture to the saucepan, whisking constantly. Return the pan to the stove and heat over medium heat for 2 minutes. Strain the mixture through a fine sieve and cool over an ice bath.

3. Freeze the cooled mixture in an ice cream machine according to the manufacturer's instruction. Remove the ice cream from the machine and place in the freezer until service.

LINZER COOKIES

1. Using the paddle attachment of an electric mixer, whip the butter and sugar together until the sugar is dissolved and the mixture is smooth. Add the cinnamon and egg. Mix until incorporated, about 2 minutes. Using a plastic bowl scraper, scrape down all sides of the bowl.

2. Add the cake flour, hazelnut flour, baking powder, and crushed pecans. Mix until incorporated.

3. Remove the dough from the mixing bowl and wrap it in plastic wrap. Chill in the refrigerator for about 30 minutes.

4. Preheat the oven to 350°F.

5. Roll the chilled dough to about ⅛ in. thick. Cut the dough into desired shapes using a cookie cutter or a small knife. Place the cookies on a lined baking sheet and bake until golden brown. Remove from the oven and allow to cool.

BERRIES AND SYRUP

1. Combine the sugar, water, and cloves in a small saucepan and bring to a boil. When all the sugar is dissolved, remove the syrup from the heat and reserve.

2. In a large skillet, combine the berries and vanilla bean. Add the clove syrup and gently heat the berries.

3. Place the berries and syrup in a serving dish and garnish with linzer cookies and vanilla bean ice cream.

Simply Sinful

SERVES: 4

VANILLA BEAN CRÈME BRÛLÉE

1½ cups heavy cream

½ cup, plus extra for garnish, granulated sugar

Seeds from ½ vanilla bean

½ cup egg yolks

CHOCOLATE TRUFFLE

2 oz dark chocolate

⅛ cup heavy cream

1 oz dark chocolate

TUILES

¼ cup all-purpose flour

¼ cup granulated sugar

2 Tbsp egg whites

2 Tbsp butter, unsalted, melted

RASPBERRY SAUCE

1 cup raspberries

¼ cup granulated sugar

½ cup water

CHEESECAKE POP

3½ cups cream cheese

1¾ oz butter, unsalted

2¼ cups granulated sugar

2 Tbsp cornstarch

1 tsp vanilla extract

1 egg

½ cup heavy cream

2 cups chocolate, melted (white, milk, or dark)

1 Tbsp vegetable oil

VANILLA BEAN CRÈME BRÛLÉE

1. Preheat the oven to 310°F.

2. In a heavy-bottomed saucepan, combine cream, ½ cup sugar, and vanilla bean seeds. Bring to a boil over medium heat; then remove from the heat.

3. In a medium mixing bowl, gently whisk the egg yolks. Add 1 cup of the hot cream mixture, whisking constantly.

4. Add the egg yolk mixture to the saucepan. Heat gently over medium heat for 2 minutes, stirring constantly. Strain the mixture through a fine sieve and divide evenly among 4 ramekins.

5. Place the ramekins in a shallow baking dish and set the dish in the oven. Pour enough warm water into the baking dish to come halfway up the sides of the ramekins. Bake until the custard sets, 25–40 minutes. Remove the ramekins from the baking dish and refrigerate.

CHOCOLATE TRUFFLE

1. Combine the chocolate and cream. Make a ganache. Allow the ganache to set. Scoop or pipe into small balls.

2. Roll the balls in tempered chocolate as a first coat. Let set.

3. Dip the whole truffle in the tempered chocolate again for an even finish. Let set.

TUILES

1. Combine the flour and sugar. Add the egg whites; mix by hand to break down any lumps.

2. Add the melted butter. Mix until thoroughly incorporated and totally smooth. Refrigerate until set.

3. Using a small offset spatula, spread the tuile mixture evenly over a rectangle stencil onto a Silpat. Par bake at 350°F just until the batter loses its shine, about 2 minutes. Remove from the oven and cool.

4. Bake a second time until golden brown. Pull the cookies from the Silpat and shape into teardrops.

RASPBERRY SAUCE

1. Combine the raspberries, sugar, and water in a small saucepot. Cook over medium heat until the raspberries are broken down.

2. Strain the seeds out and cool the sauce. Adjust it for sweetness if necessary.

CHEESECAKE POP

1. Cream the cream cheese and butter together.

2. Combine the sugar and cornstarch and incorporate with the creamed mixture, scraping the sides of the bowl.

3. Add the vanilla and eggs in 2 stages, scraping the sides of the mixing bowl in between. Add the cream. Do not overmix.

4. Pour the batter into a greased hotel pan to a depth of about ¾ in. Set in a water bath and bake at 310°F until set.

5. Freeze the cheesecake until firm.

6. Cut the cheesecake into 1½-in. squares. Place a stick in the center of each square. Refreeze.

7. Melt high-quality white, milk, or dark chocolate and thin with vegetable oil. The more oil is added, the thinner the coating on the pop. For about 2 cups melted chocolate, start with 1 Tbsp oil.

8. Dip frozen pops into coating. Scrape lightly against a screen to remove excess from the bottom. Place on a parchment-lined sheet pan and refreeze until service. Serve frozen.

13

Trilogy

My concepts of trilogy cuisine and its food philosophy are simple: Showcase organic seasonal foods along with the finest cuts of meat, game, vegetables, and seafood to members and guests.

Our club's trilogy cuisine runs the gamut from pure comfort food to globally inspired contemporary cuisine that I have learned through my culinary travels. The focus for each menu item is always on just one item. For example, the Trilogy of Lobster includes a Lobster Cappuccino, Tempura Lobster, and Lobster Cassoulet. The presentation is always simple and elegant.

Layers of flavor and trilogy cuisine go hand in hand. Consider the Tasting of Tomatoes. That trilogy includes a delicate Tomato Mousse, Tomato Water, and Olive Oil Tomatoes. All of these items are surrounded by accoutrements that compliment and bring out the characteristics of the tomatoes used.

It all starts with the purchase and selection of the freshest ingredients and items. We even grow herbs and some vegetables in our chef's garden and ensure we purchase from many local farmers and those who have passion about supplying food. The highest standards are in place for every step, from the way the food is handled, to the way it is stored and prepared for cooking.

The flavors and textures in trilogy cuisine food are designed to wake up the senses. They display to the palette how one item and the many ways in which it is prepared can come together to create culinary pleasure. Trilogy cuisine is a perfect synergy of ingredients, passion, fun, and flavor that gives you both a variety of flavors and textures and a small tasting all on one plate. Try creating and working with one product to develop it into a special dish that features a trilogy of preparations and flavors that will please your customers.

MENU

Trio of Salmon: A Tasting of Salmon Roasted, Poached, and Grilled with Spinach and Potatoes Parisienne

Trilogy of Lobster: A Tasting of Maine Lobster—Lobster Cappuccino, Tempura Lobster, Lobster Cassoulet

Trilogy of Summer Asparagus—Asparagus Tempura, Eight-Hour Asparagus Spears, Asparagus Cappuccino with Truffle Foam and Fennel Croutons

A Tasting of Tomatoes— Tomato Water, Olive Oil Poached Tomatoes, Tomato Syrup, Tomato Pulp, and Tomato Mousse with Basil Reduction and Balsamic

Foie Gras—Candied Foie Gras Pops, Seared Foie Gras with Cherry Jam, Seared Foie Gras with Quail Egg on Cherry Brioche Toast

Trio of Salmon:
A Tasting of Salmon Roasted, Poached, and Grilled with Spinach and Potatoes Parisienne

SERVES: 4

ROASTED SALMON

Four 3-oz salmon mignons, skin removed

4 Tbsp extra-virgin olive oil

1 Tbsp finely minced fresh Italian parsley

To taste, sea salt

To taste, freshly ground black pepper

POACHED SALMON

Juice of 2 limes

Four 3-oz salmon mignons, skin removed

1 tsp Spice de Cosette

To taste, coarse kosher salt

To taste, coarsely ground black pepper

1 cup pinot noir

1 cup fish broth

¼ cup diced fennel

¼ cup diced celery

2–3 Tbsp butter, unsalted, ice cold

GRILLED SALMON

½ cup walnut oil

¼ cup lime juice

¼ cup red vermouth

2 Tbsp minced shallot

1 Tbsp lemon honey

1 tsp dill

½ tsp soy sauce

To taste, freshly ground black pepper

Four 3-oz salmon mignons

ASSEMBLY

4 oz sautéed spinach or other vegetable

36 small potatoes parisienne

As needed, lime juice

As needed, extra-virgin olive oil

As needed, Mustard Cream (see Chef's Pantry)

ROASTED SALMON

1. Brush the salmon mignons with the olive oil, parsley, then season with salt and pepper.

2. Place the filets skin side down on a lightly oiled roasting rack.

3. Roast in a 365°F oven for 2–3 minutes, until the salmon is just pink in the middle.

POACHED SALMON

1. Squeeze the lime juice over the top of the salmon. Sprinkle with the spice, salt, and pepper.

2. In a stainless-steel pan large enough to hold the liquid while covering the salmon, place the wine, broth, fennel, and celery; bring to a simmer. Reduce the heat to low; check temperature for about 160°F.

3. Add the salmon and poach until cooked through, 5–7 minutes. Remove the salmon from the liquid and reserve.

4. Strain the liquid and return to a clean stainless-steel saucepan. Boil the liquid until reduced to about ⅓ cup. Remove pan from heat. Whisk in the butter. Strain the sauce and season with salt and pepper to taste. Pour the sauce over the salmon just before serving.

GRILLED SALMON

1. In a small bowl, whisk together the oil, lime juice, vermouth, shallot, honey, dill, soy sauce, and pepper. Toss the salmon in the marinade. Cover the dish or Cryovac the salmon and marinade. Let sit at room temperature for 2 hours.

2. Drain the salmon well and pat dry. Reserve the marinade.

3. Oil a grill rack. Grill the salmon 2–3 minutes on each side, brushing often with marinade.

ASSEMBLY

1. Divide 1 oz fresh sautéed spinach or your favorite vegetable into 3 portions and place on plate. Place 1 serving of each type of cooked salmon on the spinach. Add small roasted potatoes or a scoop of Potatoes Parisienne (see Chef's Pantry).

2. Spoon mustard cream over the roasted salmon. Spoon sauce over the poached salmon. Spoon lime juice and extra-virgin olive oil over the grilled salmon.

Trilogy of Summer Asparagus—Asparagus Tempura, Eight-Hour Asparagus Spears, Asparagus Cappuccino with Truffle Foam and Fennel Croutons

SERVES: 4

The start of spring is a great time to showcase the sweet tenderness of asparagus. This tasting highlights spears simply cooked at a slow temperature, a creamy soup, and crisp tempura.

EIGHT-HOUR ASPARAGUS

24 medium to large asparagus spears, woody ends removed and trimmed

1 small shallot, very thinly sliced

3 Tbsp extra-virgin olive oil

6–8 Tbsp butter, unsalted, cold and diced

To taste, kosher salt

To taste, cracked black pepper

1 cup Giancarlo's Brodo (see Chef's Pantry)

ASPARAGUS CAPPUCCINO

3 Tbsp butter, unsalted

2 Tbsp olive oil

2 garlic cloves, thinly sliced

1 yellow onion, diced small

1 cup peeled, small-diced Yukon Gold potatoes

5 cups high-quality vegetable broth

3 cups heavy cream

2 Tbsp chopped fresh tarragon

½ lb asparagus, woody ends removed, trimmed, and cut into 1-in. pieces

1 cup English green peas, frozen or fresh

½ cup high-quality butter, unsalted, ice cold and diced

To taste, sea salt

TRUFFLE FOAM

1 cup heavy cream

½ Tbsp gelatin powder

1 Tbsp truffle oil

To taste, salt

To taste, freshly ground black pepper

ASSEMBLY

16 asparagus spears, trimmed

As needed, Tempura Batter (see Chef's Pantry)

As needed, truffle

As needed, Tomato Syrup (see Chef's Pantry)

EIGHT-HOUR ASPARAGUS

1. Preheat the oven to 140°F.

2. Lay the asparagus in a single straight layer across a sheet of baking paper placed on a baking pan. Distribute the shallot, olive oil, butter, salt, and pepper over the asparagus.

3. Fold the paper at all ends to close the package; turn it seam side down. Pour the broth over the package. Bake for 8 hours. Check the pan occasionally; if it dries out, add more broth.

Alternatively, simply blanch the asparagus spears and sauté them in butter, if you prefer.

ASPARAGUS CAPPUCCINO

1. Melt the butter and oil in a heavy stainless-steel saucepan over low heat. Add the garlic and onion; cook until translucent.

2. Add the potatoes, broth, cream, and tarragon; bring to a full boil. Add the asparagus and simmer until tender, 15–20 minutes. Add the peas, simmer for about 2 minutes, remove from the heat, and cool slightly.

3. Carefully blend the soup in a high-speed blender, then strain it twice through a chinois.

4. Return the soup to the stove, bring to a low simmer, whisk in the butter, and add salt to taste.

TRUFFLE FOAM

1. Add the gelatin to the cream. Whisk well and let sit for 10 minutes.

2. Place the gelatin cream in a copper or stainless-steel saucepan; add the truffle oil. Bring to a simmer for 2 minutes and season with salt and pepper.

3. Place the mixture in a whipped cream canister or foam gun with one cartridge, shake well, and top each serving of soup with foam.

ASSEMBLY

1. Blanch asparagus spears and fry them tempura-style. Place them on plates with the eight-hour spears. Divide the cappuccino among espresso cups. Shake the foam canister and top each cup of soup with foam. Shave a little truffle over each cup.

2. Garnish the plate with Tomato Syrup and truffle foam.

Trilogy of Lobster: A Tasting of Maine Lobster— Lobster Cappuccino, Tempura Lobster, Lobster Cassoulet

SERVES: 4

Three 1½–2-lb lobsters

LOBSTER CAPPUCCINO

1½ Tbsp olive oil

1 onion, medium, cut in half, sliced into ¼-in. slices

1 carrot, small, peeled, chopped into ½-in. pieces

1½ tomato paste

3 Tbsp cognac

¾ cup white wine

2 cups heavy cream

2 cups Lobster Essence (see Chef's Pantry)

1 garlic clove

3 sprigs thyme

4 sprigs tarragon

4 Tbsp tomato sauce

To taste, salt

To taste, cayenne

2 Tbsp fava beans, fresh or frozen, blanched and outer skin removed

2 oz picked lobster meat

As needed, warm frothed milk

As needed, dry, pulverized lobster coral

LOBSTER CASSOULET*

2 cups dried great northern beans or other
   white beans

4 Tbsp butter

6 cloves, whole

1 onion, cut in half

2 cups Lobster Essence (see Chef's Pantry)

2 cups Giancarlo's Brodo (see Chef's Pantry)

6 oz slab apple smoked bacon (unsliced)

3 garlic cloves, crushed

1 bouquet garni**

2 shallots, diced small

¼ cup clarified butter

¼ cup carrots, blanched and diced

¼ cup fennel, diced and cooked

½ cup Roma tomatoes, peeled, seeded, and diced

½ cup porcini mushrooms, diced

1 vanilla bean, split

4 Tbsp whole butter

1 lb picked fresh lobster meat, diced medium

8 white fresh or black truffles, sliced thin

1½ cups panko bread crumbs

*Begin preparing the cassoulet one day in
advance.

**In a double-thickness cheesecloth square,
tie together 2 bay leaves, 2 parsley sprigs,
2 thyme sprigs, ½ tsp coriander seeds, and
1 tsp peppercorns.

1. Blanch and remove the meat from the lobsters, reserving the shells. Reserve 4 claws for the tempura and the rest of meat for the preparations that follow.

LOBSTER CAPPUCCINO

1. Chop the reserved lobster bodies into medium pieces.

2. In a heavy-bottomed, stainless-steel soup pot, heat the oil over medium-high heat. Add the lobster shells and let cook, moving infrequently, until a crust forms on the bottom, 10–12 minutes.

3. Add the onion and carrot and cook until caramelized, about 10 minutes. Add the tomato paste and cook for 4–5 minutes, stirring constantly. Add the cognac and deglaze, scraping the bottom to release the crust.

4. Bring the mixture to a simmer. Add the cream, broth, garlic, thyme, and tarragon. Bring to a boil, then simmer about 30 minutes.

5. Season with the tomato sauce, salt, and cayenne. Strain twice through a fine sieve.

6. At the last moment before serving, warm the fava beans and the lobster meat in the soup and spoon into cappuccino cups, topped with a little warm frothed milk and sprinkled with dry pulverized lobster coral (the red roe sometimes found in female lobsters).

LOBSTER CASSOULET

1. Cover the dried beans with 3 times their volume of water and let stand overnight.

2. Drain the beans well.

3. In a sauté pan, heat the butter and brown the bottom half of the onion very well. Stick the cloves in the onion halves.

4. In a large saucepan, place onions, beans, stock, brodo, bacon, garlic, and bouquet garni. Bring to boil, skim off any foam, cover, and simmer for 1 to 1½ hours or until beans are tender.

5. Drain, reserving cooking liquid. Remove bacon and cut into 8 pieces; set aside. Discard bouquet garni and onion.

6. Add diced shallots and butter to skillet; cook for 2 minutes or until tender. Add carrots, fennel, tomatoes, porcinis, and the reserved bacon. Cook 2–3 minutes more, then add the vanilla bean.

7. Combine this mixture with the beans and place in a 4-qt stainless casserole or Dutch oven. Cover with the reserved broth and butter and bake in a 360°F oven for 1 hour.

8. Remove from the oven. Discard the vanilla bean.

9. Divide about one-quarter of the beans among 4–6 small cast-iron pots or casseroles. Add equal amounts of lobster meat, then the truffle, and then fill with the remaining beans.

10. In a sauté pan, melt the butter and lightly sauté the panko crumbs. Top each pot with bread crumbs and pack firmly. Finish baking in a 360°F oven for 10–12 minutes and serve.

A Tasting of Tomatoes—Tomato Water, Olive Oil Poached Tomatoes, Tomato Syrup, Tomato Pulp, and Tomato Mousse with Basil Reduction and Balsamic

SERVES: 6

With all the new varieties and sizes of tomato, a tomato tasting plate is a wonderful and flavorful concept that will please your customers. It is also a great vegetarian item.

TOMATO WATER

8 very ripe large tomatoes, chopped

1–2 tsp kosher salt

As needed, extra-virgin olive oil

TOMATO MOUSSE

5 large, ripe tomatoes, cut into thirds

1 tsp kosher salt

2 tsp Worcestershire sauce

¼ tsp freshly ground black pepper

¼ tsp minced mint

½ tsp minced basil

2 tsp sugar

2¼ oz gelatin powder

½ cup tomato juice

1 cup heavy cream

As needed, extra-virgin olive oil

PETITE OLIVE OIL TOMATOES

12 small red cherry tomatoes, peeled

6 small yellow cherry tomatoes, peeled

1 cup extra-virgin olive oil

8 large basil leaves

TOMATO PULP

4 large vine-ripe tomatoes or heirloom tomatoes

To taste, sea salt

6 Tbsp extra-virgin olive oil

To taste, freshly ground black pepper

1 tsp minced parsley

ASSEMBLY

As needed, Tomato Syrup (see Chef's Pantry)

As needed, extra-virgin olive oil

As needed, balsamic vinegar

As needed, Basil Reduction (see Chef's Pantry)

6 Crostini, 1 in. by 3 in.

TOMATO WATER

1. Chop the tomatoes in a food processor. Strain for 24 hours in cheesecloth with a pan set underneath to catch the tomato water, or press with a weight in a colander set over a pan.

2. Combine the strained tomato water and salt, whisk briskly, and set aside.

3. Serve in a glass with a few drops of olive oil.

TOMATO MOUSSE

1. Chop the tomatoes in a food processor. Strain them for 24 hours in cheesecloth with a pan underneath to catch the tomato water.

2. Combine the tomato water, salt, Worcestershire sauce, pepper, chervil, basil, and sugar. Whisk briskly and set aside.

3. Sprinkle the gelatin over the tomato juice; let stand 5 minutes to bloom. Set over a hot water bath to dissolve gelatin; this will occur at about 90°F. Add the gelatin mixture to the tomato water mixture and mix well. Keep stirring and chill until it reaches 60°F.

4. Place the cream in a mixing bowl and beat until stiff. Fold the whipped cream into the tomato mixture.

5. Lightly oil a small square pan with olive oil and pour in the tomato mixture. Set until firm in a refrigerator 1–2 hours, unmold, and cut into desired shapes.

For layers, repeat the recipe with yellow tomatoes and yellow tomato juice. Let 1 layer of red tomato mousse set. Top with a layer of yellow tomato mousse and let set. Finish with a second layer of red tomato mousse.

TOMATO PULP

1. Cut out the center pulp of fresh ripe garden tomatoes with a ½-in. by 2-in. cutter; toss with sea salt, olive oil, parsley and pepper.

ASSEMBLY

1. On long plates, set portions of the tomato mousse and drizzle Tomato Syrup, Basil Reduction, and balsamic vinegar around the mousse.

2. Place the crostini with 3 olive oil tomatoes, 2 red and 1 yellow; drizzle with some extra virgin olive oil. Place center pulp of tomato next to the olive oil tomatoes. Garnish with basil.

3. On the last spot, place a shot glass of the tomato water, and top the glass with a crostini.

Foie Gras—Candied Foie Gras Pops, Seared Foie Gras with Cherry Jam, Seared Foie Gras with Quail Egg on Cherry Brioche Toast

SERVES: 4

What a better way to showcase foie gras than with a tasting of foie gras and cherries? The sweetness, the sourness, and the richness are tantalizing to the taste buds.

CANDIED FOIE GRAS POPS

1 cup foie gras mousse or your favorite terrine

2 cups sugar

2 cups corn syrup

⅓ cup chopped red lollipops

1 cup cherry juice

¾ tsp ground cinnamon

½ tsp vanilla extract

¼ tsp ground cloves

½ tsp red paste food coloring (optional)

SEARED FOIE GRAS AND CHERRY JAM

1 lobe grade A foie gras

2 cups pitted, diced fresh black or Rainier cherries

3 cups sugar

1 cup anise honey

1 tsp citric acid

2 Tbsp powdered pectin

¾ cup cherry juice or nectar

½ vanilla bean

SEARED FOIE GRAS WITH QUAIL EGGS AND CHERRY BRIOCHE

Six 2-in. slices cleaned foie gras

6 quail eggs

2 Tbsp butter

6 slices cherry brioche, 2 to 2½ in.

6 tsp Cherry Jam

CANDIED FOIE GRAS POPS

1. Place the mousse in candy or lollipop molds, insert lollipop sticks, and freeze.

2. Combine the sugar, corn syrup, lollipops, and water in medium-sized stainless-steel or copper sugar pan. Stirring constantly, cook until the lollipop pieces dissolve. Do not boil.

3. Add the cinnamon, vanilla, cloves, and food coloring. Mix thoroughly.

4. Set a candy thermometer in the mixture and continue cooking, without stirring, until the temperature reaches 290–300°F, 18–25 minutes. In the meantime, lay a Silpat on a baking tray; if no Silpat is available, then generously coat a baking sheet with cooking spray.

5. As soon as the candy mixture reaches 290°F, dip the frozen foie gras pops into it to coat. Set the coated pops, standing on their bottoms with the sticks pointing up, on the Silpat.

Substitute magic sugar for the sugar and corn syrup. Prepare following the same procedure.

SEARED FOIE GRAS AND CHERRY JAM

1. Clean the foie gras, cut into desired pieces, score them, season with salt, and then sear on both sides.

2. Combine the diced cherries, sugar, honey, and citric acid. Let stand 20 minutes, stirring occasionally.

3. Combine the pectin and juice in a small stainless-steel saucepan. Bring to a boil and boil 1 minute, stirring constantly. Add the cherry mixture and the vanilla bean; let simmer for 5 minutes. Cool over an ice bath.

4. Serve the foie gras over the jam in individual spoons or plates.

Seared Fois Gras and Cherry Jam makes a great starter.

SEARED FOIE GRAS WITH QUAIL EGGS AND CHERRY BRIOCHE

1. Clean, season, and sear foie gras as for the Seared Foie Gras and Cherry Jam recipe.

2. Cook quail eggs in butter gently; take care to keep them whole.

3. Lightly toast slices of cherry brioche. Spread a little Cherry Jam on each slice; top with seared foie gras and then a quail egg.

ASSEMBLY

1. On a plate or a platter, place the 6 candied foie gras pops, then the spoons with the jam and foie gras, and then the cherry brioche slices.

14

Guest Chefs

It is increasingly common for clubs and restaurants to invite guest chefs into the kitchen. A top chef comes in and prepares a special meal, teaching and working with the kitchen crew and providing a wonderful dining experience for those who are lucky enough to dine at the time.

Every year my club holds a food and wine festival, and I invite several master chefs to come into my kitchen and cook. We each select a station to showcase our cuisine, and at the end of the day we relax with some nice wine and conversation and sample each other's food. It is a great evening of friendship and cooking that makes lasting memories.

This chapter is special because the guest chefs who submitted recipes are my friends and long-time colleagues. Just like me, they are consumed with the art of cooking and live and breathe it daily. I appreciate their kindness in contributing their valuable time and knowledge to this book.

Please enjoy these dishes, their flavors, and the approach each chef brings to his art. I respect these guest chefs, and I always look forward to stepping into the kitchen with them and doing what we all love to do: cook.

TOP: *Chef Leonard with friend Charles Carroll of River Oaks Country Club, outside the Westchester Country Club.*

MIDDLE: *Chef Leonard with friends Joachim Buchner of the Chevy Chase Club and Chef Joe Faria of Quail Valley.*

BOTTOM: *Chef Buchner placing the finishing touches on a dish.*

CLUB CUISINE

MENU

Chef Joe Faria

Jumbo Lump Crab and Avocado Salad

Whole Roasted Young Piri Piri Chicken

Lemongrass-Skewered, Tempura-Fried
Yellowtail Snapper with Teriyaki Glaze

Chef Charles Carroll

Bacalao

Foie Gras, Tarte Tatin with Pear, Cherries,
and Apple, Jícama, and Butternut Slaw

Shrimp and Crab en Croute

Spice-Rubbed Texas Black Buck Antelope
with Mushroom and Herb Farce, Foie Gras
Sausage, and Truffle Potato Sauce Laced
with Wine Merchant

Chef Joachim Buchner

Pan-Roasted Salmon with Salted Ham,
Wine Sauerkraut, Sautéed Fingerling
Potato, and Shallot Butter Sauce

Glazed Squab Breast and Red Wine Pear,
Blue Cheese Potato Gratin,
and Sautéed Mushroom

Grilled Basil and Garlic-Marinated
Beef Tenderloin, Grilled Polenta,
and Vegetable with Tomato Chutney

Chef Reimund Pitz

Arugula Napoleon Salad, Goat Cheese
Oven-Dried Plum Tomato, Pineapple Compote

Roosevelt Salad

Blackened Mahi-Mahi, Crispy Potato Cake,
Watercress, Mandarin, and Pineapple Salad

Jumbo Lump Crab and Avocado Salad

SERVES: 4

DRESSING

2 cups fresh orange juice

2 cups fresh grapefruit juice

1 cup fresh lemon juice

1 Indian River orange, large

1 Indian River grapefruit, large

1 cup canola oil

1 cup extra-virgin olive oil

1 oz rice wine vinegar

2 tsp chopped parsley

1 tsp white sugar

ASSEMBLY

2 Florida avocados, large

1 lb jumbo lump crabmeat

DRESSING

1. In a medium saucepan, place the orange, grapefruit, and lemon juice and reduce by half. Chill.

2. Zest the orange and grapefruit and set aside. Remove the skin and segment each fruit section. Set aside.

3. Add the canola and olive oils and the vinegar to the chilled juices, slowly blending the mixture with a hand blender until emulsified.

4. Add citrus zest, chopped parsley, and sugar to taste.

ASSEMBLY

1. Skin and halve each avocado. Slice off a small portion of the bottom of each half so it will stand on a plate. Stuff each avocado half with lump crabmeat.

2. Drizzle dressing over the crabmeat. Garnish with citrus segments and parsley sprigs.

Whole Roasted Young Piri Piri Chicken

SERVES: 4

PIRI PIRI SAUCE

1 red bell pepper, ribs and seeds removed, diced

1 Yellow bell pepper, ribs and seeds removed, diced

1 green bell pepper, ribs and seeds removed, diced

1 Spanish onion, large, diced

6 garlic cloves, large, peeled

1 jalapeño, stem removed

1 Tbsp paprika

1 tsp crushed red pepper

To taste, salt

To taste, freshly ground black pepper

½ cup extra-virgin olive oil

¼ cup white balsamic vinegar

CHICKEN

Two 2-lb whole young chickens

To taste, salt

To taste, freshly ground black pepper

PIRI PIRI SAUCE

1. In a medium saucepan, combine the peppers, onion, garlic, and jalapeño. Add the paprika, red pepper, salt, pepper, and olive oil. Place over medium heat and bring to a simmer. Simmer for 30 minutes or until the vegetables are fully tender.

2. Add the vinegar and simmer 30 more minutes. Remove from heat and let cool for 30 minutes.

3. Blend the mixture with a hand blender or tabletop blender until smooth; set aside. If using a tabletop blender, cool for 1 hour before blending.

CHICKEN

1. Remove the neck and giblets from the chickens if necessary. Rinse the chickens in cold water and towel dry. Place in a mixing bowl.

2. Lightly add salt and pepper to taste. Rub the chickens inside and out with 6 oz of the Piri Piri sauce.

3. Place the chickens in a roasting pan and bake in a 325°F oven for 35 minutes. Raise temperature to 475°F and bake another 10 minutes.

ASSEMBLY

1. Quarter the chickens and place 2 quarters on each of 4 plates. Brush on additional Piri Piri sauce for garnish. Serve with your favorite starch and vegetables.

Lemongrass-Skewered Tempura-Fried Yellowtail Snapper with Teriyaki Glaze

SERVES: 4

TEMPURA BATTER

½ cup sifted cornstarch

½ cup sifted all-purpose flour

Pinch baking soda

Pinch salt

Pinch freshly ground black pepper

1 egg yolk

½ cup ice water

TERIYAKI GLAZE

2 Tbsp chopped lemongrass

2 Tbsp chopped fresh ginger

4 garlic cloves, peeled

½ cup chopped onion

4 Tbsp sesame oil

¼ cup brown sugar

½ cup pineapple juice

½ cup teriyaki sauce

1 cup sake

SNAPPER

Four 6-oz filets of yellowtail snapper, scaled, with skin left on

5 pieces lemongrass

4 Tbsp sesame oil

BATTER

1. In a bowl, combine the cornstarch, flour, baking soda, salt, and pepper.

2. Add the egg yolk and ice water, mix well, and set aside.

TERIYAKI GLAZE

1. Combine the lemongrass, ginger, garlic, and onion with 1 Tbsp of the sesame oil. Sweat this mixture in a sauté pan until golden brown. Add the brown sugar, pineapple juice, teriyaki sauce, and ½ cup of the sake.

2. Bring to a boil, decrease to a simmer, and reduce by one-quarter. Thicken the sauce if needed with a small quantity of cornstarch and water. Let simmer 5 more minutes.

3. Remove from heat. Add the remaining sesame oil and sake. Let steep for 30 minutes, and then strain.

SNAPPER

1. Place the filets skin side down on a cutting board. Remove the belly sections and pin bones.

2. Move the filets to a plate, skin side up. Cut two relief cuts in each so the fish will not curl.

3. Skewer each filet from tail to head with a lemongrass skewer, piercing the skin and meat on both sides of the fish.

4. Dredge the filets in the batter and fry in oil heated to 350°F. To prevent the fish from sticking to the basket, hold it by the lemongrass until it starts to float. Remove when golden brown and allow to drain.

ASSEMBLY

1. Place each skewered filet on a plate with a starch and vegetable. Drizzle with teriyaki glaze.

Bacalao

SERVES: 4

1½ lbs salt cod

1 qt milk

3 Tbsp butter, unsalted

3 oz onion, medium diced

1 Tbsp roasted garlic puree

½ cup olive oil

To taste, freshly cracked black pepper

1 cup cooked and riced Yukon Gold potatoes

⅓ cup hummus

1 cup lightly sautéed spinach

4 slices hard-cooked egg

½ cup julienne prosciutto, sautéed

½ oz Osetra caviar

4 slices black truffle

2 Tbsp snipped chives

2 Tbsp Chive Oil (see Chef's Pantry)

3 Tbsp cooked and minced egg yolk

3 Tbsp cooked and minced egg white

1. Soak the salt cod in water for two days, changing the water twice a day.

2. Simmer the salt cod in the milk with the butter, onion, and garlic until the fish flakes apart. Remove the fish from the milk and place in a stainless-steel bowl, reserving the milk.

3. Add the olive oil and cracked pepper to the flaked fish. Add just enough riced potato to bind the mixture. Adjust the seasoning and spoon into a ring mold. Heat in a 325°F oven till hot.

4. For each serving, place 1 Tbsp of the hummus in the center of a plate and add a small amount of spinach and a cod potato timbale. Place 1 slice of egg, ⅛ cup sautéed prosciutto, and a caviar garnish on top. Garnish with 1 slice of truffle, ½ tbsp chives, ½ tbsp chive oil, pepper, 1½ tbsp egg yolk, and 1½ tbsp egg white around the edge of plate.

Foie Gras Tarte Tatin with Pear, Cherries, and Apple, Jícama, and Butternut Slaw

SERVES: 4

1 qt milk

6 juniper berries, crushed

2 bay leaves

3 sprigs thyme

2 Tbsp spice blend, toasted

2 tsp freshly cracked black pepper

2 Tbsp cognac

8 oz foie gras

3 Tbsp butter, unsalted

1½ Tbsp acacia honey

½ cup fresh orange juice

1 Tbsp orange zest, blanched

1 tsp ground coriander

Pinch salt

1 pear, peeled and sliced

2 Tbsp minced dried cherries

½ bulb Fennel, julienne, roasted

1 sheet puff pastry

As needed, egg wash

1. Combine the milk, juniper berries, bay leaves, thyme, spice blend, pepper, and cognac. Soak the foie gras in this mixture for 24 hours. Remove from the liquid and air-dry for 6 hours in a cooler. Cut four 2-oz portions from the lobe.

2. Score the pieces of foie gras and season with salt and pepper. Just before searing, freeze for 15 minutes.

3. Sear when needed in hot pan for about 30 seconds on both sides.

4. In a saucepan, combine the butter, honey, orange juice, zest, coriander, and salt. Reduce by two-thirds, adjust seasoning, and set aside.

5. Line the bottom of a nonstick tart pan with small, thin, uniform slices of pear. Sprinkle the chopped dried cherries over the pear slices and then the fennel over the cherries.

6. Pour the orange reduction into the tart pan. Cover with parchment. Bake at 350°F for 15–20 minutes.

7. Remove the tart from oven and cool. Cover with puff pastry and trim any excess from around the edges. Make 2 slits in the pastry, brush with egg wash, return to the oven, and bake until the pastry is golden brown 12-15 minutes.

Shrimp and Crab en Croûte

SERVES: 8

½ lb shrimp, peeled, deveined, and diced

6 oz heavy cream

½ lb lump crabmeat

1 Tbsp lemon zest, blanched and chopped

1 tsp snipped chives

1 tsp chopped dill

1 tsp chopped tarragon

1 Tbsp brunoise red bell pepper

1 oz black Trumpet mushroom, chiffonnade

1 oz spinach, chiffonnade

To taste, salt

To taste, freshly ground black pepper

1 Tbsp fresh lemon juice

1 sheet puff pastry

As needed, egg wash

1. Puree the shrimp in a Robo Coupe until smooth, scraping the sides as needed. Add the cream and pulse until well incorporated.

2. Pass the farce through a tamis and fold in the crab, zest, chives, dill, tarragon, red pepper, mushroom, spinach, salt, pepper, and lemon juice. Wrap the mixture in plastic to make a sausage. Tie the ends, then wrap with foil. Poach at 170°F until the internal temperature reaches 125°F. Chill in an ice bath.

3. Unwrap the chilled sausage and dry well. Wrap the sausage in puff pastry, using a little egg wash as an adhesive. Brush the outside of the pastry with egg wash as well.

4. Bake at 450°F for 8–10 minutes or until the pastry is golden brown.

5. Serve with baby greens, Roasted Pepper Relish (see Chef's Pantry), and Whole-Grain Mustard Sauce (see Chef's Pantry).

Spice-Rubbed Texas Black Buck Antelope with Mushroom and Herb Farce, Foie Gras Sausage, and Truffle Potato Sauce Laced with Wine Merchant

Serves: 4

ANTELOPE

2 antelope loins, cleaned

1 tsp tricolor peppercorn mélange

1 tsp kosher salt

1 tsp toasted spice blend

CHARRED PORTOBELLO MUSHROOMS

4 portobello mushrooms

¼ cup extra-virgin olive oil

As needed, Chef Leonard's Balsamic Vinaigrette

To taste, tricolor peppercorn mélange

To taste, kosher salt

MUSHROOM AND HERB FARCE

1 Tbsp chopped garlic

1 Tbsp minced shallots

Antelope trim from loins

4 oz ground pork

½ oz apple-smoked bacon, minced

Portobello trimmings, diced fine

4 portobellos, diced fine

½ cup Madeira

½ cup Marsala

2 Tbsp brandy

½ cup heavy cream

1 tsp chopped fresh thyme

1 tsp chopped fresh rosemary

2 Tbsp chopped fresh parsley

To taste, kosher salt

To taste, tricolor peppercorn mélange

As needed, caul fat

FOIE GRAS SAUSAGE

1 qt milk

6 juniper berries, crushed

2 bay leaves

3 sprigs thyme

2 tsp toasted spice blend

2 tsp tricolor peppercorn mélange

2 Tbsp cognac

1 lobe grade A fois gras

1 lb pork trim, ground fine

1 tsp chopped fresh thyme

1 tsp chopped fresh rosemary

1 Tbsp chopped fresh parsley

To taste, tricolor peppercorn mélange

To taste, kosher salt

TRUFFLE POTATO SAUCE

2 lb Idaho potatoes, peeled and quartered

8 oz yellow onion, large dice

As needed, chicken stock

To taste, heavy cream

2 Tbsp truffle oil

To taste, tricolor peppercorn mélange

To taste, kosher salt

ASSEMBLY

½ cup Wine Merchant Sauce (see Chef's Pantry)

½ cup roasted morel mushrooms

½ cup roasted wild asparagus tips

½ cup baby pearl red onions

ANTELOPE

1. Season the antelope with the peppercorn mélange, salt, and toasted spice. Set aside.

CHARRED PORTOBELLO MUSHROOMS

1. Remove the stem and gills from the mushrooms. Using a circle cutter, punch a 3½-in. disk from the middle of the mushrooms. Finely chop the remaining mushroom and set aside.

2. Brush the disks with olive oil and balsamic vinaigrette, and season with salt and pepper. At service time, char-grill on both sides.

MUSHROOM AND HERB FARCE

1. Sauté the garlic and shallots, then cool.

2. Grind the antelope trim, pork, bacon, garlic, and shallots through a small die, then grind a second time. Set aside; keep cold.

3. Sauté the mushrooms in a heavy saucepan. Add the Marsala, Madeira, and brandy. Cook until all the wine is reduced and the mushrooms are dry. Cool.

4. In a chilled Robo Coupe, mix the ground antelope mixture until smooth, scraping down the sides a few times. Add enough cream for a light consistency. Pass the mixture through a tamis into a chilled mixing bowl.

5. Add the sautéed mushroom mixture and mix on second speed until well incorporated. Add the thyme, rosemary, and parsley, and season with salt and pepper.

6. Onto a piece of plastic wrap, pipe an even layer of farce the length of the loin. Smoothe with a palette knife until the farce is about a ½ in. thick. Lay the loins on the farce, one on top of the other, and wrap, twisting the ends to make a uniform shape, tie. Chill for 1 hour to firm the roulade.

7. Unwrap the loin and rewrap it in caul fat. Place on a wire rack and roast in a 400°F convection oven for about 12 minutes. Let rest before slicing.

FOIE GRAS SAUSAGE

1. Combine the milk, juniper berries, bay leaves, thyme, toasted spice, peppercorn mélange, and cognac. Soak the foie gras in this mixture for 24 hours.

2. Remove the foie gras from the liquid and air-dry for 6 hours in a cooler.

3. Place the foie gras in the freezer for 30 minutes before mixing.

4. In a chilled mixing bowl, mix the pork trim, thyme, rosemary, parsley, peppercorns, and salt on third speed for about 1 minute. Transfer to a stainless-steel bowl. Fold in the diced foie gras and gently mix until well incorporated.

5. Using the sausage attachment, stuff the mixture into hog casing by hand so as not to break up the foie gras chunks. Roast in a 350°F convection oven 8–10 minutes.

TRUFFLE POTATO SAUCE

1. Place the potatoes and onions in a saucepot and add enough chicken stock to cover. Simmer until tender and puree in a blender until smooth. Add a little heavy cream to adjust consistency.

2. Add truffle oil and season with salt and pepper. Strain through a fine sieve.

Pan-Roasted Salmon with Salted Ham, Wine Sauerkraut, Sautéed Fingerling Potato, and Shallot Butter Sauce

SERVES: 6

SALMON

12 salmon filets

To taste, salt

To taste, freshly ground black pepper

Juice of 1 lemon

12 strips cured ham

2 oz olive oil

3 oz butter, unsalted

WINE SAUERKRAUT

3 oz onion, sliced fine

2 oz bacon fat or vegetable oil

18 oz sauerkraut

1 cup vegetable stock

1 cup good white wine

1 spice sachet (bay leaf, juniper berry, cloves)

½ apple, shredded

4 oz potato, shredded

To taste, salt

To taste, freshly ground black pepper

FINGERLING POTATOES

2 oz clarified butter

3 oz shallots, sliced thin

18 fingerling potatoes, cooked and peeled

1 oz whole butter, unsalted

1 oz chopped chives

To taste, salt

To taste, freshly ground pepper

SHALLOT BUTTER SAUCE

3 oz shallots, diced

1 sprig thyme

1 bay leaf

2 peppercorns

6 oz good white wine

6–8 oz butter, unsalted

To taste, fresh lemon juice

To taste, salt

To taste, freshly ground black pepper

SALMON

1. Trim filets as needed. Season with salt, pepper, and lemon juice. Roll up and wrap with the ham.

2. Heat the oil and sauté the filet. Add the butter to the pan and baste the fish with the hot butter and oil mix.

3. Finish roasting in the oven.

WINE SAUERKRAUT

1. In a heavy pot, sauté the onion in the fat. Add the sauerkraut and mix well.

2. Add the stock, ½ cup of the wine, and the spice sachet. Cook for about 20 minutes. Add the shredded apple and potato to the sauerkraut to thicken it. Continue to cook until the sauerkraut is tender. Remove the spice sachet and adjust the seasoning with salt, pepper, and the remaining ½ cup wine.

FINGERLING POTATOES

1. In a sauté pan, heat the clarified butter and sauté the shallots and the potatoes until they are heated through and nicely colored.

2. Discard most of the clarified butter. Add the whole butter and the chives. Season with salt and pepper.

SHALLOT BUTTER SAUCE

1. In a small saucepot, simmer the shallots, thyme, bay leaf, peppercorns, and wine until the wine is reduced by two-thirds and the shallots are tender. Remove the thyme, bay leaf, and peppercorn.

2. Slowly whisk in the butter. Season with lemon juice, salt, and pepper.

Glazed Squab Breast and Red Wine Pear, Blue Cheese Potato Gratin, and Sautéed Mushrooms

SERVES: 6

SQUAB DIPPING AND DRYING

1 cup soy sauce

1 cup honey

1 cup dark molasses

3 cups balsamic vinegar

SQUAB

6 squab breasts

To taste, kosher salt

3 oz vegetable oil

RED WINE PEAR

1 star anise

1 cinnamon stick

6 peppercorns

1 bottle red wine

3 ripe pears, peeled, halved, seeds removed

2 oz butter, unsalted

2 oz red wine

12 oz poultry demi-glace

To taste, salt

To taste, freshly ground black pepper

BLUE CHEESE AND POTATO GRATIN

2 cups heavy cream

2 lbs Yukon Gold potatoes, peeled and sliced thin

4 oz sweet onion, sliced thin

1 oz butter, unsalted

To taste, salt

To taste, freshly ground black pepper

To taste, ground nutmeg

4 oz good-quality blue cheese

SAUTÉED MUSHROOMS

1 oz oil

1 oz butter, unsalted

6 oz assorted fresh mushrooms

1 oz shallots, diced

1 garlic clove, diced

To taste, salt

To taste, freshly ground black pepper

1 Tbsp chopped fresh herbs

SQUAB DIP

1. In a saucepan, combine the soy sauce, honey, molasses, and vinegar. Bring to a boil and skim off the impurities.

SQUAB

1. Dip the squab breasts in the hot brine 3 times and hang to dry in the refrigerator for 3–4 days.

2. In a large sauté pan, heat the oil and sear the squab breasts until the skin is crisp and golden. Finish roasting in a 320°F oven. Let the squab rest before carving.

RED WINE PEAR

1. In a heavy stainless-steel saucepot, combine the star anise, cinnamon stick, peppercorns, and wine. Simmer until the liquid is reduced by one-third. Add the pears and simmer until they are soft. Let the pears cool overnight in the liquid. Remove the pears from the liquid and cut into wedges.

2. In a sauté pan, heat half of the butter and warm the pear wedges. Deglaze with the fresh red wine and add the demi-glace. Bring to a simmer, stir in the rest of the butter, and adjust the seasoning with salt and pepper.

BLUE CHEESE AND POTATO GRATIN

1. In a heavy pot, heat the cream, then add the potato, onion and butter. Season with salt, pepper, and nutmeg and simmer for 10 minutes.

2. Transfer the potato mixture to a buttered baking dish. Sprinkle the blue cheese over the potato and bake in a 350°F oven until golden and well cooked.

SAUTÉED MUSHROOMS

1. In a sauté pan, heat the oil and butter. Add the mushrooms, shallots, and garlic, and sauté for 2 minutes. Season with salt and pepper. Finish with the herbs.

Grilled Basil and Garlic-Marinated Beef Tenderloin, Grilled Polenta, and Vegetable with Tomato Chutney

Serves: 6

BEEF TENDERLOIN

1 oz fresh lime juice

2 garlic cloves

4 oz olive oil

1 Tbsp cumin seed

1 tsp crushed black pepper

1 Tbsp kosher salt

3 Tbsp steak seasoning

6 beef tenderloin medallions

GRILLED POLENTA

2½ qt vegetable stock

1 Tbsp salt

1 lb coarse yellow cornmeal

2 oz herb and pepper oil

GRILLED VEGETABLES

1 onion, cut in rings or wedges

1 red bell pepper, quartered, seeds removed

1 yellow bell pepper, quartered, seeds removed

1 zucchini, cut in ¼-in. slices

1 squash, cut in ¼-in. slices

2 oz roasted garlic oil

To taste, seasoning blend

TOMATO CHUTNEY

5 oz rice vinegar

2 Tbsp sugar

3 oz white wine

4 oz onion, diced

2 Tbsp honey

1 lb tomatoes, peeled, seeded, and diced

2 Tbsp finely sliced basil

To taste, salt

To taste, freshly ground black pepper

BEEF TENDERLOIN

1. In a blender, combine the lime juice, garlic, and oil. Blend until smooth.

2. Combine the cumin, pepper, salt, and steak seasoning; set aside.

3. Brush the meat with the lime oil mixture and season with the seasoning mix. Let marinate for 20 minutes. Grill over hot charcoal to the desired doneness.

GRILLED POLENTA

1. Bring the stock to a boil, add the salt, and then add the cornmeal in a thin stream, stirring constantly. Cook over moderate heat, stirring constantly, for about 35 minutes.

2. Pour the polenta into a lined pan and cool thoroughly. Cut into shapes, brush with oil, and grill.

GRILLED VEGETABLES

1. Place the onions, red and yellow peppers, zucchini, and squash on a cookie tray. Brush the vegetables with the oil and season with the seasoning blend on both sides. Grill over hot charcoal until tender and golden.

TOMATO CHUTNEY

1. In a stainless-steel pot, combine the vinegar, sugar, wine, onion, and honey. Bring to a boil and simmer until the liquid is evaporated. Add the tomatoes and continue to cook for 5 minutes. Add the basil and salt and pepper to taste.

Arugula Napoleon Salad, Goat Cheese, Oven-Dried Plum Tomato, and Pineapple Compote

SERVES: 4

RED WINE VINEGAR REDUCTION

2 cups red wine vinegar

½ cup brown sugar

PINEAPPLE COMPOTE

1 oz vegetable oil

½ Maui onion, small, sliced

½ pineapple, small, ripe

2 Roma tomatoes

6 basil leaves, chiffonade

ARUGULA SALAD

4 oz arugula

1 oz goat cheese

1 Tbsp balsamic vinegar

1½ tsp vegetable oil

To taste, salt

To taste, cracked black pepper

RED WINE VINEGAR REDUCTION

1. Reduce the red wine vinegar by nearly half. Add the brown sugar. Continue to reduce at a low heat until syrupy. Set aside.

Roosevelt Salad

SERVES: 4

BASIL OIL

¼ cup basil leaves

¾ cup extra-virgin olive oil

To taste, salt

ORANGE PEEL DUST

6 oranges

2 cups simple syrup

SALAD

1 European cucumber

1 tub microgreens

1 muscovy duck breast

PINEAPPLE COMPOTE

1. Heat a pan over medium heat. Add the oil and onion and cook until the onion is golden brown. Cool.

2. Cut the pineapple and tomatoes into thin slices. Put the slices on a sheet pan and slowly bake at 250°F. Remove the pineapple when it is nearly dry. Cool. Allow the tomatoes to continue cooking until they are dry. Cool.

3. Put the onion, pineapple, tomatoes, and basil in a bowl and drizzle with vinegar reduction. Set aside.

ARUGULA SALAD

1. Immediately before plating, toss the arugula and the flowers with the oil and vinegar. Season with salt and pepper.

ASSEMBLY

1 pt blackberries

¼ lb gourmet Italian salami, julienne

1 pt cherry tomatoes, quartered

4 oz Blackberry Vinaigrette

1 pt rose petals, small

As needed, Fried Noodles

BASIL OIL

1. Blanch and shock the basil leaves. Place them in a blender with the olive oil and puree until well blended.

2. Strain the basil oil through a fine mesh filter or coffee filter; reserve until needed.

1. Peel the outer layers from the oranges. Boil the peels in the syrup for 10 minutes.

2. Transfer to a sheet pan and dry the peels in a 200°F oven for 1 hour or until very crisp.

3. Puree the peels in a coffee grinder.

SALAD

1. Using a mandoline, cut the cucumber lengthwise into long thin ribbons. Roll the ribbons into cylinders and fill each cylinder with 2 oz microgreens.

2. Score the duck breast liberally and sauté skin side down for 8–10 minutes or until the skin is very crisp. Turn over and cook for 4 more minutes. Let the breast rest for 2 minutes, then slice.

ASSEMBLY

1. Place a cucumber roll in the center of each plate and arrange the duck slices, blackberries, salami, and tomatoes around it. Drizzle the vinaigrette around the plate and garnish with basil oil, rose petals, and fried noodles.

Blackened Mahi-Mahi, Crispy Potato Cake, Watercress, Mandarin, and Pineapple Salad

SERVES: 4

PINEAPPLE CHIPS

4 thin pineapple slices

PAPRIKA OIL

4 oz vegetable oil

2 oz paprika

POTATO CAKES

3 russet potatoes, grated

MAHI-MAHI

2 lb mahi-mahi filets

WATERCRESS SALAD

6 oz mandarin orange segments

1 bag watercress, stems removed

1 pineapple

1 oz black sesame seeds, toasted

1 oz white sesame seeds, toasted

1 oz rice wine vinegar

2 oz extra-virgin olive oil

2 oz blackening seasoning

PINEAPPLE CHIPS

1. Place the pineapple slices on a Silpat and bake at 275°F until crisp, about 2 hours.

PAPRIKA OIL

1. Steep the paprika in the oil, then strain through a coffee filter. Reserve until needed.

POTATO CAKES

1. Add the oil to a nonstick pan. Cook the potatoes in a 5-in. round metal ring until crisp on both sides.

MAHI-MAHI

1. Season the fish with blackening mix and sear until blackened, then place in a 400°F oven for 12 minutes.

WATERCRESS SALAD

1. Combine oil, vinegar, and sesame seeds. Toss with watercress and orange segments.

ASSEMBLY

1. Place a potato cake in the center of each plate. Top with the fish and watercress salad. Garnish with a pineapple chip and paprika oil.

15

Chef Leonard's Pantry

Apple Cider Dressing

SERVES: 4

3 Tbsp butter, unsalted

1 small Fuji apple, peeled, cored, and chopped

4 Tbsp high-quality apple cider vinegar

1 cup high-quality apple cider

½ cup grapeseed oil

1 tsp allspice

½ tsp sage, minced

To taste, kosher salt

1. In a small saucepan, melt the butter over medium heat. Add the apple and cook, stirring, until it begins to caramelize, 4–5 minutes. Deglaze with the vinegar and cider and bring to a soft boil. Continue to cook until the mixture is reduced by half and the apple is very soft. Remove from the heat and allow mixture to cool for 10 minutes.

2. Place the cooled mixture in a blender and puree. While the blender is running, slowly add the grapeseed oil. Strain through a fine strainer.

3. Adjust seasoning to taste. Cool completely before using.

Arugula Jus

1 cup arugula leaves

4–6 Tbsp extra-virgin olive oil

1 Tbsp honey

2 tsp Giancarlo's Brodo (see below)

To taste, sea salt

1. Blanch the arugula in boiling salted water, shock in ice water, and wring dry.

2. In a high-speed blender add arugula, then slowly drizzle oil while blending on medium speed.

3. Next add the honey and brodo to the arugula mixture. Blend on high speed for 2–3 minutes.

4. Strain the mixture, then season to taste with salt.

Asparagus Emulsion

2 soft-boiled eggs

1 garlic clove

½ cup diced cooked asparagus

2 tsp green peas, frozen

½ cup extra-virgin olive oil

2 Tbsp blanched mint

4–8 Tbsp Giancarlo's Brodo (see below)

To taste, sea salt

1. Place the eggs, garlic, asparagus, and peas in a blender. Blend on high, then drizzle in oil.

2. Add the mint, blend 2–3 minutes more, then strain well. Add brodo, if needed, for a thinner consistency, and season with salt.

Balsamic Reduction

YIELD: ½ CUP

2 cups high-quality balsamic vinegar

4 Tbsp high-quality clover honey

1. In a stainless-steel saucepan, combine the balsamic vinegar and honey. Place over medium heat and slowly reduce to ½ cup.

2. Allow to cool to room temperature before using. If the mixture is too thick, add some vinegar until you get the consistency you desire.

Barley Jus

2 Tbsp butter, unsalted

2 oz bacon lardoons

1 minced shallot

1 garlic clove, minced

1 cup cooked barley

½ cup Demi de Cosette

To taste, salt

To taste, freshly ground black pepper

2 Tbsp extra-virgin olive oil

1. Place the butter and bacon in a saucepan and render. Add the shallot and garlic; cook until soft.

2. Add the barley, mix well, and cook 1–2 minutes. Add the demi and simmer 3–5 minutes.

3. Blend on medium speed for 1 minute, then on high speed for 2–3 minutes. Strain well, and season with salt and pepper. Stir in the olive oil.

Basil Reduction

1 large bunch basil leaves, very fresh, stems removed

½ cup flat-leaf parsley, stems removed

½ cup white balsamic vinegar

3 Tbsp sugar

½ cup seltzer

¼ cup honey

½ cup extra-virgin olive oil

1 garlic clove, peeled, germ removed

To taste, sea salt

1. Wash and dry the basil and parsley.

2. In a 1-qt stainless-steel or copper saucepot, place the basil, parsley, balsamic vinegar, sugar, seltzer, and honey. Bring to a boil, then simmer until reduced by half. Let the liquid cool slightly.

3. Transfer the basil liquid to a high-speed blender and add the olive oil, garlic, and salt. Process until smooth. Strain well through a mesh strainer.

4. Pour into a clean squeeze bottle and store in the refrigerator. Store under refrigeration for up to 1 week.

Chef Leonard's Pantry

Beef Brodo

2½ lbs beef shank, cut in 2-in. pieces

8 oz short rib

1 onion, small

½ cup chopped leek

2 carrots, peeled and chopped

3 Roma tomatoes, diced

1 bouquet garni

1. Trim away any fat from the meat and place in a stainless-steel stockpot. Add the onion, leek, carrot, tomatoes, and bouquet garni. Add enough cold water to cover the meat and vegetables by 2 in.

2. Bring to a boil, skim, then simmer slowly for 12 hours. Strain through a chinois and cool.

Butter-Poached Asparagus Spears

2 cups Giancarlo's Brodo (see below)

½ lb butter, unsalted

1 Tbsp sea salt

1 tsp minced shallots

20 asparagus spears

1. In a shallow baking or roasting pan, heat the brodo to a simmer. Add the butter, salt, and shallots.

2. Add the asparagus spears, ensuring the buttery broth covers them. Place a buttered piece of parchment paper on top.

3. On a very low simmer, cook the asparagus until tender, 15–20 minutes. Be sure the asparagus retains its color. Remove and serve.

Candied Garlic

2 cups water

1 cup sugar

1 cup garlic cloves, peeled and cleaned

1. Bring the water and sugar to a boil and simmer 5 minutes. Add the garlic and simmer until tender, 4–5 minutes.

2. Drain the garlic, place on a Silpat, and bake in a 375°F oven until a very light color is achieved.

Candied Tomatoes

1 lime, cut in half

8 large Roma tomatoes, peeled

1 Tbsp sea salt

6 Tbsp brown sugar

2 Tbsp extra-virgin olive oil

¼ cup bar sugar

1. Rub the lime over the peeled tomatoes.

2. Combine the salt and brown sugar. Roll the tomatoes gently in the salt mixture and place on a rack set over a baking pan.

3. Using a small bottle, drizzle the olive oil over the tomatoes. Sprinkle the bar sugar over the tomatoes.

4. Slow-roast the tomatoes in a 160°F oven for 5–6 hours, until slighty firm and candied.

CLUB CUISINE

Cashew Salt

2 cups cashews

½ cup sea salt coarse

2 Tbsp brown sugar

1. In a dry nonstick pan, toast cashews lightly for 3–5 minutes over medium heat, tossing frequently.

2. In a food processor, add nuts, salt, and sugar and pulse 10–15 seconds.

3. Place salt on a baking tray and let dry in an oven set at 145°F for 1 hour.

4. Put salt through a sieve and place in a shaker.

Chef Ed's Satay Sauce

4 Tbsp roasted peanut oil

1 tsp red curry paste

1 tsp ChefNique Curry Powder

2 Tbsp Knorr Satay Paste

1 Tbsp brown sugar

⅔ cup rice vinegar

1 cup coconut milk

½ cup cream of coconut

4 Tbsp peanut butter

1. In a stainless-steel saucepan, heat the oil, add the curry paste, and cook for 30–45 seconds.

2. Add the curry powder, satay paste, brown sugar, and vinegar; simmer until the mixture is reduced by half.

3. Add the coconut milk and cream of coconut, mix well, and simmer 2–3 minutes.

4. Whisk in the peanut butter. Simmer until the mixture is slightly thickened, and then strain through a chinois.

Chef Leonard's Basic Vinaigrette

4 Tbsp quality aged red wine vinegar

⅜ tsp salt

⅛ tsp sugar

Pinch, freshly ground Tellacherry black pepper

1 tsp Creole mustard

4 Tbsp extra virgin olive oil

8 Tbsp grapeseed oil

1. Whisk together well all the ingredients except the oils.

2. Slowly incorporate the oils by droplets. If you're using a food processor, blend in the oil in a slow, steady steam until blended. Serve at once.

Chef Leonard's Special Sauce

1 pt mayonnaise

4 medium-boiled eggs, diced

6 oz Westchester Country Club Cocktail Sauce (see below)

½ cup sweet relish

2 oz minced onion, sautéed

3 oz sour cream

2 Tbsp extra-virgin olive oil

2 Tbsp chopped parsley

1. Mix all items well and let sit for 1 hour prior to using.

Chicken Brodo

3 lbs chicken carcasses, clean, trimmed of fat, and chopped

10 oz chicken legs, with fat removed

2 onions, peeled and chopped

1 cup celery, diced

1 carrot, peeled and chopped

3 sprigs thyme

1 sage leaf

3 sprigs parsley

1. Place all the chicken in a stainless-steel stockpot. Add cold water to cover by 3 in. Bring to a boil, skim, and simmer for 2 hours. Skim once again.

2. Add the onions, celery, carrot, thyme, sage, and parsley. Simmer for 1 hour.

3. Strain well into a clean pan. Simmer for another 2 hours, skim again, and then strain through chinois and cool.

Chicken Jus

2 Tbsp grapeseed oil

3 chicken necks, cut in pieces

3 chicken thighs, chopped

4 chicken wings, chopped

2 Tbsp duck fat

2 shallots, chopped

1 garlic clove, sliced thin

4 cups Chicken Brodo (see above)

1. In a pan, heat the oil and sauté the chicken necks, thighs, and wings until nicely browned. Remove the chicken pieces and drain off the extra fat.

2. Add the duck fat and then the shallots and garlic. Caramelize the vegetables and juices.

3. Return the chicken pieces to the pan. Deglaze with 1 cup brodo and reduce by half. Add another 3 cups brodo and simmer for 1 hour. Strain well and cool.

Chive Oil

⅓ cup grapeseed oil

⅓ cup olive oil

4 oz chives

1 tsp minced parsley

1. Lightly heat the grapeseed and olive oils. Pour into a jar and add the chives and parsley. Infuse for 5 hours. Strain well.

Cinnamon Honey

1 pt grade A clover honey

12 cinnamon sticks

1. Place the cinnamon sticks in a sterilized 1-pt mason jar.

2. Place the honey into a heavy-bottomed 1-qt saucepan. Set the pan over medium heat and cook until the honey begins to bubble.

3. Pour the heated honey into the mason jar with the cinnamon sticks. Wipe the rim clean and seal with the lids.

4. Place the jar on a wire rack in the bottom of a deep stockpot. Add enough water to cover the jar by at least 2 in. Bring to a boil over high heat and continue to boil for 10 minutes. Remove the jar from the pot, set on a wire rack, and allow to cool.

5. Place the honey in a cool, dark place and allow to sit for 1 week before using.

Court Bouillon

4 qt water

1 cup dry white wine

3 limes, cut in half

2 Tbsp sea salt, coarse

1 Tbsp crushed black peppercorns

2 carrots, peeled

1 onion, peeled

3 shallots, peeled

2 celery ribs

2 fennel stalks

2 celery leaves

3 sprigs flat-leaf parsley

2 sprigs thyme

2 bay leaves

2 Tbsp Old Bay Spice or Spice de Cosette

A court bouillon, meaning "short boil," is an acidulated broth with vegetables. The vegetables are cooked with aromatics for a short time to create a flavorful vegetable broth, and then an acidic wine, vinegar, or lemon juice is added. The main purpose of using a court bouillon to cook things in is to preserve and enhance their flavor. If you use plain water, the flavor of the foods leaches out. The osmotic pressure of the vegetable stock keeps flavors in the food being cooked, while the acid firms and whitens the flesh of the chicken, fish, or shellfish.

1. Place water and wine in a shallow stainless-steel pan, squeeze in the juice from the limes, and add the limes along with the salt and pepper.

2. Coarsely chop all the vegetables and add them to the water along with the parsley, thyme, bay leaves, and seasoning.

3. Bring to a boil and then simmer at 140–160°F. Poach items to be used for other recipes as directed.

Chef Leonard's Pantry

Demi de Cosette

2-lb oxtails, cut in 1-in. pieces

2 lb beef shoulder meat, diced in 2-in. pieces

2 chickens (3 lb each), cut into 12 pieces each

3 onions, chopped

4 carrots, peeled and chopped

3 leeks

2 bay leaves

8 parsley stems

2 cloves

½ oz sea salt

2 cups white wine

3 qt quality veal stock

3 qt quality chicken stock

Use as a finish to pan sauces, to glaze meat prior to roasting, or as a glaze for flavor infusion on a plate.

1. Roast oxtails, beef, and chicken pieces until brown. Drain off fat.

2. Remove the skin from the chickens and scrape off any skin left in the roasting pans.

3. Add all items in a stainless-steel pot.

4. Bring to a boil. Then lower to a medium heat, skimming off any fat or impurities as it simmers.

5. Let simmer for 2 hours.

6. Strain well, and place back on the stove with a new pot. Bring to a simmer and reduce to half the amount.

7. Strain well.

8. Place Demi in an ice bath to cool, and store in the refrigerator until ready to use.

Crab Broth

3 Tbsp olive oil

4 Tbsp butter

½ cup chopped onions

1 small garlic clove, chopped

2 Tbsp tomato paste

4 lb blue crab, cleaned and chopped

⅔ cup white wine

6 fresh parsley stems

2 sprigs fresh thyme

½ tsp crushed red pepper flakes

3 diced Roma tomatoes

16 oz cold spring water, or enough water to cover

1. Heat olive oil and butter in heavy-bottomed pot over medium-high heat.

2. Add onion and garlic and sauté 2–3 minutes. Add tomato paste and crabs.

3. Add wine and stir while cooking for another minute more, then add remaining items.

4. Let simmer 40 minutes. Strain twice through a fine-mesh strainer, reserve, and use as needed.

Demi de Edward Christopher

2 oz butter, unsalted

1 Tbsp olive oil

4 Tbsp diced onion

1 garlic clove, sliced

3 Tbsp diced carrot

2 Tbsp all-purpose flour

1 Tbsp tomato paste

3 cups veal stock, cold

To taste, kosher salt

To taste, freshly ground black pepper

1. Heat the butter and oil in a saucepan. Add the onion, garlic, and carrot. Cook until soft.

2. Mix in the flour and tomato paste. Cook for 2–3 minutes.

3. Add the stock. Mix well and simmer for 1 hour. Strain and season with salt and pepper.

Dried Orange Zest

2–3 oranges, or as many as needed for recipe

2 tsp bar sugar

This recipe can be used for lemon and lime zest as well. Zest is the outer colored portion of the citrus peel. Freshly grated orange, lime, or lemon zest packs a flavor infusion that no store-bought zest can match.

1. Use a citrus zester to obtain long, thin strands of citrus zest. The zester will have five tiny cutting holes that create threadlike strips of peel. Lightly zest the oranges, being careful not to zest the bitter white pith.

2. Toss the zest lightly with bar sugar, and spread on a baking tray lined with a Silpat.

3. Dry with the oven door slightly open and the oven temperature at 140°F.

4. Zest should be crisp in 1 to 1¼ hours.

Duck Confit

SERVES: 4

1½ Tbsp kosher salt

1 tsp freshly cracked black pepper

½ tsp ground cardamom

1 Tbsp brown sugar

4 duck legs, thighs attached

10 garlic cloves

4 sprigs thyme

4 bay leaves

4 cups duck fat, melted

1. In a small mixing bowl, combine the salt, pepper, cardamom, and brown sugar and mix well. Evenly coat the duck legs with the mixture and place them on a platter. Cover with plastic and refrigerate for 12 hours.

2. Preheat the oven to 200°F.

3. Remove the duck from the refrigerator. Rinse the duck legs gently to remove excess salt mixture and pat dry with paper towels.

4. Place the garlic, thyme, bay leaves, and shallots in a heavy-bottomed pan or casserole with cover. Add the duck legs and melted duck fat. Cover and bake until tender, 8–10 hours. The meat can be served on the bone or removed from it, depending on the application.

Chef Leonard's Pantry

5. Allow the confit to cool while submerged in the duck fat. Store in the refrigerator for up to 1 month.

Fried Onions

As needed, onions

1 egg, well beaten

1 cup buttermilk

1 cup all-purpose flour

½ tsp cayenne pepper

1 tsp Old Bay Seasoning

1 tsp baking powder

¼ tsp kosher salt

Fat for deep frying

1. Cut off the root ends of the onions; slip off the loose skins. Cut onions in half, then slice them thin on a bias.

2. Combine the egg and buttermilk in a bowl, and beat until thoroughly blended.

3. Add onions and let soak for 20 minutes.

4. Blend well the flour, pepper, seasoning, baking powder, and salt.

5. Take the onions from the milk mixture and coat them with flour mix.

6. Heat the fat to 375°F. Deep-fry onions in fat until golden brown and crisp, 2–3 minutes. Place on paper towels to absorb grease.

Fried Sage Leaves

30 sage leaves, washed and dried

1 cup flour

2 Tbsp salt

1 Tbsp cinnamon

½ tsp pepper

1. Mix all spices with the flour and sift.

2. Dust sage leaves in flour and deep-fry at 325°F until crisp.

Fruit Compote

¾ cup apple juice or berry water

½ cup sugar

½ cup blueberry, raspberry, or lavender honey

2 Tbsp fresh lime juice

1 Tbsp sage leaves

1 vanilla bean, split

4 Tbsp butter, unsalted, diced

1 sheet gelatin, soaked for 15 minutes, then squeezed

4 cups seasonal fruit*

*If using hard fruits such as pears and apples, peel and dice.

1. In a small saucepan, place the apple juice, sugar, honey, lime juice, sage, and vanilla bean. Bring to a boil, stirring occasionally. Boil until the sugar is dissolved.

2. Add the butter and gelatin to the sugar mixture. Add the fruit, bring to a boil, and let simmer until the fruit is just tender. The time will vary with the type of fruit. Let cool.

For cranberry compote, use 3 cups cranberries and 1 cup diced pears or apples. Cook until the cranberries are soft, then fold in 1–2 cups high-quality pear puree.

Garlic Jus

8 garlic cloves, peeled and thinly sliced

3 Tbsp olive oil

3 tsp tomato paste

½ cup merlot

½ cup Giancarlo's Brodo (see below)

4 Tbsp raisins

2 sprigs thyme

1 tsp ground cardamom

8 coriander seeds

To taste, salt

To taste, freshly ground black pepper

1. In a pan, sauté the garlic in the oil until soft. Add the tomato paste, cook for 30 seconds, and then deglaze with the wine.

2. Add the brodo, raisins, thyme, cardamom, and coriander. Simmer until the liquid evaporates and turns to a very light syrup. Strain and season with salt and pepper.

Giancarlo's Brodo

¼ cup diced leeks

4 garlic cloves, diced

¼ cup white button mushrooms, cut in quarters

3 shallots, diced

½ cup high-quality extra-virgin olive oil

2 star anise

2 bay leaves

3 whole cloves

1 qt spring water

To taste, sea salt

1. In a stainless-steel saucepan, place the leeks, garlic, carrots, mushrooms, shallots, olive oil, star anise, bay leaves, cloves, water, and salt. Bring to a boil, then simmer for 40 minutes. Strain and cool.

Hollandaise Sauce
YIELD: ABOUT ⅔ CUP

1 cup butter, unsalted

3 egg yolks, large

1 tsp vinegar

1 Tbsp fresh lime juice

1 tsp fresh lime juice

⅛ tsp salt

1–2 dashes cayenne or hot pepper sauce

1. Heat the butter in a heavy saucepan until hot and foamy but not browned.

2. Ladle off the clear butter and place in a container.

3. In a small stainless-steel bowl, whisk or beat the egg yolks with the vinegar, lemon juice, salt, and cayenne until foamy.

4. Place the bowl over a pan of low-simmering water and whisk quickly to thicken the egg yolks. Do not let the mixture get too hot, as the eggs will scramble.

5. When the yolks start to thicken, remove the bowl from the heat and slowly whisk in ½ cup of the clear butter.

6. Return the bowl to the saucepan and beat over very low heat until the mixture is slightly thickened. Adjust the seasoning with salt and hot sauce if desired. Serve immediately or let stand over warm heat.

Lime Jam

12 limes, peeled and sectioned, with juice

8 Tbsp sugar

½ tsp gelatin

1 tsp Chinese chili paste

1 vanilla bean, split

2 Tbsp minced shallot

1. In a stainless-steel saucepan, place the limes, sugar, chili paste, vanilla bean, and shallots. Cook for 6–8 minutes, then let steep for 30 minutes. Remove the vanilla bean.

Lobster Essence

YIELD: 2 CUPS

6 lobster carcasses, roasted, crushed, and chopped

2 stalks fennel

1 onion, diced

1 cup chardonnay

¼ cup tomato paste

1 qt Giancarlo's Brodo (see above)

6 peppercorns

1 bay leaf

1. In a stainless-steel pot, place the lobsters, fennel, onion, wine, tomato paste, brodo, peppercorns, and bay leaf. Bring to a boil, reduce heat, and simmer for 1 hour.

2. Strain the liquid through a fine sieve, return it to the pot, and simmer until reduced to 2 cups, skimming occasionally.

Maple Vinegar Reduction

1 cup muscat vinegar

2 Tbsp bar sugar

3 Tbsp maple syrup

2 Fine zest of 2 limes

Juice of 1 lime

1. Mix the vinegar, sugar, maple syrup, lime zest, and lime juice together and let sit for 5 minutes.

2. Bring the mixture to a boil, reduce the heat, and let simmer until reduced to a thin syrup. Strain and cool.

Maple Vinegar Reduction can be used at room temperature or warm.

Mashed Potatoes, Simply the Best

Serves: 4

1½ lb Yukon Gold potatoes, scrubbed but not peeled

As needed, spring water, cold

As needed, kosher salt

½ cup heavy cream

½ cup milk

3 oz high-quality butter, unsalted, diced

To taste, sea salt

1. Place the potatoes in a large stainless-steel pan. Cover with cold spring water by 2 in. Add 1 Tbsp kosher salt for every 4 cups water.

2. Bring to a boil, reduce heat, and simmer until potatoes are tender. Drain the potatoes immediately and place on a clean kitchen towel.

3. In a saucepan, combine the cream and milk; bring to a boil. Set aside.

4. When the potatoes are cool enough to handle, peel and cut them into pieces. Pass the potatoes through a ricer twice and then transfer them to a heavy-bottomed stainless-steel saucepan.

5. Place the pan over low heat and beat with a wooden spoon for 3–5 minutes. A little at a time, stir in the butter, beating well until it is incorporated and the potatoes are fluffy. Slowly stir in the scalded cream and milk. Season with salt.

Mushroom Essence

Yield: 1 cup

⅔ cup dried cèpes

½ cup dried morels

4 cups Giancarlo's Brodo, very warm (see above)

2 cups Giancarlo's Brodo, cold (see above)

½ cup diced shiitakes

½ cup diced portobellos

2 shallots, peeled and chopped

6 peppercorns

1 mace blade

8 tarragon leaves

½ bay leaf, small

To taste, salt

1. Combine the cèpes and morels in a bowl with the warm brodo. Push the mushrooms under the surface and weigh them down with a china saucer. Let soak overnight.

2. Strain the soaked mushrooms into a container, squeezing out and reserving as much liquid as possible. Dice the mushrooms.

3. In a 4-qt stainless-steel saucepan, place the diced reconstituted mushrooms and the shiitakes, portobellos, shallots, peppercorns, mace, tarragon, and bay leaf. Bring to a simmer.

4. Strain the mushroom soaking liquid twice through a moist cheesecloth and a chinois. Add to the pan, bring back to a boil, and simmer for 20 more minutes.

5. Strain the mixture well, return it to the pan, and reduce to 1 cup. Season with salt.

Mustard Cream

1 shallot, minced

½ cup dry white wine

1 tsp mustard seed

4 oz butter, unsalted, cold, diced

½ cup heavy cream, warm

2 tsp Lemon-infused honey

2 Tbsp Dijon mustard

To taste, sea salt

1. In a saucepan, place the shallot, wine, and mustard seed. Bring to a boil, reduce the heat, and simmer until the wine is almost evaporated.

2. Whisk in the butter a little at a time. Add the cream, honey, and Dijon mustard and simmer for 2–3 minutes. Strain twice and season with salt.

Olive Oil Tomatoes

4 tomatoes

2 garlic cloves, sliced thin

4 Tbsp extra-virgin olive oil

1 tsp sugar

2 tsp kosher salt

1 tsp crushed red pepper flakes

1 cup extra-virgin olive oil

1. Place the tomato petals in a bowl. Gently toss with the garlic, 4 Tbsp olive oil, sugar, salt, and pepper. Lay the tomatoes evenly in a 2-cup stainless-steel baking pan. Add 1 cup olive oil. Place in a 140°F oven and bake for 6 hours.

2. Carefully remove the tomatoes from the pan.

3. Store the remaining oil in the refrigerator. Use for dressings and flavoring vegetables.

Pecan Cream

½ cup whole fresh milk

½ cup heavy cream

4 Tbsp caramel sauce

½ cup roasted pecan pieces

4 Tbsp pecan oil

1 tsp pecan salt

1. In a small copper or stainless-steel pan, combine the milk, cream, caramel sauce, pecan oil, and pecan salt. Bring to a simmer.

Pomegranate Syrup

YIELD: ½ CUP

2 cups pomegranate juice

¼ cup Pomegranate molasses

2 Tbsp clover honey

1. In a stainless-steel saucepan, combine the juice, molasses, and honey. Bring to a simmer over medium heat. Allow to reduce to about ½ cup. Cool and reserve for use.

If you cannot find pomegranate molasses, boil pomegranate seeds in corn syrup for 10 minutes and then strain the syrup.

Potatoes Parisienne

4 large Yukon Gold potatoes peeled

To taste, salt

3 Tbsp olive oil

3 Tbsp butter

1 tsp minced shallots

1 garlic clove, minced

To taste, kosher salt

To taste, black pepper, freshly ground

2 Tbsp parsley, chopped finely

1. Using a Parisienne scoop, make rounded balls from large peeled potatoes. Make full, round balls and place in a stainless steel pan filled with salted water.

2. Bring the water to a boil and simmer for 2–3 minutes. Drain the potatoes and dry well.

3. Heat a cast iron skillet on medium heat. Add the olive oil and butter.

4. Add shallots and garlic and sauté until soft, for 1–2 minutes.

5. Add the potato balls in a large frying pan and sauté until golden brown.

6. Sprinkle with parsley and serve.

For a low-fat version, simply boil potatoes until tender and sprinkle them with parsley.

Profiteroles

Yield: 4 to 6

½ cup water

¼ cup butter, unsalted, cut into pieces

1½ tsp sugar

Pinch salt

½ cup all-purpose flour

2 eggs, large

1. Line a heavy baking sheet with parchment paper.

2. Combine the water, butter, sugar, and salt in a heavy medium saucepan. Bring to a boil, stirring until the butter melts. Add the flour and stir over medium heat for 1 minute. Remove from the heat and allow to cool for 5 minutes.

3. Crack 2 eggs into a measuring cup. Using a wooden spoon, beat both eggs into the mixture, one at a time.

4. Drop the mixture ¼ cup at a time onto the lined sheet pan, leaving 2 in. between each. Place in a preheated 375°F oven and bake until amber brown, about 50 minutes. Remove from the oven and allow to cool before serving. Unused pastries may be stored in the freezer for up to 1 month.

Pumpkin Butter

This butter may be stored in the refrigerator for up to 1 week or in the freezer for up to 1 month.

One 15-oz can pumpkin puree

½ tsp allspice

Pinch kosher salt

1 lb butter, unsalted, softened

1. Place the pumpkin puree in a heavy-bottomed stainless-steel saucepan and set it over medium heat. While stirring with a wooden spoon, cook for about 10 minutes to remove all moisture.

2. Remove from the heat and add the salt and allspice. Allow to cool completely in the refrigerator.

3. Dice the butter and place in a small electric mixer. Add the cooled puree and use the paddle attachment to combine well.

4. Place the pumpkin butter on a piece of parchment paper and roll it tightly to form a log about 1½ in. in diameter. Place the log in the refrigerator and allow to harden. Once hardened, the pumpkin butter is ready for use.

Raspberry Coulis

½ cup raspberries

¼ cup sugar

2 Tbsp lime juice

1 vanilla bean, split

2 Tbsp raspberry liqueur

¼ cup sparkling water

1. In a stainless-steel or copper saucepan, combine the raspberries, sugar, lemon juice, vanilla bean, liqueur, and sparkling water. Simmer until the sauce reduces to a light syrup consistency. Strain and cool.

Roasted Garlic

2 cups garlic cloves, peeled

2 Tbsp orange honey

1 cup olive oil

½ cup clarified butter

1 tsp sea salt

½ tsp red pepper flakes

1. Preheat the oven to 350°F. In a glass baking dish large enough to hold them in a single layer, place the garlic cloves and the honey, olive oil, clarified butter, salt, and red pepper. Cover the dish with aluminum foil and bake for 1½–2 hours, or until the garlic is soft.

2. Remove from the oven and cool. Drain before using.

Save the oil in the refrigerator and use for cooking, salad dressing, or marinades.

Roasted Red Pepper Relish

½ cup V-8 juice

1 Tbsp powdered gelatin

3 large roasted red peppers

2 cloves garlic, minced

2 shallots, finely minced

2 Tbsp grated candied ginger

1 tsp sea salt

1 cup dark brown sugar

2 Tbsp molasses

¾ cup rice wine vinegar

1. Mix juice and gelatin and let sit for 10 minutes.

2. Dice the peppers finely.

3. In a stainless-steel saucepan add peppers, gelatin, and the remaining items.

4. Bring to a boil and simmer for 45 minutes.

5. Place in sterilized jars and seal.

Sage Potato Butter

1 cup Giancarlo's Brodo, cold (see above)

2 tsp arrowroot or clear jell

4 oz cooked Yukon Gold potatoes, riced twice and mashed, warm

3 oz high-quality butter, unsalted

1 Tbsp high-quality extra-virgin olive oil or white truffle oil

1 tsp sea salt

1 tsp chopped fresh sage

1. In a stainless-steel pan, combine the arrowroot with the brodo. Bring to a light simmer and then whisk in the mashed potatoes. Place over medium heat and bring to a low simmer. Quickly beat in the butter and oil.

2. Remove from the stove. Season with the salt and sage.

Seafood Brodo

2 Tbsp butter, unsalted

1 Tbsp olive oil

1 cup shrimp shells

14 Prince Edward Island mussels

1 onion, diced

¼ bulb fennel, diced

2 lb bones from snapper or sole, washed and chopped

1 celery stalk, diced

3 Tbsp diced white mushrooms

2 Roma tomatoes, diced

¼ cup white wine

2 sprigs flat-leaf parsley

1 sprig thyme

As needed, spring water, cold

1 tsp sea salt

¼ tsp white pepper

1. Heat the butter and oil in shallow stainless-steel pan. Add the shrimp shells, mussels, onion, and fennel. Sweat for 4–5 minutes.

2. Add the fish bones, celery, mushrooms, tomatoes, wine, parsley, and thyme. Cook for 3–5 minutes. Just cover with cold spring water and bring to a low boil.

3. Skim well. Add the salt and pepper, then simmer for 20–25 minutes only. Strain well through a chinois.

Sweet and Sour Reduction

¼ cup merlot wine vinegar

2 Tbsp raisins

6 Tbsp bar sugar

3 cloves

1. Mix the vinegar, raisins, sugar, and cloves with a whisk.

2. In a small stainless-steel saucepan, bring the mixture to a boil, then simmer until it reduces to the consistency of syrup.

Tempura Batter

1 egg

1 cup ice water

1 cup all-purpose flour

2 tsp Spice De Cosette seasoning

1. Beat the egg in a bowl.

2. Add ice water to the bowl.

3. Mix flour with seasoning. Then add flour to the bowl with the egg and ice water and mix lightly.

Use ice cold water for the batter, the colder the better. This is really important to prevent the batter from absorbing too much oil. Do not make the batter ahead of time.

Do not overmix the batter, and avoid coating ingredients with too much batter.

If you are frying seafood, meat, and vegetables, fry the vegetables first, then the meat, then the seafood. Fry vegetables at 340°F, meat at 360°F, and seafood at 350°F.

To check the temperature of frying oil, drop a little batter into the oil. If the batter comes up right away instead of sinking to the bottom of the pan, it's about 360°F. If the batter goes halfway to the bottom and comes up, it's about 340°F. This is said to be the right temperature to fry tempura. The best way to gauge the temperature is to use a frying thermometer.

Three-Herb Oil

⅔ cup grapeseed oil

2 oz parsley, minced

2 oz basil, minced

2 oz sage, minced

1. In a saucepan, heat the oil, then add the herbs.

2. Store in an airtight container.

Tomato Confit 1

8 Roma tomatoes, ripe but firm, peeled, seeded, and halved

To taste, sea salt

To taste, freshly ground black pepper

8 garlic cloves, peeled and thinly sliced

8 sprigs thyme

4 Tbsp extra-virgin olive oil

2 tsp ground cloves

1 tsp ground cumin

½ tsp ground cinnamon

2 tsp finely minced parsley

1. Preheat the oven to 180°F. Arrange the tomatoes, cut sides up, on a baking tray lined with a Silpat.

2. Season the tomatoes generously with salt and pepper. Scatter the garlic and thyme over the tomatoes. Drizzle with the oil.

3. Sift together the cloves, cumin, and cinnamon, and place in a mesh shaker. Sprinkle the spice mixture evenly over the tomatoes.

4. Bake, uncovered, until the tomatoes are soft but firm, 1½–2 hours. Discard the thyme and garlic. Sprinkle parsley over tomatoes. Store the tomatoes with the olive oil in a closed container for up to 1 week.

Tomato Confit 2

4 Roma tomatoes, peeled and seeded

1 Tbsp ground cumin

½ Tbsp ground coriander

To taste, kosher salt

2 garlic cloves, thinly sliced

6 oz olive oil

1. Cut the tomatoes into quarters and lay them on a lightly oiled pan. Season with the cumin, coriander, and salt. Place 2–3 slices of garlic on each tomato quarter. Drizzle the tomatoes with the oil.

2. Bake at 200°F until the tomatoes are soft but still slightly firm, 40–45 minutes.

3. Serve with chicken dishes, fish, or veal, toss with pasta, or use as a garnish or vegetable.

Tomato Emulsion

2 fresh organic eggs, soft-boiled

1 garlic clove, minced

1 Tbsp olive oil

½ cup diced, peeled, and seeded ripe Roma tomatoes

2 tsp tomato paste

3 Tbsp high-quality balsamic vinegar

½ cup extra-virgin olive oil

2 Tbsp blanched basil

4–8 Tbsp tomato water

To taste, sea salt

1. In a blender, place the eggs and garlic. Puree on low for 2 minutes.

2. In a stainless-steel sauté pan, cook 1 Tbsp olive oil and the tomatoes and tomato paste for 3 minutes. Add the vinegar and remove from the stove. Add to the mixture in the blender and blend on medium speed while drizzling in ½ cup olive oil. Add the basil and blend on high speed for 1–2 minutes. Strain well.

3. Add tomato water to obtain desired consistency. Season with salt.

Tomato Syrup

⅓ cup olive oil

8 Tbsp brown sugar

2 Tbsp bar sugar

4 tsp honey

1 tsp kosher salt

1 tsp red pepper flakes

1 lb Roma tomatoes, overripe, peeled

4 garlic cloves, sliced thin

¼ cup blanched basil leaves

3 cups tomato water or tomato juice

1. Mix the oil, brown sugar, bar sugar, honey, salt, and red pepper well. Coat the tomatoes well with this mixture.

2. Sauté the tomatoes in a seasoned cast-iron pan until nicely caramelized and juicy.

3. Add the garlic, basil, and tomato water. Cook for 45 minutes, then press through a chinois.

Vanilla Oil

Vanilla oil can be used as a base for vinaigrettes or as a marinade for roasted pork chops or chicken breasts.

6 vanilla beans, split and chopped into ½-in. pieces

½ cup grapeseed oil

⅛ tsp salt

1. Combine the vanilla beans, grapeseed oil, and salt in a stainless-steel saucepan and heat to 180°F. Shut off heat and let steep for 20 minutes. Place in a blender and process until fine. Strain through a fine-mesh sieve twice and set aside.

2. Place in a squeeze bottle to use as a flavoring oil on plates or to make a dressing. Store in the refrigerator.

Veal Demi Glace

1 qt quality veal stock made from clean, fresh veal bones with some knuckle

3 Tbsp diced, cold high-quality butter

To taste, kosher salt

1. Place the stock in a heavy bottomed stainless-steel 2-qt saucepan.

2. Set over medium heat. Bring the stock to a very gentle simmer. Reduce the heat and simmer until the stock is reduced by half, 1½ to 2 hours.

3. From time to time, using a ladle, skim off any foam that appears on the top of the stock to keep the sauce pure and untainted.

4. Transfer the stock to a 1-qt clean saucepan and continue to simmer until the stock is reduced to a light syrup, about 30–45 minutes longer.

5. Whist in 3 Tbsp very cold diced butter. Season with salt to taste, cool down, and place in the refrigerator until ready to use.

Be careful not to overcook, as Demi then will be sticky and have a bitter taste.

Welsh Rarebit Sauce

8 oz cheddar cheese, grated (yellow or white
Wisconsin or English cheddar, sharp in flavor)

2 oz butter

1 tsp dry Colman's English mustard

⅓ cup Brown Ale

3 dashes Worchestershire sauce

Pinch, black pepper, freshly ground

Pinch, salt

1. Place all ingredients in a thick-based stainless-steel saucepan, and heat gently until a creamy mixture is formed. Be careful not to burn.

2. Incorporate all of the sauce to dry the ingredients.

Westchester Country Club Cocktail Sauce

MAKES: 2 CUPS

½ cup chili sauce

1 cup Heinz Ketchup

5 limes, for juice

½ cup Tanqueray

2 Tbsp hot sauce

2 Tbsp walnut oil

2 oz prepared horseradish

2 oz mushroom soy sauce

1 Tbsp finely chopped parsley

1 Tbsp finely chopped sage

1. Mix all items well and let sit for 4 hours.

Westchester Country Club Ketchup

2 onions, medium, diced

3 garlic cloves

1 carrot, peeled and diced

6 Tbsp olive oil

6 Tbsp tomato paste

⅔ cup dark brown sugar

½ cup cider vinegar

2 lb tomatoes, overripe, peeled and diced

½ tsp kosher salt

1 tsp celery salt

1 cinnamon stick

½ vanilla bean

½ tsp ground allspice

5 cloves

1. In a heavy-bottomed pan, sauté the onions, garlic, and carrot in the oil until well caramelized. Add the tomato paste and sugar, and cook 2–3 minutes. Deglaze the pan with the vinegar.

2. Add the tomatoes and the kosher salt, celery salt, cinnamon stick, vanilla bean, allspice, and cloves. Cook for 2–3 hours on slow heat or in a 260°F oven until rich and thick. Press through a sieve or chinois.

Whole-Grain Mustard Sauce

3 slices minced pancetta

3 Tbsp olive oil

1 cup diced small onion

2 cloves minced garlic

1 Tbsp mustard seed

1 cup chicken broth

1 cup heavy cream

½ cup grain mustard

3 Tbsp diced cold butter

2 tsp diced chives

1 tsp minced parsley

To taste, kosher salt

1. Render the pancetta until crisp with the olive oil.

2. Sauté the onions, garlic, and mustard seed for 2–3 minutes.

3. Add the broth, cream, and mustard. Bring to a simmer, and cook for 5 minutes.

4. Puree the sauce until smooth in a high-speed blender. Strain well.

5. Whisk in butter, chives, and parsley. Adjust seasoning with salt.

Wine Merchant Sauce

4 Tbsp butter

3 fresh shallots, minced

1 cup quality dry red wine

1 cup Demi de Edward Christopher (see above)

2 Tbsp balsamic vinegar

2 Tbsp cold diced butter

1. Melt butter in a stainless-steel saucepan. Add shallots.

2. Cook, stirring, for 3 minutes.

3. Stir in red wine; simmer for 15 minutes until reduced by half.

4. Stir in Demi de Edward Christopher and vinegar; simmer for 3 to 4 minutes more.

5. Just before serving, whisk in remaining butter.

ABOUT THE AMERICAN CULINARY FEDERATION

The tenderness of a well-braised lamb shank, the lightness of a velvety lemon mousse, or the crispness of finely blanched asparagus all can inspire culinarians to reach new heights in their profession. The American Culinary Federation, Inc., (ACF) is an organization that supports the infusion of that passion into the food industry throughout the world.

For members of the ACF, cooking well is its own passion, one that requires a desire to become the best culinarian one can be. The appreciation for the art of cooking has been significantly raised through the efforts of the ACF and its more than 20,000 members. ACF is the largest and most prestigious professional organization of chefs and cooks in North America today, and the pioneer responsible for elevating the position of chef from service status to true professional.

In addition to a large network of colleagues in the United States, every ACF member is simultaneously enrolled in the World Association of Cooks Societies (WACS), a worldwide association of millions of cooks and chefs representing 54 nations across five continents. As an authority and opinion leader on food, WACS is a global voice on all issues related to the culinary profession.

One of the most acclaimed programs of the ACF, Culinary Team USA is led by Chef

Edward G. Leonard, CMC as captain. The team represents the United States in major international culinary competitions, including the Culinary Exhibition, or Culinary Olympics, held every four years in Germany. In 2004, the United States was named World Champion in the hot food, or restaurant-style, division of the Culinary Olympics, beating 31 nations for the honor and is currently ranked third in the world as of 2005.

The culinary arts profession continues its ascent toward becoming one of the most well-respected professions in the United States. Only by creating an environment where restaurant and foodservice industry chefs can be educated and celebrated can the industry thrive. The ACF's role in this growth is to focus on member development through continuing education, apprenticeships, and accreditation programs.

Much like the maestro of a symphony, chefs may become masters in their profession. The ACF is the only certifier of U.S. Master Chefs and Master Pastry Chefs. Certification is a high honor among culinarians; there are currently only 53 Master Chefs and 10 Master Pastry Chefs in the entire United States. ACF also certitifies other levels, such as certified executive chef, chef de cusine, and culinary educaters to name a few. Individual certification is awarded to culinarians after a rigorous evaluation of industry experience and professional education and testing. Candidates for ACF certification must have a high level of exemplary work and educational experience and pass both a written and practical cooking/baking examination. In addition, they must complete coursework in food safety, nutrition, and supervisory management.

One of the most dynamic and important elements of the ACF membership is professional development. ACF sponsors opportunities for competition and professional recognition as well as access to educational forums with fellow culinarians at events around the country. In addition, ACF hosts regional and national conventions to allow chefs to enhance culinary skills, learn new techniques, and network with fellow culinarians. ACF national conventions host the largest gathering of professional cooks in the nation while addressing the needs of its members at various stages in their careers.

The ACF's appetite for excellence led to the creation in 1976 of a global apprenticeship/training program for cooks and pastry cooks, ensuring that novice cooks could learn practical applications of the trade. The two- or three-year program combines both education and experience and currently serves more than 1,300 apprentices through 69 programs at sponsoring operations nationwide. Upon completion of the apprenticeship program, recognized by the

U.S. Department of Labor, graduates are granted ACF's Certified Culinarian status. The ACF is proud to have graduated more than 3,500 culinary and pastry/baking apprentices since 1976.

Expanding its reputation as a program pioneer, the ACF established the accreditation commission in 1987 as the U.S. foodservice industry's gold standard for accrediting culinary and pastry/baking programs at institutions around the world. Each year, the national accrediting staff makes nearly 100 site visits to high school and post-secondary institutions to ensure compliance with established accrediting commission standards. Certified by the Council for Higher Education Accreditation (CHEA), the commission has accredited 266 foodservice training programs at 75 high schools nationally and 152 post-secondary institutions worldwide.

For members who wish to keep in touch with industry news and the latest culinary trends and techniques, the ACF publishes monthly editions of *The National Culinary Review* (*NCR*) and *Center of the Plate* (*COP*). These publications are a vital resource for culinarians around the globe. For up-and-coming chefs, *Sizzle* is an exciting publication geared toward breaking into the world of professional foodservice and hot new trends in the field.

While the ACF helps culinarians become better chefs, it also helps them become better stewards to the communities' youth. ACF Chef and Child Foundation

(CCF) is the voice of the American Culinary Federation in its fight against childhood hunger. ACF chapters across the country work in their local communities to provide nutrition-based education programs to children in preschool through grade five, where many children are fighting childhood obesity. CCF's mission is to educate and assist families in understanding proper nutrition, which is vitally important to a child's development.

Established in 1929, the principal goal of the ACF's founding chefs remains true today: to promote the professional image of American chefs worldwide through education among culinarians at all levels, from apprentices to the most accomplished certified master chefs. Whether you are a seasoned professional or a whiz kid with a whisk, the ACF provides the necessary resources for you to infuse the culinary world with passion and professionalism.

Chef John Kinsella,cmc
President
American Culinary Federation

ABOUT THE CLUB MANAGERS ASSOCIATION OF AMERICA

I could not be more thrilled that Chef Leonard is finally publishing a book on club cuisine!

As an accomplished, award-winning club chef and a true expert in this niche, Chef Leonard's creativity and flair are unrivaled. This is surely a treat for all gourmets! His impact on the culinary world and the club industry has resulted in high new standards and an awareness of quality for all to emulate.

Private clubs offer the finest in classic and cutting-edge cuisine, and I am delighted that he is shining a well-deserved spotlight on some of the most delectable dishes available at exclusive clubs.

Chef Leonard's work with the U.S. Olympic Culinary team and with the American Culinary Federation are visionary. I applaud his passion, and I hope that many people enjoy this fantastic book from a passionate chef.

The Club Managers Association of America (CMAA) is the professional association for managers of clubs. Its mission is to advance the profession of club management by fulfilling the educational and related needs of its members.

In the early 1920s, professional club managers recognized the impact clubs had on the American way of life and the need for a professional association for managers of these clubs. A Boston group pioneered the movement to establish such an association, limited to that geographic area. Detroit and New York managers followed and established two organizations, one for city club managers and one for country club managers.

By February 1927, the first annual meeting of these groups took place in Chicago, where the organization and bylaws were created for what is now the Club Managers Association of America. From 1927 to 1949, all business operations were handled by the Association's elected officers. The first national headquarters opened in 1949 in St. Louis, Missouri, and in 1959 the organization moved to its current location in the Washington, D.C., area.

CMAA represents and responds to the needs of all its members and is a strong and effective advocate for professionalism in club management.

In addition to the services and resources available through the CMAA National Headquarters, the association draws on hundreds of its members to participate in national committees and focus groups. Committee members willingly contribute their time and energy to enhancing the effectiveness of the association, which acts as a clearinghouse for the exchange of ideas and the means of working together for the mutual benefit of all members.

Committees are charged with the responsibility of shaping creative ideas into new programs; these must be approved by the National Board of Directors and implemented by the national staff. They are also responsible for working with and providing direction to the 50 CMAA senior chapters and approximately 39 student chapters and colonies throughout the world.

The Association's Club Foundation supports the advancement of the club management profession. The Club Foundation sponsors research, funds industry education programs, provides financial assistance to educational institutions, and awards scholarships to outstanding students interested in the club management profession.

CMAA recognizes the importance of an exceptional culinary experience to the members of clubs.

CMAA members are encouraged to be well versed in the intricacies and nuances of fine dining.

CMAA members can receive extensive training in food and beverage operations from a marketing and business perspective and have many resources at their disposal to maintain a thriving operation.

CMAA recognizes and appreciates the professionalism of the chefs who work at clubs. They have a tough audience and must maintain a high level of excitement and freshness with repeat diners—a formidable task!

A good general manager or chief operating officer of clubs entrusts the creation of appropriate menus and the overall culinary experience to trained professional chefs and their aspiring staff. I myself still wear my Certified Executive Chef designation proudly.

We at CMAA have a great respect for professional chefs and those who are passionate about food and beverage and the enjoyment of a good culinary experience.

James Singerling, CEC, CCM
President and CEO
Club Managers Association of America

CERTIFIED MASTER CHEF

Formation of the Program

In the 1970s, right after the establishment of the American Culinary Federation's (ACF) Certification Program for cooks, a special committee set out to create the highest level of certification: Certified Master Chef.

I was fortunate to serve as the chairman of the committee charged with researching, developing, and implementing a program that would withstand all possible challenges on both the national and international levels.

Logically, we looked toward those countries in Europe that had established successful programs. We began to study the pros and cons of each, adopting the best elements while adjusting them to the culinary profession in the United States.

What we learned was astonishing. While some countries offered a serious program, which in some cases required the candidate to take a full-time six-month preparatory

course, others simply awarded a Master Chef designation without any obvious criteria and certainly without any practical or theoretical test.

Because of this great diversity among programs, the committee soon understood the need to create one that would be above reproach, as it would certify a chef at the profession's highest level. It was equally clear that there was no room for compromises or shortcuts if the program was to be and remain unchallengeable.

As the result of that philosophy, we can proudly look back on 23 years of Master Chef exams, which since 1982 have brought forth 62 ACF members as U.S. Certified Master Chefs. Today, the foodservice and hospitality industry recognizes the Certified Master Chef status and offers commensurate compensation and benefits.

What Is a Master Chef?

By definition, a Master Chef is a master of his or her craft and all the elements, functions, responsibilities, and requirements associated with that. First and foremost, however, he or she is an excellent, passionate cook, versed not only in a microcosm of regional cooking but also familiar with many emerging global cuisines.

A Master Chef must be able to do all the tasks he or she asks staff members to perform and must be able to motivate and guide others to do them.

A Master Chef must be a leader and as such must lead by example, as a true master inspires and encourages others to attain the same professional designation.

This by no means implies that even a Certified Master Chef has omniscient and detailed knowledge of every aspect of all cuisines around the world. Far from it, as no one on earth can stake that claim. It simply recognizes the vast and evolving pool of knowledge that is attainable only through commitment to continuing education, a requirement for maintaining the Certified Master Chef status.

Ferdinand Metz
Certified Master Chef
Past President the
Culinary Institute of America
President of the World Cooks Society

INDEX